Nazi Occultism, Jewish Mysticism, and Christian Theology in the Video Game Series *Wolfenstein*

THEOLOGY, RELIGION, AND POP CULTURE

Series Editor
Matthew Brake

The *Theology, Religion, and Pop Culture* series examines the intersection of theology, religion, and popular culture, including, but not limited to television, movies, sequential art, and genre fiction. In a world plagued by rampant polarization of every kind and the decline of religious literacy in the public square, *Theology, Religion, and Pop Culture* is uniquely poised to educate and entertain a diverse audience utilizing one of the few things society at large still holds in common: love for popular culture.

Select titles in the series

Nazi Occultism, Jewish Mysticism, and Christian Theology in the Video Game Series Wolfenstein, by Frank G. Bosman

The Last of Us and Theology: Violence, Ethics, Redemption?, edited by Peter Admirand

Fantasy, Theology, and the Imagination, edited by Andrew D. Thrasher and Austin M. Freeman, with Fotini Toso

Theology and Wes Craven, edited by David K. Goodin

Theology and the DC Universe, edited by Gabriel Mckee and Roshan Abraham

Theology and Star Trek, edited by Shaun C. Brown and Amanda MacInnis Hackney

The Spirit and the Screen: Pneumatological Reflections on Contemporary Cinema, edited by Chris E. W. Green and Steven Félix-Jäger

Theology and the Avett Brothers, edited by Alex Sosler

Bob Dylan and the Spheres of Existence, by Christopher B. Barnett

Theology and Protest Music, edited by Jonathan H. Harwell and Heidi M. Altman

Animated Parables: A Pedagogy of Seven Deadly Sins and a Few Virtues, by Terry Lindvall

Nazi Occultism, Jewish Mysticism, and Christian Theology in the Video Game Series *Wolfenstein*

Frank G. Bosman

LEXINGTON BOOKS/FORTRESS ACADEMIC
Lanham • Boulder • New York • London

Published by Lexington Books/Fortress Academic
Lexington Books is an imprint of The Rowman & Littlefield Publishing Group, Inc.
4501 Forbes Boulevard, Suite 200, Lanham, Maryland 20706
www.rowman.com

86-90 Paul Street, London EC2A 4NE, United Kingdom

Copyright © 2024 by The Rowman & Littlefield Publishing Group, Inc.

All rights reserved. No part of this book may be reproduced in any form or by any electronic or mechanical means, including information storage and retrieval systems, without written permission from the publisher, except by a reviewer who may quote passages in a review.

British Library Cataloguing in Publication Information Available

Library of Congress Cataloging-in-Publication Data

Names: Bosman, Frank G., 1978– author.
Title: Nazi occultism, Jewish mysticism, and Christian theology in the video game series Wolfenstein / Frank G. Bosman.
Description: Lanham, Maryland : Lexington Books/Fortress Academic, [2024] | Series: Theology, religion, and pop culture | Includes bibliographical references and index. | Summary: "The video game series Wolfenstein incorporates various, contractionary narrative elements and inspirations, including Nazi occultism, Jewish mysticism, and Christian theology. In this monograph, the game theologian Frank G. Bosman analyses the series critically, focusing on the portrayal of the fictional Jewish Da'at Yichud organization"—Provided by publisher.
Identifiers: LCCN 2024013014 (print) | LCCN 2024013015 (ebook) | ISBN 9781978715516 (cloth ; acid-free paper) | ISBN 9781978715523 (epub)
Subjects: LCSH: Wolfenstein: the New Order (Game) | National socialism and occultism. | Mysticism—Judaism. | Video games—Religious aspects—Judaism. | Video games—Religious aspects—Christianity.
Classification: LCC GV1469.35.W64 B67 2024 (print) | LCC GV1469.35.W64 (ebook) | DDC 794.8/4—dc23/eng/20240411
LC record available at https://lccn.loc.gov/2024013014
LC ebook record available at https://lccn.loc.gov/2024013015

♾️ The paper used in this publication meets the minimum requirements of American National Standard for Information Sciences—Permanence of Paper for Printed Library Materials, ANSI/NISO Z39.48-1992.

In 2016, my esteemed colleague Dr. Leon Mock and I wrote the article "We do not pray, we invent. Jews, Judaism and Jewish mysticism in the video game 'Wolfenstein: The New Order'" published in the academic series Jewish Christian Perspectives by Brill (Leiden). It was this friendly and fruitful collaboration that sparked the research cumulating in the monograph you are reading now, published in 2024. On August 31, 2023, while we were participating in the bi-annual conference of the European Society of Catholic Theology in Pécs (Hungary), the sad news reached us that Leon Mock had suddenly and unexpectedly passed away back home.

Therefore, I dedicate this monograph to the one who inspired me to write it in the first place, Leon Mock. May his memory be a continuous blessing for us all.

Contents

Introduction	1
PART I: PRELIMINARIES	9
Chapter 1: Why Nazis are Fun: Nazi Glorification	11
Chapter 2: From Blavatsky to Himmler: Ariosophy	15
Chapter 3: Hitler's Deal with the Devil: Nazi Occultism	25
Chapter 4: The Kabbala: Jewish Mysticism	31
Chapter 5: Shooting Nazi Zombies: An Overview of the Series	37
PART II: ANALYSIS	49
Chapter 6: Daggers, Spears, and Medallions: The SS Paranormal Division	51
Chapter 7: Don't Pay Any Attention, Please: To Disclaim or Not to Disclaim	71
Chapter 8: Celebrating Streicher's Purim: The Revenge of the Jews	79
Chapter 9: The Good, the Bad, and the Ugly: The Wrath of the Degenerates	117
Chapter 10: Failing Gloriously: Wolfenstein's Theodicy	139
PART III: EVALUATION	153
Chapter 11: Playing the Jew: Consequences for the Player	155
Chapter 12: Playing the War: Wolfenstein's Esotericisms	161

Bibliography	167
Index	183
About the Author	187

Introduction

Wolfenstein: The New Order (MachineGames 2014) is quite the exceptional game. Belonging to the legacy of games infested with and criticized for their profuse use of Nazi occultist tropes, it treats adult and controversial topics with a level of serenity almost dissonant to its violent and relentless gameplay, which is primarily dominated by the killing of hundreds of Nazi henchmen, whether they be organic, artificial, or occult in nature. When the series' immortal hero, the American soldier William "B.J." Blazkowicz, is crawling through the sewers of Berlin in search of secret Nazi technology, his love interest Anya Oliwa reads entries from the diary her friend and cousin Ramona out to him over the radio (even though it is heavily implied that it is altogether Anya's story). This "Ramona," through Anya, describes her life from 1940 to 1960; a life focused on killing as many Nazis as she can, usually by exploiting her sexual prowess. In August 1941, she realizes she is pregnant with a "Nazi baby" and she clumsily but successfully aborts it. Some players praised *Wolfenstein* for portraying a woman choosing to abort her fetus without condemning her (Sheldon 2021):

> It's a difficult and terrifying part of her story, things that happened when she was very young and in the crisis of the war. I appreciate that the game does not frame her as a villain for these things—while she does seem to struggle with the violence she did, it's framed as something she did that is no different than the violence B.J. does to seek freedom.

Other gamers thought differently and were even so appalled by the inclusion of an abortion (and the absence of any moral rejection of it) in the game that they contemplated to stop playing the game all together (Godofwarlover 2018):

> I don't know if I should continue playing the game or not because I am Catholic and pro-life, and there is also the fact that some people make abortion into a joke, when it is a horrifying subject and also a sin. (. . .) I just think they shouldn't have added this in the game because it's a very controversial subject and I don't know if I will continue playing the game or not.

Other controversial topics include the Holocaust, a topic only very few games have dared to address, and then usually unsuccessfully. One of the levels of *Wolfenstein: The New Order* takes place in a fictional concentration camp in Croatia, called Belica (probably portraying the Jasenovac concentration camp in erstwhile Croatia). B.J. volunteers to be captured by the Nazis to infiltrate the facility in search of a Jewish scientist called Set Roth. While the gamer is positioned—at least temporarily—as a powerless victim of the Nazi regime, the set-up of the game informs the same player that B.J. will anyway soon find a way to escape his confinement (Hughes 2017). Critics accused developer MachineGames, therefore, of dishonoring the memory of the real victims, turning the Holocaust into mere entertainment, and ignoring the principle hopelessness of the historical camp prisoners (McKeand 2018, Widmann 2020).

In the same prisoners' camp, after Blazkowicz finds his Jewish scientist, both witness a Nazi robot torturing and killing a (presumably also Jewish) female inmate. Set Roth knows her and is reverently talking about the strength of her faith. "I can't believe with such certainty," he confides to B.J., who replies with "Maybe [God] is testing us." To which Roth sarcastically remarks: "If He is testing us, we are failing gloriously." The theological conundrum of the theodicy (Bosman 2019, 130–38) is casually discussed in the midst of a *Wolfenstein* game. The series has come a long way indeed since *Wolfenstein 3D* (1992) defined the genre of the 3d shooter game in 1992 (Fox 2013, 135; Sharp 2014, 112), together with id Software's other iconic games like *Doom* (1993) and *Quake* (1996).

The series has been praised for its ludic qualities. Up until the release of *Wolfenstein: The New Order*, it was criticized for neglecting the Jews as World War II's primary victims (Hayton 2012, 211), and for the omission of the Holocaust (Hayton 2015, 260–65). Other critiques included the series' continuous flirtation with occultism, including references to historical groups like Theosophy and Ariosophy and the use of "popular" occult objects like the Spear of Destiny and the Thule Medallion (Hite 2013, 76). Also, its halo of Nazi glorification (Cullinane 2009), its supposed trivialization of violence (Chapman 2020, 104–106), and even its supposed inclination toward colonialist traits (Ensslin 2012, 40) are mentioned by critics.

Nevertheless, with the release of *Wolfenstein: The New Order* the game series makes a decisive turn in narrative tone and material. In *The New Order*, in its prequel *Wolfenstein: The Old Blood* (2015), as well as in its sequel *Wolfenstein II: The New Colossus* (2017), the series now incorporates an allohistorical timeline in which the Nazis won the Second World War in 1946, many more or less explicit Jewish characters (exclusively heroes who fight against the Nazis), the aforementioned concentration camp, an ancient Jewish organization called the Da'at Yichud, various references to Jewish mysticism (or Kabbala), the tragic fate of those dubbed *Untermenschen* by the Third Reich (including people of color, Jews of all races, and Romani), as well as of other undesirables (such as mentally and physically challenged people, communists, and LGBTQ+ people), and a remarkable nuancing of "the Germans" as an evil collective (i.e., by including several German resistance fighters).

Furthermore, with the release of *The New Order*, developer MachineGames and publisher Bethesda Softworks included a disclaimer to the installments:

> *Wolfenstein: The New Order* is a fictional story set in an alternate universe in the 1960's. Names, characters, organizations, locations, and events are either imaginary or depicted in a fictionalized manner. The story and content of this game are not intended to and should not be construed in any way to condone, glorify, or endorse the beliefs, ideologies, events, actions, persons, or behavior of the Nazi regime or to trivialize its war crimes, genocide, and other crimes against humanity.

As I will explain later on, disclaimers contain very paradoxical communication in and of themselves: they draw scrutiny to what they want to avoid being scrutinized. Apparently, according to the disclaimer, there may be people who could be offended by these games, but—as the developer and publisher state—without real cause or reason. The truth of this supposition, however, has yet to be decided.

This change, set in motion with the arrival of *The New Order* and continued in its successors, does not, however, mean that the series has abandoned its old fascination with Nazi occult themes, persons, and objects. Neither has it become immune to the old criticism of Nazi glorification, as both critics and MachineGames' disclaimer attest. And even more pressing, the inclusion in the later installments of an ancient but technologically very advanced group of predominantly or maybe even exclusively Jewish scientists (the Da'at Yichud) superficially functions as a counterweight to the initial criticism of the structural exclusion of the Jews from the series. At a deeper level, however, this Da'at Yichud resembles the (both historical and contemporary) idea of a secret Jewish world-government (Konda 2019, 47–87) a bit too closely to be comfortable, especially within the context of the Second World War. This uncomfortable connection is strengthened by the fact that Set Roth, the only living member of the Da'at Yichud, involves himself with all kinds of medical experiments of very questionable ethical nature, usually associated precisely with the Nazi regime itself.

THE FOCUS: OCCULTISM, MYSTICISM, AND THEOLOGY

In this monograph, I want to focus on the development of the series' narrative and world lore in regard to the notions of Nazi occultism and Jewish mysticism, both from a Christian historical-theological perspective. By this I mean that both this occultism and mysticism function within the larger historical context of Western society, predominantly that of the nineteenth to the twenty-first century, also through the persisting Christian influence within this society (Bosman 2019). The theological perspective comes into play especially in the case of the in-game discussion of the theodicy conundrum, as well as regarding the various occult objects and historical figures originating from the Christian and Jewish traditions that feature in the series' installments.

This historical-theological analysis of the *Wolfenstein* series will provide insight into the continuous appropriation of the Second World War as a self-explanatory background for the creation of thrilling and compelling stories in novels, films, and games, but also show the possible problematic consequences of that appropriation in terms of the trivialization of violence in connection to the glorification of the Nazi era. Finally, this analysis will shed light on the continuous cultural processing of the Holocaust in our contemporary society *and* on the continuation of (implicit) Jewish stereotypes, potentially leading to anti-Judaism or even anti-Semitism.

Part I: Preliminaries. To do so, I present five preliminary chapters in which the monograph's constituent parts are introduced, being: (1) the topic of Nazi glorification as a cultural phenomenon, especially in relation to the medium of digital games; (2) the development of a series of interrelated forms of esotericism collectively known as Ariosophy prior to and during the Second World War; (3) the alleged connection between Hitler and the Nazi regime and occult or satanic powers (called "Nazi occultism") during and after the Second World War; (4) the concept of Jewish mysticism that is or is not to be equated with Jewish mysticism; and (5) an overview of the *Wolfenstein* series' narrative, including its multiple reboots, the problems these form for the series' internal continuity, and the creative way the developers have tried to reconcile these. This overview will give the reader the possibility to place all later discussed in-game (historical, fictional, or hybrid) objects, characters, and organizations within the greater context of the series.

Part II: Analysis. After this, in the second part of my monograph, I present five analytical chapters. The first of these is dedicated to (6) Nazi occultism within the *Wolfenstein* series, structured by the various occult objects and characters the player comes across. This occultism increases the danger of the series being a trailblazer for possible anti-Semitist sentiments, but also, quite paradoxically, is a basis for the series' later inclusion of other forms of (Jewish) esotericism. Surprisingly perhaps, this means that Kabbala and Nazi occultism exist side-by-side in the same series and even in the same games.

In the next chapters I discuss various narrative novelties that have entered the game series since the release of *The New Order*, countering or balancing the continuous societal and scholarly criticisms toward the cultural use of Nazi occultist traits in general and toward games appropriating the Second World War specifically: (7) an in-depth discussion on MachineGames' new disclaimer appearing from *The New Order* onwards; (8) the complex depiction of Jews, Judaism, and Kabbala in the series; (9) the narrative emancipation of Jews and other victims of the Nazi regime; and (10) the in-game discussions on the theodicy, in the context of the Second World War in general and in that of the Holocaust especially.

Part III: Evaluation. Lastly, I will discuss (11) the ramifications of all this for and from the perspective of the player of the series' games, especially because of the unique communication property of digital games: the entanglement between the Text-Immanent Reader/Player and the player's avatar as a character on the textual stage of the game (see next section). I conclude with an overall evaluation of *Wolfenstein*'s multiple esotericisms and their interactions (12).

METHODOLOGY: COMMUNICATION-ORIENTED ANALYSIS

In this monograph, as a methodology, I will make use of the Communication-Oriented Analysis of texts. This method was initially developed by Archibald van Wieringen for the purpose of the analysis of biblical and classical texts, but was later further developed and considerably broadened for the analysis of other kinds of "texts," including digital games, by—again—Van Wieringen in close collaboration with myself (Bosman and Van Wieringen 2022). This method distinguishes—fundamentally—between the text-immanent communication (= the communication in the textual world) on the one hand, and the text-external communication (= the communication in the real world) on the other.

This results in a strict distinction between the characters (and the accompanying props) on the textual stage and a Text-Immanent Author directing these characters and communicating the narrative to a Text-Immanent Reader. Outside the text, the Real Author and the Real Reader exist. But in both cases, the first communicates to the second by means of the text "between them" (see figure I.1).

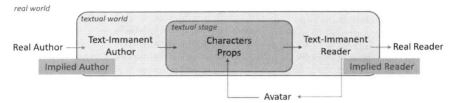

Figure I.1. The basic outline of the Communication-Oriented Method of text analysis (Bosman and Van Wieringen 2022). *Bosman and Van Wieringen 2022.*

Although the Real Author, who belongs to the real word, never coincides with the Text-Immanent Author, who belongs to the textual world, and the Real Reader, who belongs to the real world, never coincides with the Text-Immanent Reader, who belongs to the textual world, they are all nevertheless related. This relationship is mediated by the set of socio-historical data that makes the existence of both the Text-Immanent Author and the Real Author on the one hand, and the Text-Immanent Reader and the Real Reader on the other, plausible; these entities are called the "Implied Author" and "Implied Reader." These Implied Author and Implied Reader anchor the necessary conditions for the communication to take place in the first place: for example, the practical knowledge of how to read a book, watch a film, or play a game.

In the case of video games, the Real Author is the game developer or the game developing team, and the Real Reader the actual player behind his pc or console playing the actual game. The Implied Author and Implied Reader anchor the technical knowledge of how to run and interact with the game on a practical-technical and a ludic level, the understanding of the implicit rules of games as a medium, of the genre a game belongs to, and of the game in question specifically.

Digital games, such as the *Wolfenstein* series, have—however—a special communication characteristic, which I have to address here especially. In video games, players intervene in the unfolding of the story. Without the player's input, the game will not commence, neither in its ludic nor its narrative capacities. If seen from the perspective of the Communication-Oriented Analysis, what happens in a video game is the entanglement of the position of the Text-Immanent Reader/Player with that of a character on the stage, that is, the game's protagonist (narrative property)/player's avatar (ludic property). Via the Text-Immanent Reader, the player (as Real Reader) has access to the game by being present on stage in the Text-Immanent Reader's avatar.

In other words: the Text-Immanent Player is the one the story is told *to* (by the Text-Immanent Author to the Text-Immanent Reader), the one the story is—partially—told *by* (the Text-Immanent Reader as far as is allowed by the Text-Immanent Author), and the one the story is told *about* (the Text-Immanent Reader's in-game character/avatar). On several occasions in the monograph, I will refer to this methodology and its communicative instances. What the ramifications are for the player of *Wolfenstein*, I will return to explicitly at the end of this monograph.

SOME REMARKS

In this monograph, I will very frequently refer to the different installments of the *Wolfenstein* series. So, for convenience's sake, I will use proper names and their abbreviations interchangeably (see table I.1). I will largely ignore the first two installments of the series, *Castle Wolfenstein* (1981) and *Beyond Castle Wolfenstein* (1984), since the state of technology in the 1980s more or less prevented any narrative significance to begin with. They will only be discussed shortly in the overview of the series.

Secondly, I will also ignore altogether the installment *Wolfenstein: Enemy Territory* (2003); its ludic quality as an exclusively multiplayer game prevents the game from having any serious narrative significance. In multiplayers, the gamers "create" the game story together. Or in communication terminology, the Real Readers of the game have to identify voluntarily with the Text-Immanent Reader, at the invitation and under the authorial control of the Text-Immanent Author, in order to take up their appropriate position on the textual stage of the game in the form of their in-game avatars. Because of this genre property and the relative "withdrawal" of the Text-Immanent

Table I.1. A list of *Wolfenstein* games discussed in this monograph including their abbreviations.

Abbr.	Title	Developer	Year
CW	Castle Wolfenstein	Muse Software	1981
BCW	Beyond Castle Wolfenstein	Muse Software	1984
W3D	Wolfenstein 3D	id Software	1992
SoD	Spear of Destiny	FormGen	1992
RtCW	Return to Castle Wolfenstein	Grey Matter Interactive	2001
WET	Wolfenstein. Enemy Territory	Splash Damage	2003
WRPG	Wolfenstein RPG	id Software	2008
W09	Wolfenstein	Raven Software	2009
WNO	Wolfenstein. The New Order	MachineGames	2014
WOB	Wolfenstein. The Old Blood	MachineGames	2015
WNC	Wolfenstein II. The New Colossus	MachineGames	2017
WYB	Wolfenstein. Youngblood	MachineGames/Arkane Studios	2019
WCP	Wolfenstein. Cyberpilot	MachineGames	2019
W3	Wolfenstein III	MachineGames	TBP

Author to the fringes of the game text, extracting any meaning out of the game beyond the individual experiences of individual Real Readers, a.k.a. the players of flesh and blood, becomes very difficult if not impossible.

Thirdly, even though *Wolfenstein III* has been announced as being in production, no reliable release date has been given at the time of the writing of this monograph (Faulkner and Nicol 2022). For that reason, I had to leave out the final act of the trilogy that started with *The New Order* and *The New Colossus*.

If I quote the Hebrew Bible or the New Testament, I will use the New American Standard Bible translation of 2020.

This monograph did not start in and of itself; it has its origin in an article I wrote together with my esteemed colleague Leon Mock, titled "We do not pray, we invent" (Bosman and Mock 2016a). In many ways it formed the first public phase of my research into Nazi occultism, Jewish mysticism, and the *Wolfenstein* franchise. I recall this article and the collaboration with Leon with great gratitude (see also p. v).

PART I

Preliminaries

Chapter 1

Why Nazis are Fun

Nazi Glorification

In 1971 Disney produced its 1971 film *Bedknobs and Broomstricks*, directed by Robert Stevenson. The film combines live-action and animated sequences just like its predecessor *Mary Poppins* (1964), directed by the same Stevenson, and was based on the children's novels *The Magic Bedknob; or, How to Become a Witch in Ten Easy Lessons* (1943) and *Bonfires and Broomsticks* (1947) by Mary Norton (Everett 2020). The story takes place in 1940, during the Blitz on London. Three children are evacuated to the little town of Peppering Eye near the Dorset coast, to be placed under the care of Miss Eglatine Price (Angela Lansbury), a not very successful amateur witch. After a lot of adventures, Price and the children defeat a secret Nazi invasion force that happened to land on the Dorset coast (Long 2021).

The film is light in tone, is full of wizardry and magic, and has the perfect Disney touch for a younger audience. Despite all its magical adventures, the film begins and starts with the cold-hard reality of the Second World War in England. At the start of the film, the war is hinted at: road signs are painted black to prevent Nazi invaders from navigating too easily through the countryside and flocks of young evacuees are placed with local families. At the end of the film, the magic learned during the adventures is used to stop a very real-time Nazi invasion, complete with a German submarine and German soldiers wearing the swastika on their uniforms. And even though the Nazis are defeated by enchanted knight's armor from the local museum, the film ends with Mr. Emelius Browne, once a trickster and a gentle fraud, now enlisting in the home guard ready to defend his country.

The Nazi regime is a standard device that has been used in countless cultural productions since World War II. The most well-known are the heroic movies about the Allies' victory against Nazi Germany, from classic ones like *The Longest Day* (Ken Annakin/Andrew Marton/Bernhard Wicki 1962) and *A Bridge too Far* (Richard Attenborough 1977) to *Saving Private Ryan* (Steven

Spielberg 1998) and *Valkyrie* (Bryan Singer 2008). War simulation games also fall in this category, like *The Call of Duty* installments *Finest Hour* (2004), *WWII* (2017), and *Vanguard* (2021), but also *The Saboteur* (2010), *Sniper Elite* (2005), and *Sniper Elite V2* (2012). Second are the Nazi films and games only loosely based on the historical Nazis: films like *Inglorious Basterds* (Quentin Tarantino 2009), Marvel's *Captain America: The First Avenger* (Joe Johnston 2011), and Spielberg's first and third Indiana Jones films, *Raiders of the Lost Ark* (1981) and *The Last Crusade* (1989).

The third category is the most problematic one: the so-called sexploitation films and games drawing inspiration from the Nazi era. Films like the sex- and torture-filled *Ilsa, She Wolf of the SS* (Don Edmonds 1975), portray a

> flagrant disregard for historical accuracy, pornographic and misogynistic tendencies, graphic violence, and all-around tastelessness and lack of ethical sensitivity to the twentieth-century's deadliest war and most notorious genocide. (Magilow 2012, 7)

Some games also fall in this category, especially the ones including Nazi soldiers, like *Zombie Army Trilogy* (2015) or *Call of Duty: World at War*'s (2008) "Nazi zombie mode." Games and films like these

> violate a central taboo of Holocaust representation: they visualize and exaggerate atrocities in ways that claim to make them comprehensible, even as Holocaust survivors insist non-participants simply cannot comprehend them if they were not there. (idem 8)

The problematic nature of cultural, "entertaining" artifacts appropriating the Second World War, the Nazi regime, and the Holocaust, has been summarized by the much-quoted German philosopher Theodor W. Adorno. In his 1951 *Kulturkritik und Gesellschaft*, Adorno speaks about the impossibility to "do" art after Auschwitz: "Nach Auschwitz ein Gedicht zu schreiben, ist barbarisch." This famous line might be interpreted in two different if not interrelated ways in the English language (Rowland 1997). (1) After the Second World War, writing poetry, as *pars pro toto* for all forms of art, has become virtually impossible. The shock was simply too great to overcome: art and its associations with beauty and truth is fundamentally "broken" by the horrors of the Shoah. (2) After the Second World War, using Auschwitz, as *pars pro toto* for the Holocaust, as a source of artistic inspiration is in principle unethical.

This artistic, ethical, and philosophical problem of art after Auschwitz materialized in the so-called "Lanzmann-Spielberg controversy" (Kearney 2002, 50–60). In 1985, French filmmaker Claude Lanzmann directed his celebrated

Holocaust documentary film *Shoah*. Eight years later, in 1993, Hollywood legend Steven Spielberg made his epic historical drama *Schindler's List*. Both films revolve around the Jewish victims of the Nazi death machinery, but the first is a documentary, the second a historical drama.

Lanzmann did not take kindly to his American colleague's work. In a 1994 essay, entitled "Holocauste. La representation impossible," the French director accused Spielberg of turning the Holocaust into a "kitsch melodrama." The Shoah, according to the French director, prohibits its own visual representations, not for religious reasons *per se* ("Thou shalt have no graven images"), but for moral ones, to prevent voyeurism or *Schadenfreude*. Lanzmann:

> The Holocaust is first and foremost unique in that it builds around itself, in a circle of flames, the limit not to be crossed, because a certain absolute of horror is incommunicable: to pretend crossing it is to become guilty of the most serious transgression. Fiction is a transgression, I feel deeply that there is a prohibition of representation. (Transl. by Kearney 2002, 52)

Wolfenstein fits this discussion perfectly. Margit Grieb (2009, 194) argues that games such as *Wolfenstein* only deal with Nazism in a very shallow way: exaggeration, irony, and artificiality negate the weight of the historical context in favor of a light-hearted piece of entertainment. She argues further that through (s)exploitation films and games, the (appalling) Nazi ideology has become separated from its (appealing) aesthetics.

Jeff Hayton (2012), in his analysis of the series, points to what he deems to be problematic aspects of *Wolfenstein* as a series (even though the fourth cycle had not yet been released at the moment of his writing, see chapter 5). In the first place, Hayton argues, the backdrop of the Second World War makes possible the elimination of B.J.'s countless enemies beyond any ethical reasoning or questioning: one can kill Nazis without any need for further explanation. In the series, at least up to and including the third cycle, all Germans are Nazis, with only some very minor exceptions (German civilians and a few Kreisau Circle members). When these non-combatants are shot, the game immediately ends with a "game over," thus removing the moral choice on the part of the player and disregarding the historical fact that wars do not distinguish very consistently between soldiers (to be killed) and civilians (to be spared).

The second observation Hayton makes is the absence of the War's primary victims, the Jews. They are not depicted or not even referred to in the series until—again—the fourth cycle, which marks a radical change in tone of voice and inclusion of Judaism. "Jews exist as silent haunting ghosts, for without the annihilation of the Jews, the Nazis are no different from the

Allies" (Hayton 2012, 211). In multiple installments, B.J. comes across allied soldiers, either being tortured or being slaughtered by the Nazis: cages and pools of blood in the first *Wolfenstein*, the torture-by-electricity in the opening scene for *Return to Castle Wolfenstein* or the blindfolded prisoners-of-war in *Wolfenstein* (2009).

Wolfenstein operates in an already tension-filled domain where the fundamental inability of conveying the experiences of the victims of the Second World War collides with our collective, cultural fascination with the Nazis and their regime.

Chapter 2

From Blavatsky to Himmler
Ariosophy

To understand what was happening in Germany, and to a lesser degree also in Austria, at the beginning of 20th century, one of the most important things to consider is the cultural dominance of Romanticism. The term 'Romanticism' (*Romantisme* in French, *Romantik* in German) denotes a specific intellectual movement that started at the end of the 18th century as a protest against the mechanical worldview of the Enlightenment, the politics of the *ancien régime*, the dominance of the neo-classical aesthetic, and the practical superiority of Western capitalism (Alsen 2001; Travers 2001). The Romantics materialized this protest by the idealization (or "Romanticization") of the "other," either in geographical, psychological, or historical sense: the child, the animal, the exotic, the monster, the lunatic, the primitive, the peasant, and the naïve (Berlin 1999, 6–18). These "others" were imbued with notions of spiritual, ethical, and moral superiority in stark contrast to the industrialized, urbanized, and desensitized modern citizen living in the major cities of the Western world. The current surge in the popularity of everything 'medieval' in the form of an idealized depiction of the Middle Ages in novels, films, and games also belongs to this romanticization phenomenon, just as re-enactments of 'historical' events do (Elliott 2017; Apel 2012, 47–76). So, in as far as Ariosophy is related to Romanticism, we must understand it as a *protest* against the societal and intellectual status quo of its time.

Geopolitically speaking, Germany found itself continuously confronted with difficult issues and developments. Germany's unification process was a slow and painful one, ending formally on January 18, 1871 with the founding of the German Empire and the proclamation of the Prussian king as the German Kaiser of the Second Reich (Peaple 2002, 2–11) by Chancellor Otto von Bismarck. The unification had been looked forward to by many Germans ever since the pre-Romantic *Storm und Drang* ("storm and urge") movement had idealized a common Germanic past and culture in defiance of any political unity (Karthaus 2007). However, as Goodrick-Clarke (2005, 3) summarizes, the "idealistic anticipation of unity had nurtured utopian and messianic expectations, which could not be fulfilled by the prosaic realities of public administration." Especially Bismarck's administrative separation between the German Empire and the Austro-Hungarian Empire meant a forceful blow to any pan-Germanic efforts (Goodrick-Clarke 2005, 4). To complicate things even more, after the end of World War I, Austria and Hungary were also forcibly split into two nations by the allied forces, which again was a blow for any pan-Germanic ideology.

Because of its domestic problems, Germany was one of the last European countries to extend its power into a network of colonies, leading to political anxiety in Berlin that the newly formed Empire would lose out in the race to world dominance vis-à-vis France's and Britain's colonial might (Millet, 2017, 78–97). Of course, the defeat in The Great War strengthened the already existing collective inferiority complex, especially after the Treaty of Versailles—displeasingly referred to as the *Diktat* by many Germans during the Interbellum—placed incredibly high war restitutions on the defeated country (Neiberg 2017). Even more, the defeat of Germany in 1918 was quickly (and quite preposterously) credited to a stab-in-the-back operation by Jewish and communist powers (Watson 2008, 184–230). Needless to say, the German army was not defeated by Jews or communists, but because of its serious lack of resources and reserve, and especially because of the involvement from the United States by late 1918.

So, in as far Ariosophy is connected to the geopolitical circumstances of early 20th century Germany, we must understand it as a *Germanic* philosophy, that is, intrinsically connected to the (failed) ideal of a political, historical, and cultural unity between the German-speaking countries and communities in Western Europe, especially in the face of continuous external (France, England) and (perceived) internal threats (communists, socialists, Jews) to that unity.

Next, turn-of-the-century Germany was under the spell of social Darwinism, as was the rest of the Western world. Social Darwinism is the translation or transition of Charles Darwin's biological-evolutional principles, especially the (often mis-quoted or misinterpreted) notion of the survival of the fittest, into the social-political domain, not infrequently leading to ethnic profiling and racism, including anti-Semitism (Gasman 2017[1971]; Mees 2008, 23–26). Social Darwinism was by no means a German invention, nor was its popularity restricted to the German speaking world: it had its fair share of fans in the Anglo-Saxon world too (Bannister 2010). But in the German context of the 1910s and the following years, Social Darwinism, as advocated by zoologists like Ernst Haeckel, fitted nicely into the nationalist framework.

The rise of Social Darwinism is not an independent phenomenon but belongs to a longer line of "pseudo-sciences" gaining popularity quickly: new scientific methods and subjects retrospectively dubbed as "pseudo" by today's scientific standards. Serious scientists and scholars went about inventing new and retrospectively problematic domains like *Sinnbildforschung* ("symbol research"); *Rassenkunde* ("racial theory"); craniofacial anthropometry (that is the science of measuring the shapes of heads, usually to determine the owner's mental and racial qualities); parapsychology; and eugenics (that is the science of the improvement of the genetic quality of a certain group) (Lawrie 2005, 84–87; Kurlander 2017, 22–32). From 1935, Himmler would institute a specialized division, the SS Ahnenerbe, targeted at concentrating and developing these kinds of "sciences" for the "discovery" of the ancient and powerful ancestry of the German people and for the obvious benefit of the creation of a stronger Germany in the present and future (Pringle 2006).

So, in as far Ariosophy is connected to the scientific context of the end of the 19th and the beginning of the 20th century, we have to understand that this philosophy did not arise as an isolated phenomenon, but that it is embedded in a much broader one, dedicated to the allegedly *scientific* feasibility of racist theories and to the accompanied vision of a once all-powerful Germanic people looking for nothing more than its rightful rehabilitation in the contemporary world.

THEOSOPHY: MADAME BLAVATSKY

Ariosophy as a specific Germanic, racist philosophy in the era up to and during the Second World War is severely indebted to Theosophy and the founder of the first Theosophical Society, Helena—or "Madame"— Blavatsky. Theosophy and Blavatsky are in their turn indebted to the larger hermetic-esoteric tradition of the Western world. Everyone interested in Ariosophy or Nazi occultism will have to quickly become familiar with interrelated notions like "esotericism," "hermeticism," and "Gnosticism." Frequently these notions seem to be synonyms, but that is unjust and undeserved. A quick primer is necessary to make sense of the dense web that is esotericism in the Western word.

Esotericism as a notion is very difficult to define. The fact that both a Jewish esoteric and a Nazi esoteric tradition can exist, is proof of that. Modern esotericism—in this context—refers to the re-emergence of the esoteric tradition in the 19th and 20th century Western world, leading to a spike in interest in "occult" phenomena and spiritualism (Deveney 2006). Esotericism is a container notion incorporating a vast amount of historical and contemporary beliefs and practices that (1) deviated or deviate from dominant or "orthodox" religious beliefs in the Western world and (2) focus on individual spiritual enlightenment, (3) often by initiation into otherwise secret knowledge (Hanegraaff 2006a). Now within esotericism, two major branches have been developed: a hermetic one (hermeticism) and a Gnostic one (Gnosticism).

The hermetic-esoteric tradition (or hermeticism) maintains a holistic worldview in which the macrocosmos and microcosmos are intimately intertwined and connected to one another (Van den Broek 2006a; Lucentini & Compagni 2006; Faivre 2006). Historical examples include (forms of) Neo-Platonism (Shaw 2006; Leijenhorst 2006a, 2006b), medieval alchemy (Principe 2006), Theosophy (Santucci 2006), Anthroposophy (Leijenhorst 2006c), and Kabbala (Hanegraaff 2006b), or rather a "Christian Kabbalah," that is, a Christianized version of Jewish mysticism (Dan 2006). The gnostic-esoteric tradition (or Gnosticism), on the contrary, postulates a radically dualistic worldview in which everything that exists is categorized as belonging to one of two cosmic forces, light versus dark (Van den Broek 2006b). Historical examples include the so-called Gnostic gospels (Van den Broek 2006c), Valentinianism (Holzenhausen 2006), Marcionism (May 2006), Manichaeism (Van Oort 2006), and Catharism (Bozoky 2006).

As explained above, Blavatsky's Theosophy is part of the hermetic-esoteric tradition (Santucci 2006; Goodrick-Clarke 2005, 18–25), and no discussion of Ariosophy can succeed without paying due attention to this influential woman. Helena Petrovna Blavatsky (1831–1891), self-proclaimed clairvoyant and founder of the Theosophical Society (in 1875) plays an important role in the development of what is later known as Nazi occultism. Not because Blavatsky was in any shape or form a sympathizer with the Nazi regime, but her esoteric doctrine influenced more than one generation of German and Austrian "Ariosophists." It is therefore important to sketch, however briefly, her most important doctrines, even though a systematic overview is difficult because of the many contradictions in Blavatsky's writings.

Blavatsky's first book, *Isis Unveiled* (1877), is—as Goodridge-Clarke summarizes (2005, 18)—"less an outline of her new religion than a rambling tirade against the rationalist and materialistic culture of modern Western civilization." She was clearly intrigued by "mysterious" ancient Egypt, introduced to that specific perspective by Edward Bulwer-Lytton's novel *The Last Days of Pompeii* (1834), which revolved around, amongst other things, the impact of the cult of Isis in the Roman Empire during the first century AD.

Blavatsky's second book, *The Secret Doctrine* (1888) forms, however, the heart of her theosophical system. The author presented the book as a commentary of another text, called the *Stanzas of Dzyan*, which Blavatsky claimed to have read in a subterranean Himalayan monastery, where she was initiated into ancient, secret doctrines by two spiritual guides, Morya and

Koot Hoomi. The *Doctrine* effectually is an alternative interpretation of the origin and history of humanity, fashioned after cyclical processes that repeat themselves eternally. The first volume, "Cosmogenesis," tells the story of the universe emanating from the primal unity of an unmanifested divine being. In the *Doctrine*, Blavatsky included a range of esoteric symbols, including the swastika, probably derived from Hinduism, but later adopted as the symbol of the Nazi party by Hitler himself.

The second volume, "Anthropogenesis," tells the story of the origin and history of humanity. It is in this context that Blavatsky introduces her famous theory of the seven consecutive "root races": the first four become increasingly entangled with the material world, while the last three ascend again in spiritual quality. The first root race was an Astral one, beings of pure energy and consciousness. The second race were the Hyperboreans (probably from the Greek *hyper borea*, "beyond Boreas," being the personification of the North wind), who dwelled on a now disappeared polar continent. Third were the Lemurians, who lived on a now sunken continent in the Indian ocean (as proposed by zoologist Philip Sclater in 1864). The fourth ones are the Atlanteans (derived from Plato's *Timaeus*), again once living on a now disappeared continent, lying off the coast of Africa. The fifth root race are supposed to be the Aryans, who in later Ariosophical circles were identified with the Germanic peoples.

This amalgam of Egyptian mysticism, Hinduism, and American spiritualism found its way into German and Austrian intellectual circles through its appeal to the Wilhelmian *Lebensreform*, a mid-19th century, German-romantic movement striving to return to the "natural" world, that is, a construction and idealization of pre-industrial, rural life. Other conduits into the Germanic world were laid by the efforts of Wilhelm Hubbe-Schleiden (1846–1916), a senior civil servant in Hamburg and first president of the German Theosophical Society in 1884 and publisher of the monthly periodical *Die Sphinx*. It was through this periodical's installments that many internationally prominent spiritists and occultists, and Blavatsky herself of course, received a German-speaking audience for the first time. Also, very helpful to Blavatsky's popularity was the German translation of her *Doctrine* as *Die Geheimlehre* (1897–1901). All this led to the first generation of Ariosophists in Austria and Germany, amongst whom can be found Guido von List, Rudolf von Sebottendorf, and Jörg Lanz von Liebenfels.

If the hermetic-esoteric tradition in the Western world is an hourglass, Blavatsky can be located in the narrow neck: her teachings connect the pre-modern esotericism of Antiquity, the Middle Ages, and the Renaissance with that of modernity. Her Theosophy was an attempt to harmonize the outcomes of modern (empirical and world-immanent) science with (new forms of) spirituality and transcendence from Western *and* Eastern traditions. As Romanticism was ultimately a protest movement against the mechanical worldview of the Enlightenment, the politics of the *ancien régime*, the dominance of the neo-classical aesthetic, and the practical superiority of Western capitalism—as argued above—then Theosophy was also a protest movement against the metaphysical reductionism of the empirical sciences, that is, the reduction of reality to its empirically verifiable forms (Chan 2003; Sitelman and Sitelman 2000). Blavatsky gave what her followers wanted: a way of fusing science and religion, to bring together the wisdom of the East and the West.

THE THEORISTS: LIST, LIEBENFELS AND SEBOTTENDORF

The term "Ariosophy" was first coined by Jörg Lanz von Liebenfels (1874–1954) in 1915, having used similar notions before like theozoology and Ario-Christianity (Goodrick-Clarke 2006a; Kurlander 2017, 20–22). Later Guido von List (1848–1919) would name his own, similar, doctrine Wotanism or Armanism (Goodrick-Clarke 2006b; Kurlander 2017, 33–35). Whether called Ariosophy or Wotanism, the doctrines of Von List, Von Liebebfels, and their followers combined aspects of Blavatsky's Theosophy with theories of Aryan supremacy and racial purity.

The Ariosophists claimed that the natural dominance of the Aryan race—blue-eyed, blond-haired people from the north—had been systematically undermined by inferior non-Aryan races, by the Jews, or by the Roman Catholic Church under the guise of democracy, liberalism, and egalitarianism. The Church was accused by the Ariosophists of prosecuting the guardians of esoteric-Aryan knowledge, like the Manicheans, Cathars, and the Knights of Solomon's Temple. The Atlanteans, Blavatsky's fourth root race, were held to be divided into super- and subhuman species, because of their ancestors' (the third root race of the Lemurians) interbreeding with inferior females, spawning apes, monsters, and demons. The knowledge and subsequent powers of the old Aryans had to be revived in order to bring the modern world back to an Aryan-led new world order.

Ariosophy entered Nazi circles by means of interconnected personal networks. Philipp Stauff (1876–1923) was a personal friend of Guido von List, founding member of the Guido-von-List-Gesellschaft (in 1908), obituarist for the *Münchener Beobachter*, and a high-ranking member of the Germanenorden ("Germanic Order"), founded in 1912 to counter the supposed Jewish dominance in Germany. The *Münchener Beobachter* was edited by Rudolf Sebottendorf (1875–1945), founder of the *völkerische* Thule-Gesellschaft ("Thule Society") in 1918, which would (in 1920) later be renamed the *Völkischer Beobachter*, ending up to be the leading Nazi party newspaper until 1945 (Kurlander 2017, 38–47). The same Sebottendorf would take over the Bavarian chapter of the Germanenorden in 1917.

Under Sebottendorf, members of the Germanenorden and the Thule Society—which sometimes appear to have been more or less the same organization—played an important role in the Bavarian counter-revolution of 1919, when the Munich paramilitary *Freikorps* smashed the independent Soviet Republic established only a year before. In that same year, members of these groups founded the Deutsche Arbeitspartei (the 'German Workers' Party'), which would be renamed the Nationalsozialistische Deutsche Arbeiterpartei (the 'National Socialist German Workers' Party') in 1920. The use of the swastika as the Nazi party symbol and subsequentially as that of the Third Reich may be traced back to Von Liebenfels' and Von List's influence in the Germanenorden and Thule Society.

As far as Hitler and Ariosophy are concerned, there is some evidence that seems to suggest that he read and collected an unspecified number of issues of the *Ostara* magazine, published by Lanz von Liebenfels during his Vienna period between 1908 and 1913 (Kershaw 1999, 49–51). Lanz von Liebenfels' idea of women as prone to copulate with impure men was mirrored in Hitler's concern that Jewish men were seducing and trafficking German girls. Hitler's love of Wagner's operas like *Parsifal* would connect to Lanz von Liebenfels' idea of medieval knightly orders committed to guard the Grail as a symbol for purity of blood, and to Lanz von Liebenfels' idea of a dualistic battle between the 'blonds' and the 'darks' for world domination is very comparable to Hitler's later racist ideology.

THE PRACTITIONERS: WILIGUT, HIMMLER, AND HITLER

The question now is, how did Ariosophy travel from a branch of Germanic Theosophy via a couple of—in all honesty—fringe figures like Von List, Von Liebenfels, and Sebottendorf to the ranks of the Nazi political elite, especially Heinrich Himmler and Adolf Hitler?

To start with the SS Reichsführer, Himmler came into contact with Ariosophy by means of his personal 'guru' and SS Brigadeführer, Karl Maria Wiligut (1866–1946), who had contacts with several members of the Order of the New Templars, founded in 1900 by Lanz von Liebenfels (Goodrick-Clarke 2005, 177–191; Kurlander 2017, 175–181). Wiligut claimed to have an extremely powerful form of clairvoyance and ancestral memory, with which he was able to recall his tribe's history back to the 7th century AD. New Templar and later Oberleutnant Richard Anders introduced the two men to one another (Goodrick-Clarke 2005, 183). Wiligut had considerable influence over Himmler: he designed the *SS Totenkopfring* and invented numerous "Aryan" ceremonies in the SS castle of Wewelsburg.

Now, Hitler's involvement with Ariosophy is more diffuse (Goodrick-Clarke 2005, 192–204; Kurlander 2017, 182–183). Himmler was almost certainly acquainted with Von Liebenfels' periodical *Ostara* in the period 1908–1913; the two even seem to have met in Vienna in 1909. The ideologies of both men seem compatible enough: the world is divided into Aryan *Übermenschen* with light skin and blond hair vis-à-vis the dark *Untermenschen* who threaten the racial purity and political world-domination of the former. In other parts, the *Über-* and *Untermensch*'s paths diverged: Von Liebenfels was hoping for a new united German-Austrian empire, while Hitler despised the Austrian dynasty, seeing what had happen to Vienna, which was a melting pot of nationalities, languages, and ethnicities; Von Liebenfels' language was full of Catholic symbolism, while Hitler had rejected Catholicism as an adult. Later, by order of the Gestapo, Von Liebenfels was even forbidden to publish and his organizations were dissolved. Hitler never mentioned Lanz von Liebenfels' name anywhere in a public speech, and only one of Von Liebenfels' books was found in Hitler's personal library, *Das Buch der Psalmen teutsch* from 1926. This book had nothing to do with Aryan ideology of any kind.

Scholars argue over the question whether the Thule Society was a historical group of any quantity and continuity or rather a fictional construction by some enthusiast Ariosophists around Rudolf von Sebottendorf, but it is historically clear that many people who associated themselves with the Thule Society's ideology were also contributing to the establishment of the D.A.P., continued in the N.S.D.A.P. (Kurlander 2017, 33–61).

To summarize (see Scheme #2), there are three lines to be distinguished. (1) From Blavatsky, through Von Liebenfels' *Ordo*, and Wiligut to Himmler. (2) From Blavatsky through Von Liebenfels' magazine *Ostara* to Hitler. And (3) from Blavatsky, through Von Sebottendorf and the Thule Society, to the D.A.P./N.S.D.A.P.

The citizens and regular soldiers of Nazi Germany in the thirties and forties of the 20th century were predominantly self-identifying Roman Catholics or Lutherans and were, at most, only moderately interested in occult matters, and even then, only in a cultural sense. However, in the upper echelons of the Nazi party and Hitler's intimate entourage, a considerable group of occultist believers and practitioners could be found, including famous figures

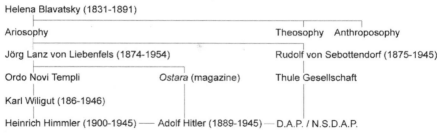

Figure 2.1. Historical lines between Theosophy, Ariosophy, and Nazism. *Bosman 2024.*

like Heinrich Himmler and Karl Wiligut. These Nazi occultists, for all their mutual differences in beliefs and practices, shared a common racist-esoteric interpretation of human history in general and of the place of the Germanic super-race within it. Many Nazi bigwigs, including Hitler and propaganda minister Joseph Goebbels (1879–1945), thought about Ariosophical notions and ideas not as a new religion for the New Germania—as Himmler probably did—but as an alternative 'civil religion' for the new Third Reich (Kurlander 2017, 74–75). Ariosophy could provide a new collective mythology or national narrative, providing an alternative for the traditional civil religion of the Christian tradition, which was—of course—far less suitable for such a purpose.

Chapter 3

Hitler's Deal with the Devil

Nazi Occultism

In *Raiders of the Lost Ark* (Spielberg 1981), the first part of the original trilogy with Harrison Ford playing the main character, Indiana Jones is tasked by two US intelligence employees to locate and secure an ancient artifact before the Nazis do so first, harnessing its power for Hitler's regime (Morris 2007, 73–83; Barrowclough 2016; McGowan 2020). The film takes place in 1936, the period in which the Nazi party and Hitler were well established as the unrivalled leaders of the German *Reich*. The artifact Jones and the Nazis are competing to find is the Ark of the Covenant, the long-lost, gold-covered, wooden chest believed (in both Judaism and Christianity) to contain the two stone tablets of the Ten Commandments given to Moses by God on Mount Sinai, as described in the book of Exodus. The Ark played an important religious-strategical role in the stories connected to the conquest of the Promised Land by the Chosen People, especially in the book of Joshua: its presence at the vanguard of the invading army is said to have provided multiple decisive victories for the Israelites.

The Ark itself disappears from (biblical) history when the Babylonians destroyed Jerusalem, including Solomon's Temple, the cultic dwelling place of the Ark. The 2nd book of Chronicles mentions "some articles" that King Nebuchadnezzar took with him to Babel, but it is unclear if the Ark is included or not (36:7). The (deuterocanonical) 2nd book of Maccabees, however, suggests that the prophet Jeremiah had taken the Ark before the Babylonian invasion and had hidden it in an unidentified cave, which later no one was able to find again (2:7–6). Yet others suggest that the Roman general and later emperor Titus took the Ark with him after the sacking of Jerusalem in the year 70. His triumphal arch, still to be found near the *Forum Romanum* on the Via Sacra in Rome, depicts—among other things associated with the Temple in Jerusalem—a seven-armed menorah, suggesting the possibility that the Ark was also part of the *spolia* (already suggested by Lübke in 1878 [296]; see also Fine 2016, 1–41).

In *Raiders of the Lost Ark*, the Ark is located in Egypt, probably following yet another cryptic reference to the Ark's disappearance (Falk 2020; Barrowclough 2016). The same 2nd book of Chronicles that seems to suggest a Babylonian fate for the Ark, also describes another sacking of Jerusalem in the tenth century B.C.E. by Egyptian pharaoh Shishak, usually identified with the historical Shoshenq I (Sagrillo 2015), who ruled from 943 to 922 B.C.E.:

> So Shishak king of Egypt went up against Jerusalem, and he took the treasures of the house of the LORD and the treasures of the king's palace. He took everything; he even took the gold shields which Solomon had made. (2 Chronicles 12:9 – NASB20)

Again no explicit mention of the Ark, but it is not hard to understand the interpretation that it was also brought to Egypt by Shishak/Shoshenq. Jones locates the Ark with the help of a gold medallion—obtained from Marion, the daughter of his old mentor Abner Ravenwood—which happens to be a part of the "staff of Ra," another object frequently appearing in popular culture in connection to the magical or the occult. Unfortunately, the Ark is stolen from Jones by the Gestapo officer SS-Sturmbannführer Arnold Ernst Toht (his surname is probably a word-play on the German word *Tot*, "death").

After being transported to a remote island in the Aegean Sea by a German submarine, Marion and Jones involuntarily witness the "activation" of the artifact by the opening of it. Before the actual opening, Toht's associate, French Archaeologist René Emile Belloq, is seen dressed in a pseudo-Jewish garment, probably derived from the priestly vestments used in the Temple in Jerusalem, and praying in a sort of pseudo-Hebrew language. After the Ark has been opened, Belloq is very disappointed to find only sandy dust inside. But soon afterward, unseen powers are unleashed from the Ark, killing Toht, Belloq, and all the other Nazis present by means of electric shocks and an all-consuming fire.

In the Hebrew Bible, fire is associated with God's presence, for example in the case of Moses and the Burning Bush (Exodus 3:1–4) and the columns of fire and smoke going before the Israelites and guarding them against pharaoh's army (Exodus 13:21–22). The electric shocks are probably a reference to a scene from the 2nd book of Samuel, in which a certain Uzzah tries to touch the Ark while it is being brought to Jerusalem by David from its exile in Kirjat Jearim, only to be instantaneously be struck down by God, killing him on the spot (6:7). Only Jones and Marion survive the fiery onslaught, because—at the suggestion of Jones—they both keep their eyes shut, a reference to the praxis of closing one's eyes when communing with God. Jones delivers the Ark to the American authorities, who stash it away in a gigantic warehouse, apparently without any interest in it whatsoever.

In another film, *Indiana Jones and the Last Crusade* (Spielberg 1989), Jones is chasing after yet another famous religious artifact, the holy Grail. Unburdened by the later dominance of the Grail being interpreted as a symbol for the bloodline of Jesus and Mary Magdalene—as popularized by Dan Brown's novel *The Da Vinci Code* (2003) and its massively popular film adaption in 2006 (Ron Howard) with Tom Hanks in the main role—Jones' Grail is still a material object, associated with Wagner's opera *Parcifal* (1882)—from his opera-cycle *Der Ring der Nibelungen*, one of Hitler's favorites (Kurlander 2017, 4)—and Wolfram von Essenbach's and Chrétien de Troyes' famous medieval novels. The Grail is supposed to be one of two things or a combination of the two: (1) the cup which Jesus used during the Last Supper, urging his disciples to "drink his blood" (Mathew 26:26–28; Mark 14:22–24; Luke 22:15–20), and (2) the vessel which Joseph of Arimathea used to collect the blood of Jesus, pouring from his side on the cross, after he was pierced by an unnamed Roman soldier (John 19:34).

Just like in *Raiders*, the film *Last Crusade*, set in 1938, portrays a race between the forces of good, spear-headed by Indiana Jones—together with his father, played by Sean Connery—and the forces of evil, again the Nazis. Forced by Walter Donovan, an American businessman and scholar working for the SS, who severely wounds Jones Senior, our hero has to overcome three challenges posed to those who want to retrieve the Grail from its resting place in the Canyon of the Crescent Moon in present-day Turkey. After two initial tests, including a Hebrew word-puzzle about the Tetragrammaton and a literal leap of faith (a notion commonly attributed to the Danish theologian Søren Kierkegaard), Jones and Donovan must choose the chalice used by Jesus from a large collection of chalices. Donovan chooses a richly-decorated one, while Jones sticks to a simple, wooden one.

A Grail Knight, clearly based on the historical Templar Order and having mysteriously survived centuries to guard the true Grail, explains that Jones chose "wisely": Jesus was, after all, a simple carpenter's son. Donovan ages instantaneously into a skeleton, which then falls apart into dust. The Grail itself is lost because of the greed of Elsa Schneider, another Nazi scholar, who cannot resist taking the object for herself. Both Schneider and the Grail fall into a bottomless pit. Once all the others are safe and sound, Jones asks his father what he has discovered in all of this. "Illumination," Jones Senior answers, referring implicitly to the realm of esoterism, associated both with historical Nazi occultism and contemporary new-age spirituality.

The Ark of the Covenant and the holy Grail, together with the holy Lance (or Spear), as popularized by Trevor Ravenscroft's *The Spear of Destiny* (1972) and shortly featured in the latest *Indiana Jones* film (*The Dial of*

Destiny, 2023), identifying Hitler as the possessor of the legendary spear of Longinus who pierced Jesus' side on the cross (John 19:34; see above), are a kind of "holy trio" of occult artifacts the Nazis are said to have hunted for. In popular and often semi-scholarly books, the Ark, the Grail, and the Lance play an important role in the description of the inner dealings of the Nazi occultic circles (Yenne 2010, Hite 2013, FitzGerald 2013, Kirkpatrick 2010, Fitzgerald 2021).

However, no historical evidence has been produced to support the idea that Hitler, Himmler, or any other leading Nazi official ever tried to actually find these relics or issued any expeditions to claim them, let alone, found them. The same applies to the Ahnenerbe, the group of German scholars, who—under SS management—occupied themselves with (often pseudo-) scientific research into Germanic archaeology and history (Pringle 2006). Yes, Hitler was very fond of the operas *Lohengrin* (1850) and *Parsifal* (1882), respectively featuring the spear of destiny and the holy Grail, whose composer, Wagner, he "idolized as the greatest interpreter of the Germanic folk-spirit" (Goodrick-Clarke 2002, 119), but the Führer was definitely not "obsessed" with the occult as Ravenscroft suggests in his *Spear of Destiny*.

Yes, Hitler did read issues of *Ostara*, the periodical of Germanic occultist Lanz von Liebenfels, when he lived in Vienna (Goodridge-Clarke 2005, 198), but he denounced "*völkisch* wandering scholars" and occultists in his *Mein Kampf* whom he deemed unreliable and inefficient partners in his dream of awaking Germania (idem, 202). And even though Himmler was definitely much involved with occult matters, the only actual connection of any of the three holy relics with the SS-Reichsführer is the dedication of a study-room to the holy Grail in his castle in Wewelsburg, besides other rooms dedicated to Widukind, Henry the Fowler, Henry the Lion, and King Arthur (Goodrick-Clarke 2002, 125).

The connection between the Nazis and "the holy trio" seems to be exclusively post-World War II, and is usually made in pseudo-historical works of fiction. The Grail features, for example, prominently in Louis Pauwels and Jacques Bergier's *Le matin des magiciens* ("The morning of the magicians," 1960), who argue that no other than the famous SS-Obersturmbannführer Otto Skorzeny (1908–1975) had plans to steal the Grail. Marc Augier, under the pseudonym of Saint-Loup, wrote a book, *Nouveaux cathares pour Montségur* ("New Cathars for Montségur," 1969), claiming that SS-cultist Otto Rahn (1904–1939) searched for the Grail in the ruins of the French Château de Montségur, the last bastion of the Cathars, before they were massacred in 1244 during the Albigensian Crusade (Goodrick-Clarke 2002, 122).

The same connection between the Grail and the Cathars was also made by Michel Bertrand and Jean Angelini, under their joined pseudonym

Jean-Michel Angebert, in *Hitler et la tradition cathare* ("Hitler and the cathar tradition," 1971), which was quickly translated into English under the title *The Occult and the Third Reich* (1971). The Rahn-Skorzeny connection was recycled time and time again, and traces of it can still be found in, for example, Howard Buechner's book *Emerald Cup. Ark of Gold* (1991). Another Nazi Grail-trail was coined by Swiss engineer Erich Halik (1920–1985), who in his articles for the periodical *Mensch und Schiksal* ("Human and Destiny"), published between 1951 and 1955, identified UFOs being manifestations of the Grail and calling these "a cultic vessel used by the supreme hierarchy of Christian Gnostics" (Goodrick-Clarke 2002, 131).

The Lance turns up, also exclusively post-World War II, in the stories of Ravenscroft (which I will discuss in detail later in this monograph) and—again—in Buechner's work, who has written two books on the Lance's mythology. In *Adolf Hitler and the secrets of the holy Lance* (1988) and *Hitler's ashes. Seeds of a new Reich* (1989), Buechner claims that Hitler's ashes—after his suicide and the burning of his remains in 1945—were transported together with the holy Lance to a secret Nazi facility in Antarctica (Goodrick-Clarke 2002, 121). Russell McCloud's book *Die schwarze Sonne von Tashi Lhunpo* ("The black sun of Tashi Lhunpo," 1991) follows the same line.

Now, the Ark of the Covenant is very much absent in most of the post-War Nazi mythologies written by those who cannot resist connecting the seemingly interrelated dots between Nazism and occultism. However, the post-War period also has its defenders of the Nazi doctrine and its occult associations. A "prime" example of the latter is Wilhelm Landig (1909–1997), a former SS member, who found refuge in Vienna after the war. The group he formed around him and his Germanic mythology included the fascist philosopher and mystic Julius Evola (1898–1974), author of *Erhebung wider die moderne Welt* ("Revolt against the Modern World," 1935); the aforementioned Swiss engineer and occultist Erich Halik; and the two former Ahnenerbe members Herman Wirth (1885–1981), author of *Der Aufgang der Menschheit* ("The emergence of humanity," 1928) and *Die Heilige Urschrift der Menschheit* ("The holy primordial writing of humanity," 1931–1936); and Edmund Kiss, writer of *Das gläserne Meer* ("The sea of glass," 1930), *Die letzte Königin von Atlantis* ("The last queen of Atlantis," 1931), and *Frühling in Atlantis* ("Spring in Atlantis," 1933).

In his trilogy *Götzen gegen Thule* ("Gods against Thule," 1971), *Wolfzeit um Thule* ("The time of the wolves around Thule," 1980), and *Rebellen für Thule* ("Rebels for Thule," 1991), Landig describes the adventures of a small group of SS soldiers who try to uphold the ideas of Nazi ideology after their defeat in 1945. Unknown to both the Allied Forces and (most of) the German

High Command, two airmen, Recke ("berserker") and Reimer ("bard," literally "rhymer"), are sent to Point 103, a hypothetical Nazi stronghold in Arctic Canada. They are guided by an enigmatic SS officer with the name of Gutmann, meaning "good man," a reference to the *perfecti* of Catharism, who initiates the two into Thulean philosophy.

According to this Goodman, the Third Reich was ultimately defeated by their worst enemies, the Jews, who founded their own independent state in 1948. Now things very rapidly get complicated and utterly bizarre. According to Gutmann, who speaks with the voice of Landig himself, the Semites and the Thuleans originated in ancient times when the black magicians of Jewish origin ruled over the Aryan Atlanteans. Later on, these Semites would choose their god Baal over the Atlantean god Poseidon and then position their own Mount Sinai as a rip-off version of the Midnight Mount in the Arctic.

At a meeting with a rabbi in Toledo, Spain, Gutmann explains the conflict between Aryans and Jews as a universal battle between the forces of light against those of darkness. In this black Jewish conspiracy, the Ark of the Covenant plays an important role as an accumulator for magical energy and is located in a black center at Mount Sinai. Freemasons are somehow connected to all of this, including American president Roosevelt and UK prime minister Churchill, not incidentally the two statemen whose armies led the Allied Forces into victory over the Third Reich.

The popular idea that occultism had a decisive influence on Nazism in general and not only on Nazi leaders, and that a considerable portion of the general German population were devout occultists, is a cultural construct created *after* the end of the Second World War. This idea was equally formed by those who remained sympathetic to Nazi ideology, even after its definite political and military defeat in 1945, and by those who tried to find some rhyme and reason behind the terrible atrocities committed by the Nazis—including genocide, the system of death camps, diabolical medical experiments, and violent imperialism—as these crimes became common knowledge after the Nuremberg Trials of 1946, and were thereafter corroborated by decades of extensive scholarly and journalistic research, and by publications.

Both sides agree that Hitler must have had access to mystical, esoteric powers; his sudden rise to power seems to defy any other reasonable explanation. The two sides obviously differ in their moral judgment of these powers: most authors deem Hitler's alleged esoteric knowledge and powers as demonic, while a minority of authors revere the memory of the once great Reich that was brought to its knees by a union of Jews, communists, and other *Untermenschen*.

Chapter 4

The Kabbala
Jewish Mysticism

The word "Kabbala" means "reception" or "tradition," in the sense of what has been received through historical tradition into the present. Most kabbalists hold that the knowledge, wisdom, and practice of "Kabbala" were *not* created within human history, but have been present since the creation of the universe, may it be in a hidden form that is to be penetrated in order to understand their full meaning and potential. "Kabbala" is discovered, not written, conjured up, or created. I will discuss this idea further below when discussing the theme of the pre-existent Torah.

Frequently, "Kabbala" (and its numerous different spellings) is equated with "Jewish mysticism." In this monograph, I too use both notions interchangeably. However, I must address some conceptual difficulties surrounding this identification of Kabbala as Jewish mysticism. "Mysticism" is, to begin with, in and of itself a complex notion to define (Kourie 2015). Many definitions have been proposed, sometimes from a specifically institutionalized religious context, sometimes from a more interreligious perspective. Carmody and Carmody (1996, 10–11), for example, define mysticism as "a direct experience of ultimate reality," while Perrin (2005, 443), more poetically perhaps, talks about a "canvas upon which the soul paints in the wilderness of the heart its passionate return to Source." McGinn (2008, 47) thinks of mysticism more as transformation than as an object of knowledge: "the co-presence of God in our inner acts, not as an object to be understood or grasped, but as the transforming Other." The well-known Dutch scholar of spirituality, Waaijman (2002, 357), suggests that mysticism is "a relational process between God and man, a process which has its own language and logic."

Jewish mysticism fits these definitions quite nicely, with one important caveat: the absence of a *unio mystica*, as present in the Christian (Roman Catholic) tradition, at least in the opinion of most (but not all) scholars of kabbalist history (Laenen 2001, 121). Where Christian mysticism deals with the process of God and human becoming one, at least in the experience of the latter, Kabbala honors the fundamentally (ontologically) unbridgeable gap between God and his creation. The nearest "equivalent" notion in the kabbalist tradition is *devequth*, meaning "cleaving (to God)." *Devequth* is attained, as described by many kabbalist groups like the Ashkenazi Hasidim and the Lurianic mystics, by meditative prayer which frequently involves the manipulation of words, names, and sentences from traditional prayers.

Kabbala is also a part of the larger tradition of hermetic esotericism in the West. As I have defined earlier (see chapter 2), based on Hanegraaff (2006a), esotericism is a container notion incorporating a vast amount of historical and contemporary beliefs and practices that (1) deviated or deviates from dominant or "orthodox" religious beliefs in the Western world and (2) focusses on individual spiritual enlightenment, (3) often by initiation into otherwise secret knowledge. Kabbalist thinking frequently fits within these parameters. Both historical orthodox Judaism and those influenced by the *Haskalah*, the Jewish Enlightenment in the eighteenth century, are frequently wary of, or even hostile to kabbalist ideas, disqualifying them as heresy or blasphemy on the one hand, and as magic or superstition on the other.

The kabbalist focus is, indeed, generally on attaining spiritual enlightenment: from the Merkavah mystics of the first millennium of the common era, who penetrated the seven heavenly palaces (*hekhaloth*) for a vision of the divine throne, through the *Zohar* and its fascination with the ten sephirot, to the eighteenth century Eastern European Hasidim, who desired to restore the divine harmony by a strict observance of the *halakhah* in combination with mystical prayers. The points of secrecy and initiation are, however, somewhat more complicated in the kabbalist domain. Yes, kabbalists obviously thought, wrote, and spoke about their doctrines as "secret" in the sense of "hidden," and as "mystery" in the sense of belonging to a divine-transcendent reality. And yes, it takes some real effort to penetrate the often heavily symbolic kabbalist texts. And yes, it often requires the help of someone already familiar with the Kabbala to help the "uninitiated," but this more resembles a classical education than the magical or ritualistic one that we commonly associate with other esoteric groups. The theme of secrecy itself is ambiguous within kabbalist history: some groups were very secretive of their knowledge, not infrequently because of the social consequences of being outed as a kabbalist, while others were very open and vocal.

Christian authors have taken a keen interest in Kabbala since Giovanni Pico della Mirandola (1463–1494), Johann Reuclin (1455–1522), and Cornelius Agrippa of Nettesheim (1487–1535) started to be interested in the phenomenon. Later, Kabbala—or better, a specific appropriation of kabbalist lore—was used and discussed by "esoteric" writers, like Eliphas Lévi (Alphonse-Louise Constant, 1810–1875), Dr. Papus (Gérard Encausse,

1868–1916), the founders of the secret society "The Order of the Golden Dawn" (in 1888), S. L. MacGregor Mathers and William Wynn Westcott, and Edward Alexander Crowley (1875–1947), who joined the same order in 1898. It does not require much argumentation to posit that these writers constructed their own version of what Kabbala is supposed to be. Nevertheless, Kabbala is ultimately grounded in Judaism, as Laenen (2001, 15–16) summarizes:

> Jewish mysticism lies anchored in Judaism, in which a living God manifests himself in the whole creation, in his revelation to the people of Israel on Sinai, and in the Torah. Hebrew (. . .) God's sacred language (. . .) formed the key to the deepest secrets of the Creator and creation.

Kabbala is both a form of Jewish mysticism *and* a part of the hermetic esoteric tradition of the Western world. And even though it may have been appropriated by Christian authors, Kabbala remains a Jewish phenomenon in and of itself.

HISTORY AND KEY CONCEPTS

The history of the Kabbala is vast and complex; even its origins are shrouded in uncertainties. According to most scholars (among others Laenen 2001, Dan 2006, Scholem 2007, and Weiss 2013), Kabbala in the strict sense was preceded by what is known as "Merkavah mysticism." Ranging from the second to the tenth century, closed rabbinic circles started to contemplate the *merkavah* ("chariot") from Ezekiel 1, interpreting it as God's divine throne. These rabbis, a minority within mainstream Judaism of that time, tried to penetrate God's mystery through a spiritual journey: the mystic was to ascend (or descend, both metaphors are used) to the seven heavens and pass through the seven *hekhaloth* ("palaces," hence the term Hekhaloth literature): seven palaces for each of the seven heavens. The doors of these palaces are guarded by angels, who can only be persuaded to let the mystic through by means of magical amulets engraved with magical spells or with secret passwords, both frequently being (variations of) the names of God. Any mystic who reached the end of his soul's journey would be allowed to stand before God's throne and (often still somehow veiled) see God's glory.

The texts belonging to Hekhaloth literature are exclusively pseudo-epigraphical—the names of their authors forever lost in the mist of time—and include famous tractates like *Ma'aseh Merkavah* ("The works of the throne-chariot"), *Re'uyoth Yehezq'el* ("The vision of Ezekiel"), the *Ma'aseh Bereshith* ("The works of in-the-beginning"), and the most famous of them all, the *Sefer Yetzirah* ("The book of creation"). The *Sefer Yetzirah* is one of the core works of kabbalist lore, even though it was only identified as such later in history, when self-identifying kabbalists—both Jewish and Christian—started to write commentaries. The book describes God's original creation (cf. Genesis 1) through the idea of 32 wondrous paths of wisdom that form the basic structure of reality: the 22 letters of the Hebrew alphabet plus the 10 *sephirot*, the 10 primordial numbers. (The notion of *sephirot* would greatly change its meaning over the course of history; see below.) These 22 letters and 10 numbers are associated with several parts of the human body, with the notions of beginning/ending, good/evil, up/down, and the 4 winds; but also with the elements, the 7 planets, the 7 days of the week, the 12 months of the year, and the 12 signs of the zodiac.

The second period in the history of Kabbala is called the "classical period" and stretches from the twelfth/thirteenth until the fifteenth century. Kabbalist centers emerged in the German Rhineland (the Ashkenazi Hasidim), Provence in the south of France, and on the Iberian Peninsula. This period produced two of the most well-known books of the kabbalist tradition, the *Sefer ha-Bahir* ("The book of radiant light," cf. Job 37:21) from the middle of the twelfth century, and the *Sefer Zohar* ("The book of splendor") written by Moses de Leon at the end of the thirteenth century. The first introduces the concept of the *etz hayyim*, "the Tree of Life," as a metaphor for the ten sephirot, changing them from primordial numbers to *ma'amaroth*, utterances with which God created the world (cf. Mishnah Avoth 5:1). The *Zohar* also reworks the doctrine of the sephirot from the *Sefer Yetzirah*, but in a different way than the anonymous author of the *Bahir* did.

The ten sephirot, in the version of the *Zohar*, are presented as ten emanations (*atsiluth*), aspects, attributes or qualities of the hidden, unknowable God (called *en sof* or "without end"). The sephirot bridge the gap between the tangible, contingent, immanent world of humankind on the one hand and God's absolute transcendence on the other. Everything that exists does so because one or more of the associated sephirot are involved.

- The first ("higher") three are: *keter* ("crown") or *ayin* ("nothingness"), *hokhmah* ("wisdom"), and *binah* ("intelligence"). The last two are associated with God's ideas, archetypes or blueprints of creation.
- The second three are: *hesed* ("love" or "mercy") or *gedullah* ("greatness"), *din* ("judgment") or *gevurah* ("power"), and *tif'ereth* ("beauty"). The first represents God's love, the second God's rightful judgment, while the third guarantees the equilibrium between these two.
- The last ("lower") three are: *netsah* ("endurance"), *hod* ("majesty"), and *yesod* ("foundation"), lower manifestations of the second set of three.

- The final one is: *malkhuth* ("kingdom"): the "collection" of the other emanations and the completion of God's self-revelation in the sephirot.

The third period in kabbalist history is that of Isaac Luria (1534–72), a disciple of Moses ben Jacob Cordovero. His teachings were recorded exclusively by his pupils, like Hayyim Vital, Joseph ibn Tabul, and Israel Sarug. Luria introduced three new key concepts to kabbalist teaching: *tsimtsum* ("contraction"), *shevirath ha-kelim* ("breaking of the vessels"), and *tiqqun* ("restoration"). Luria's divine cosmology proposed a "contracting" or withdrawal of God (as *en sof*) from himself, gracefully allowing space for the universe to come into existence in the void (*tehiru*, "pure emptiness"). God shot a beam of divine light into the void, giving birth to the ten sephirot in the form of the *adam qadmon*, the "primordial human." (Already in Merkavah mysticism and in the *Zohar*, the idea of associating human body forms and functions with the sephirot was formulated.)

However, the sephirah *din*, associated in Lurian Kabbala with the concept of evil, broke free of the divine harmony, causing the divine light to "burst out" of the "vessels" of the lower seven sephirot. Both the shards of the broken vessels and the light particles fell downward, became entangled, and formed an evil realm of their own. To counter this disaster and to achieve cosmic restoration, God created a second set of ten sephirot, now called *patsufim* ("countenances"). Because of Adam—a cosmic figure in Lurian Kabbala—and his sin in the Garden of Eden, all human souls are imprisoned in a mortal form (the body), resulting in human beings as a "mixed bag" of both good and evil. Humans are tasked to release the divine sparks from their imprisonment through good deeds, the study of the Torah, keeping God's commandments, and prayer.

Lurian Kabbala developed in the period after the dramatic expulsion of the Jews from the Iberian Peninsula in 1492, resulting in a strong emphasis on messianism and exile. The forced exile of the Jewish people, both in the Hebrew Bible and in several periods in Jewish history after the destruction of the Second Temple, is mirrored in God's self-chosen exile from himself. This resulted in the idea that, even though all people have the same obligation of freeing the divine sparks from their imprisonment in matter, the Jewish people has a special responsibility in the redemption of the whole world. The messianic impulse in kabbalist history reached an all-time high in the person and teachings of Shabbetai Zevi (1626–1676), who gained notoriety in the Ottoman Empire—both under Jews and Muslims—due to his erratic behavior: he uttered the Tetragrammaton often and in public, and argued to his followers that the "exoteric" commandments of the Torah were no longer applicable since with him the messianic era had arrived. To everyone's surprise, Zevi converted to Islam in 1666 to prevent his execution by the Ottomans: many of his followers did the same, since they thought that their messiah's conversion was actually a voluntary descent into the world of darkness to liberate it.

The last historical development I will discuss here, is the emergence of the Hasidim in the eighteenth century (not to be confused with the earlier Ashkenazi ones, mentioned above). The historical Hasidim ("pious ones") and their charismatic leaders, known as *tsaddik* ("righteous") or *rebbe*, have been made famous in our times by authors like Martin Buber, Isaac Bashevis Singer, and Chaim Potok, contributing to the popular interpretation of the Hasidim as devout, singing, dancing, and story-telling orthodox Jews from Eastern Europe, including Poland (not incidentally Blazkowicz' heritage, see below). The Hasidim—like their predecessors in the history of Kabbala—practiced *devequth*, a prayer practice involving the manipulation of language—letters, words, names—in combination with either silence and motionlessness or vigorously and rhythmically moving their body.

Chapter 5

Shooting Nazi Zombies

An Overview of the Series

The *Wolfenstein* series consists of multiple instalments ranging from 1981 until the present day. Below is a concise summary of the games and the narrative they provide, circling around the American super-soldier William Joseph "B.J." Blakowicz. The series contains a couple of reboots, which I will refer to as "cycles" (all conveniently published in a separate decade). Locations, characters, and objects can feature in more than one cycle, meaning that keeping track of all the different iterations becomes a challenge in itself. The continuity of the series is under serious pressure. I, therefore, distinguish between:

- Cycle #1 – 1980s: the Muse games *Castle Wolfenstein* (1981) and *Beyond Castle Wolfenstein* (1984).
- Cycle #2 – 1990s: the id Software games *Wolfenstein 3D* (1992) and its sequel *The Spear of Destiny* (1992).
- Cycle #3 – 2000s: Grey Matter's *Return to Castle Wolfenstein* (2001) and its "sequel" *Wolfenstein* (2009) developed by Raven Software.
- Cycle #4 – 2010s: the MachineGames' series comprised of *Wolfenstein; The New Order* (2014), its prequel *Wolfenstein: The Old Blood* (2015), and *Wolfenstein: The New Colossus* (2017), including its spin-offs *Wolfenstein: Youngblood* (2015) and *Wolfenstein: Cyberpilot* (2015).

In my further discussion, I will often use abbreviations for the games' titles. *Wolfenstein: Enemy Territory* (developed by Splash Damage and published by Activision in 2003) is excluded from all of the cycles, since its exclusive multiplayer setting makes it hard to extract any narrative development from it. id Software's mobile game *Wolfenstein RPG* (developed by id Software and published by EA Mobile in 2008) is also excluded in this overview since it is—essentially—a strange mixture of narrative elements presented already in W3D, SoD, and RtCW. It does not add anything to the canon.

Calling *Wolfenstein* (2009) a "sequel" to *Return to Castle Wolfenstein* and putting them together in the third cycle is a choice one could disagree with. *Wolfenstein* could be considered a very loose continuation of its predecessor or a reboot/cycle of and on its own. For convenience's sake, I have chosen for the first option, even though the game appears to have some allohistorical narrative elements (set in 1945) that are more reminiscent of its successors, the games of the fourth cycle, than of RtCW.

MachineGames, the developers of the fourth cycle, tried to address the continuity question in a rather playful manner. In WNO, there is a mattress hidden in the attic of the Kreisau base in Berlin. After deciding to sleep on the mattress, the player is able to play the first level of the first episode of W3D. The experience is dubbed "Nightmare!," a reference to both the most difficult settings in the *Wolfenstein* series, and to the experience of Blazkowicz, who comments after awakening: "Dreaming. Strange dreams. The killing never stops. 'til I die."

Because in narrative settings, keeping dream from reality tends to be a very tricky thing to do in the first place, MachineGames seems to suggest that the previous cycles 1 through 3 are bad dreams, at least from the perspective of the reality of the fourth cycle. The other way around is—of course—also possible, making the fourth series the nightmare. This is a somewhat pleasing concept, since MachineGames' reboot series features an allohistorical narrative in which the Nazis have won the Second World War in 1946; indeed, a nightmare.

This feature is also present in the other instalments of the fourth cycle. In WOB, there are nine mattresses to be found in various locations. When sleeping on one of them, the player can play W3D, but now all the levels of the first episode are available, instead of only the first one. In WNC, an arcade machine can be found in the stolen German submarine *Eva's Hammer*. Apparently, German soldiers from an alternative timeline like to play video games just as much as we do.

The arcade machine provides the perfectly playable game *Wolfstone 3D*, a Germanized version of W3D with "Elite Hans" instead of Blazkowicz as protagonist. And in WYB, in the catacombs of Nazi-occupied Paris, the player can find *Elite Hans 2. Die Neue Ordnung*, a clear pastiche of WNO, featuring six new episodes, including bosses like Blazkowicz himself. These *Wolfstone* games are self-referential (the German title of the English localized series having been translated into proper English), and suggest a more practical and simpler "solution" to the continuity problem: they are "just" games, so loosen up.

In *Wolfenstein: Youngblood*, MachineGames suggests another, more serious "answer" to the continuity problem, dealing with cycle #4's alternative timeline at the same time. Blazkowicz learns about the existence of multiple alternative realities, including one in which the Nazis lost the war in 1945 (that is, "our" timeline). This multiverse-reality explains the existence of multiple versions of B.J.'s adventures very nicely.

In the next two chapters, I will discuss in further detail all esoteric elements found in the series' instalments.

CYCLE #1: THE EARLY YEARS OF A MODERN FRANCHISE (1980s)

The *Wolfenstein* series starts in 1981 with *Castle Wolfenstein*, developed and published by the American company Muse Software for the Apple II personal computer. The game was later ported to the Atari 8 (1982), the Commodore 64 (1983) and MS-DOS (1984). *Castle Wolfenstein* was inspired by the arcade game *Berzerk* (1980) and the famous World War II film *The Guns of Navarone* from 1961 (Bleich, Plass-Flessenkämper, and Schmid 2022). It follows the adventures of an unnamed Allied prisoner of war, captured by the Nazis and brought to Castle Wolfenstein for interrogation under threat of torture. The gamer is tasked to navigate the American private through the screen-by-screen mazes of the digital castle, preferably by sneaking past the guards or impersonating them without setting off any alarm. The Castle, and hence the whole series, is probably derived from the historical Wewelsburg near Paderborn in Westphalia, Germany, bought by Himmler in 1934 to be turned into a central SS cultic hub (Hayton 2015, 252).

The goal of the game is to escape imprisonment and find the war plans for Operation Rheingold, which are hidden somewhere in the castle. Operation Rheingold is a reference to Wagner's drama *Das Rheingold* (1869), the first part of his famous *Ring der Nibelungen* (1876), as Hitler was a great fan of the German composer (Kurlander 2017, 4), and to a military operation of the same name to mobilize German reserves for the eastern front (Hoffmann 1997, 198) during the winter of 1941. The game already features a staple of the series, the incorporation of German commands like *Halt!* ("stop!"), *Kommen Sie!* ("come here!") or—spoken at the end of the game by its own American hero—*Auf wiedersehen, Schweinhund!* ("Goodbye pig-dog!").

Three years later, in 1984, Muse released a sequel, called *Beyond Castle Wolfenstein*, with similar graphics and gameplay elements, but also with new features like the use of a (silent) knife, the possibility to bribe guards, and the introduction of a pass, a legal document giving the bearer particular rights, for example permission to be in restricted areas. It was released for the Apple II and the Commodore 64 simultaneously, and an Atari 8 and MS-DOS port soon followed. This time, the—still unnamed—American soldier is tasked to enter and reconnoiter the secret *Führerbunker* in Berlin (Lehrer 2006) in order to find a bomb case, stashed away somewhere in the complex by German resistance members, to bring it to right outside the room where Hitler and his staff are having a meeting, and to escape without being caught. The plot clearly resembles that of the well-known and very real assassination-attempt on Hitler's life on July 20, 1944 by Claus von Stauffenberg and his conspirators (Fest 1997). The failed attempt would inspire multiple retellings, including the German-Austrian film *Stauffenberg* (2004) and *Valkyrie* (2008) with Tom Cruise in the leading role.

Even if the games were well received, their most important legacy, both in terms of the history of video games and in terms of the appropriation of Nazism, is the fact that they paved the way for *Wolfenstein 3D*, the proper start of the series *and* one of the most iconic games of all time.

CYCLE #2: WOLFENSTEIN 3D AND THE SPEAR OF DESTINY (1990s)

The impact and the influence of the game *Wolfenstein 3D*, developed by id Software and published by Apogee Software, can hardly be overstated. Since its initial release for MS-DOS in 1992, it has been ported to more than a dozen other systems including SNES (1994), Game Boy Advance (2002), Xbox 360 (2009), and PlayStation 3 (2009). It was not the first game using a first-person perspective, but it was the first to show the player's gun at the bottom of the screen as gunning down hordes of enemies, now a standard aspect of every first-person shooter on the market (Scullion 2020, 240). *W3D* was "one of the most immersive, bloody, historically controversial, sharable, and memorable video games of its generation and generations to follow" (Meija, Banks, and Adams 2017, 206); "the godfather of Nazi zombie games, Wolfenstein 3D" (Fuchs 2012, 279); and meant "the birth of the modern age of video games" (Lowood 2006). As Halter (2006, 156) commented on the paradoxical nature of the game: "there is something both creepy and funny about seeing the perpetrators of the Holocaust reduced to icons of near-cuteness."

The fact that id Software released the first episode as shareware—free to distribute—also contributed greatly to its popularity and prominence (Kurtz 2002, 112). In the same year, FormGen released another game by id Software, *The Spear of Destiny*, a prequel to W3D. W3D and SoD are the first games to give the previously unnamed American private-cum-spy his iconic name, which he will stick to during the rest of the series: William Joseph "B.J." Blazkowicz.

For chronological reasons, I will start with *The Spear of Destiny*. SoD is the most explicitly occult of the two, focusing on Hilter's supposed desire to master occult powers, in this case the titular Lance of Destiny, as described in Ravenscroft's novel from 1972. Sent off to Castle Nuremberg (a real city in Bavaria, Germany, featuring three different castles), B.J. encounters, besides regular Nazi soldiers and SS officers, also his first Nazi mutants, the creations of "crazy scientist" Dr. Schabbs. After killing Nazi-enforcer Hans Grösse, an *Übermutant*, the castle's jailor Barnacle Wilhelm, and a machine-human hybrid called the *Todesritter* ("Death Knight"), Blazkowicz grabs the Spear, only to be sucked down into Hell, where the Angel of Death—a red demon—challenges our hero to prove his worth to wield the Spear's power.

Back to W3D, which features six episodes—all consisting of eight regular levels, one level featuring a boss fight, and one secret level. The second set of three episodes, collectively known as the "Nocturnal Missions," are chronologically prior to the first set of three. In this overview of the *Wolfenstein* series, I will follow, again, the internal chronological sequence. In the three Nocturnal Missions (episodes four through six), B.J. has to end the Nazis' plans to develop chemical weaponry (called *Giftkrieg* or "poison war") by killing a leading Nazi scientist Otto Giftmacher ("poison-maker"), a heavy Nazi-enforcer by the name of Gretel Grösse (the sister of Trans, whom BJ killed in SoD), located in the fortress of Erlangen (a historical building in Bavaria), and finally General Fettgesicht ("Fat Face"), hiding in Castle Heidenheim or Offenbach (both real cities in Germany).

In the first three episodes of W3D, Blazkowicz has to escape Castle Wolfenstein (again), where he is being held as a prisoner, a theme already explored in CW earlier. After killing yet another Nazi-enforcer, Hans Grösse (brother of Trans and Gretel), he successfully escapes. Afterwards, B.J. directs his attention to Operation Eisenfaust, Dr. Schabbs' efforts to create an army of Nazi mutants/super soldiers. After Schabbs' death, B.J. confronts Adolf Hitler himself in the *Führerbunker* in Berlin. Hitler seems to possess all kinds of occult powers, but is no match for our American hero.

W3D and SoD contain all the ingredients of the series as a whole. An American hero by the name of Blazkowicz escapes from Castle Wolfenstein to deal with the Nazi threat: non-occult in the form of German soldiers, SS officers, and mechanically enhanced *Übersoldaten*, and occult in the form of mutants and demons. Hitler is depicted as having forged some kind of alliance with occult powers or even with Hell itself. Himmler on the other hand is blatantly lacking from both games.

CYCLE #3: BACK TO WOLFENSTEIN (2000s)

If Himmler was missing in all four prior instalments of the *Wolfenstein* series, *Return to Castle Wolfenstein* fills in the narrative opportunity immediately. RtCW was developed by Grey Matter Interactive and published by Activision in 2001 for Windows and later ported to Linux and Mac OSx (2002), and Xbox and PlayStation 2 (2003). The game is narratively speaking a reboot, the second one in the series so far: it returns Blazkowicz to his "beloved" Castle Wolfenstein, again as a prisoner waiting for the opportunity to escape (cf. CW and W3D). But B.J. is no longer an American private; he is a member of the fictional Office of Secret Actions, a reference to the historical British secret service known as Special Operations Executive, active during World War II.

The game starts with a cinematic introduction, showing a pagan wizard from 942 C.E. successfully imprisoning a rampaging Heinrich I, "the Fowler," (c. 876–936) in a magical prison. Yes, RtCW indeed "dials up the Nazi occultism to maximum" (Hite 2013, 76). Heinrich is considered to be the founder of the medieval German state and played an important role in Himmler's and Wiligut's ideology (Kurlander 2017, 179; Black 2015, 255).

RtCW also has its own prequel, called "Cursed Sands," only available on the PS2 and Xbox ports of the game, designed by Three Waves. Again, for reasons of chronology, I will start with this prequel. In 1943, B.J. and another OSA-operative are sent to Egypt to investigate the (very fictional) German SS Paranormal Division, RtCW's most important and continuously used contribution to the series' world lore. Unfortunately, B.J. is captured and brought to Castle Wolfenstein; this is where the game's proper narrative starts.

In RtCW Blazkowicz is basically busy chasing after leading figures of the SS Paranormal Division and trying to stop their occult plans for tipping the scales of the war in favor of Germany. (1) SS-Standartenführer Helga von Bulow—together with mad scientist Prof. Zemph—tries to resurrect Olaric using a combination of occult rituals and modern science in the form of electricity, reminiscent of Shelley's famous novel *Frankenstein* (1818). The in-game Olaric is a possible reference to Alaric I (c. 370–410), the first king of the Visigoths and plunderer of Rome in 410. Olaric is the guardian of the Dagger of Warding, a "Thulian artifact" according to the game. Before B.J. can intervene and take the dagger to be studied by the OSA, Olaric kills Von Bulow.

(2) Blakzowicz goes after SS-Oberführer Wilhelm "Totenkopf" ("Death's Head," rendered in-game as "Deathshead") Strasse, head of the SS Special Project Division, who wants to launch a special V2-rocket at London, bearing an experimental bacteriological warhead. His first name is probably a

reference to the Wilhelmstrasse, the historical location of the Prussian and later Nazi government in Berlin. His nickname is probably a reference to the notorious SS-*Totenkopfring*, worn by those soldiers guarding the concentration and extermination camps. B.J. prevents the bombing and kills Strasse's *Übersoldaten*—hybrids of man and machine, powered by electricity; Strasse himself, however, escapes by rocket-plane.

(3) Finally, B.J. discovers the real end-game of the SS Paranormal Division: the resurrection of King Heinrich I from his burial place near Castle Wolfenstein. Head of the occult ritual is SS High Priestess and Oberführer Marianna Blavatsky, a reference to the real-world Helena Blavatsky, founder of theosophy and, through various Ariosophists, connected to the realm of Nazi occultism. For the ritual, Blavatsky turns three mechanically enhanced *Übersoldaten* into "undead" versions of themselves, known as Dark Knights (cf. W3D). The resurrected Heinrich, however, turns Blavatsky into a psychic slave, after which B.J. kills them all. The cinematic ending shows Heinrich Himmler, watching from afar and afterwards flying back to Berlin to report to the Führer.

Except for Von Bulow, who is depicted as a very stout, German woman, the female members of the SS Paranormal Division have very sexualized aesthetics. Blavatsky is an almost naked sorceress with massive tattoos all over her body, while the higher ranks in her army consist exclusively of attractive, slim women, clad in very tight-fitting, leather pants and jackets, and sky-high stilettos. This caused some critics to argue that games like RtCW specifically, "associat[e] sexuality with the Third Reich," and thereby "suggest that Nazi evil is related to body perversion and sexual deviance" (Hayton 2015, 257).

Wolfenstein (2009) can and cannot be regarded as RtCW's sequel. The game, developed by Raven Software and Pi Studios, and published by Activision, features a dark-haired Blazkowicz (instead of the earlier blond one), dressed in civilian clothes (instead of military fatigues). Moreover, the Normandy landings of June 6, 1944 seem not to have taken place, suggesting an alternative timeline altogether.

The Nazis, however, have discovered some new occultic item to occupy their minds: the "Veil," a mysterious dimension that can be manipulated to control the world. The powers of the Veil can be harnessed by means of a Thule medallion—a reference to the historical Thule Gesellschaft—which in its turn must be powered by *Nachtsonne* ("Night Sun") crystals, a reference to the Black Sun (*Schwarze Sonne*) symbol, a popular Nazi symbol, only surpassed by the notorious swastika. Two generals, Victor Zetta and Wilhelm Strasse (cf. RtCW), oversee the operation, and both die at B.J.'s hands.

During the game's story, Blazkowicz is introduced to the German resistance of the Kreisau Circle (cf. RtCW), including Caroline Becker, who becomes the resistance's leader in cycle #4; and later also to a group of esoteric scholars, known as the Golden Dawn, a possible reference to the historical hermetic Order of the Golden Dawn founded by William Robert Woodman, William Wynn Westcott, and Samuel Liddell Mathers in 1887 (Gilbert). Caroline, however, is later killed by Hans Grosse, one of Strasse's henchmen, posing serious continuity—again—between W09, W3D, and the games of the fourth cycle. On the other hand, at the end of the game, Strasse again survives Blakzkowicz's havoc—destroying the German Zepplin with the only access-point to the Veil dimension—allowing him to make an in-continuation appearance in the fourth cycle.

CYCLE #4: THE DAWN OF A NEW ORDER (2010s)

Things changed drastically in the year 2014. That year the first *Wolfenstein* game was released by MachineGames (development) and Bethesda Softworks (publisher) for Windows, PlayStation 3 and 4, Xbox One and 360, and (only for *Wolfenstein: Cyberpilot*) for HTC Vive and PlayStation VR. MachineGames rebooted the series dramatically, by introducing an allohistorical setting (or an alternative universe) in which the Nazis have won the Second World War in 1946 by developing (and using) the atomic bomb before the Allies did. The games within this cycle #4 take place in the 1960s–1980s of this alternative universe. The reboot also features the inclusion of Jewish mysticism, the question of theodicy, and concentration camps, and gives far more attention to the German resistance than BCW, W3D, RtCW, and W09 ever did before.

Below I will discuss the instalments of the fourth cycle in their internal-chronological order. That means I will discuss *Wolfenstein: The New Order* (2014) after its prequel *Wolfenstein: The Old Blood* (2015). The other instalments of the fourth cycle include: *Wolfenstein II: The New Colossus* (2017), *Wolfenstein: Youngblood* (2019), and *Wolfenstein: Cyberpilot* (2019).

In *Wolfenstein: The Old Blood*, the OSA (cf. RtCW and W09) sends Blazkowicz to Castle Wolfenstein—again—to retrieve information regarding the location of Strasse's secret compound from the desk of SS-Obersturmbannführer Helga von Schabbs (a double wink to the male scientist Schabbs in W3D and the female commander in RtCW). This Von Schabbs believes she is a far descendent of King Otto I (912–973), the son of Henry the Fowler (cf. RtCW *and* the famous German emperor who defeated the Magyar invasion during the Battle of Lechfeld in 955. Blazkowicz, however, is captured, tortured, and imprisoned at the castle (cf. CW, W3D, and RtCW).

After his inevitable escape, he flees to the remnants of the German resistance in Paderborn and infiltrates Von Schabbs' private quarters in the town's pub. After his cover is blown again, a massive earthquake occurs. This earthquake is caused by the Nazis' continuous excavation under the town in their search for Otto's shrine, and leads to the spilling out of a strange chemical that re-animates the dead (cf. RtCW). Eventually, B.J. finds the monstrous creature—not unlike Olaric in RtCW—that Otto used to win his (historical) war against the Magyar. The monster, however, attacks and kills Von Schabbs. B.J. kills the monster, picks up the folder he was seeking, and leaves Paderborn to join a massive allied airstrike against Strasse in 1946.

Wolfenstein: The New Order opens with the same airstrike. B.J. and a couple of his comrades manage to infiltrate Strasse's base of operation, only to be apprehended by the general, who leaves them to die in an incinerator room. The troops escape, but B.J. is injured severely to his head. Admitted to a Polish psychiatric asylum, B.J. remains in a catatonic state, until, in 1960, the Nazis shut down the facility, effectually killing all those dubbed *Untermenschen*. Blazkowicz awakens from his vegetative state and flees the facility together with his later love-interest Anya Oliwa. From her grandparents, B.J. learns that the Nazis won the war in 1948.

After having rescued the remainder of the German Kreisau Circle from a Berlin prison, Blazkowicz breaks into a Nazi facility in London, where he finds documents showing the Nazis are trying to reverse-engineer ancient technology (laser beams, artificial intelligence, super concrete, extra-terrestrial travels) derived from a secret Jewish organization, known as Da'at Yichud. It is with this technology that the Nazis were able to conquer the world.

The last surviving member of the Da'at Yichud, a man called Set Roth, is imprisoned in a concentration camp called Belica. B.J. lets himself be confined to that camp, which is led by the infamous SS-Obersturmbannführer Irene Engel, where he personally witnesses the horrors of the Holocaust, and escapes with Roth. The figure of Engel is probably based on a combination of Friedrich Engel (1909–2006), a convicted SS officer and the notorious Nazi "Angel of Death" Joseph Mengele (1911–1979).

Roth in his turn leads B.J. and the Kreisau Circle—under the leadership of Caroline Becker, who apparently was not killed (as was suggested in W09) but only paralyzed—to a secret Da'at Yichud weapons-depot on the bottom of the ocean. The necessary German submarine—*Eva's Hammer*—is stolen by B.J., after which he travels to the Nazi moon base in order to steal the secret codes with which the submarine's nuclear cannon can be unlocked. With the help of the cannon and the Da'at Yichud technology provided by Roth, the Kreisau Circle is able to infiltrate Strasse's secret facility, freeing all prisoners taken earlier.

Unfortunately, Strasse manages to set off a hand grenade before he is definitely killed by B.J., leaving our hero to die at the moment of his greatest glory. In the final seconds of the game, B.J. commands the nuclear bombing of the facility, sealing his fate for good. But *Wolfenstein* would not be

Wolfenstein if B.J. did not find a way to miraculously survive such violence. At the beginning of *Wolfenstein II: The New Colossus*, Roth, Oliwa, and other Kreisau members manage to extract B.J. and transport him back to their headquarters in *Eva's Hammer*. After five months of extraordinary medical treatment, the submarine is attacked by Frau Engel, who was disfigured by B.J. during his escape from Belica (cf. WNO).

After B.J. manages to overtake Caroline Becker's Da'at Yichud power suite—she is (again) killed, now by Engel—he succeeds in releasing the submarine from Engel's control and flees to Nazi-occupied North America. Here, the Kreisaus contact the American resistance led by Grace Walker, the first Afro-American character in the series, and with her love-interest Norman Caldwell. The latter, a benign Area 51-conspiracy theorist, travels to Roswell, New Mexico, where the German *Überkommando* is convened.

When Blazkowicz manages to detonate an atomic bomb in the *Überkommando*'s building, he takes a detour to his old home in Mesquite. Suggested earlier in WOB and WNO, B.J.'s Polish-Jewish heritage becomes explicit in WNC. In Mesquite B.J. meets his abusive, racist father, who earlier sold his Jewish wife Zofia out to the Nazis. B.J. kills his father in an act of self-defense, but is immediately taken captive by Frau Engel. After a show-trial, Blazkowicz is beheaded by Engel in front of a world-wide television audience. However, through a tantalizingly complex plan, Anya Oliwa, Set Roth, and Grace Walker succeed in surgically attaching B.J.'s head to the body of a biomedically enhanced super soldier, giving him superhuman capabilities.

After a little detour through New Orleans, now a ghetto full of people deemed inferior by the Nazis, including an anarchist-communist preacher by the name of Horton Boone, B.J. travels to the Nazi base on Venus (cf. WNO's moon), where he steals the security codes of Engel's super-airplane *Die Auschmetzer*. With the help of these codes, B.J. brings *Die Auschmetzer* under the control of the resistance. B.J. and his team then hijack a national television broadcast in California, publicly executing Frau Engel and declaring a national uprising against the Nazis.

Twenty years later, as *Wolfenstein: Youngblood* tells us, B.J. and Anya have raised twin-daughters Jessie and Zofia (named after her murdered grandmother). When Blazkowicz disappears one day to Nazi-occupied Paris, the two girls set out to find and free him, assisted by Abby, the by now grown-up daughter of Grace Walker (cf. WNC). In Paris, the girls meet up with the local resistance group under the leadership of Jacques Martel and Juju Desjardin, later revealed to be the former SS-Oberstgruppenführer Lothar Brandt; the disgraced Paris commander; and his wife Julie Brandt. Both are members of a secret society, called "The Fourth Reich," intending to stage a coup against the current Third Reich.

In a secret Nazi laboratory, Jessie and Zofia find their father, who was kept prisoner there. He tells them that when he killed Hitler in the 1960s (vis-à-vis W3D), he accidentally set off a doomsday device that will render the world uninhabitable. He travelled to Paris to prevent it from going off. In the laboratory, B.J. learned, with the help of a Da'at Yichud artifact, about the existence of multiple alternate dimensions, including a universe in which the Nazis lost the Second World War. At the end of the game, Anya, Grace, and Blazkowicz understand the threat that the Fourth Reich poses, despite the Brandt couple having been killed by the twins, and they call upon all their old allies to stop it. Jessie, Zofia, and Abby stay in Paris to defend the city.

The game *Wolfenstein. Cyberpilot*, exclusively for VR, was released simultaneously with WYB and takes place around the same time within the series' universe, but it does not do much to further the story of the canon.

PART II

Analysis

Chapter 6

Daggers, Spears, and Medallions
The SS Paranormal Division

One of *Wolfenstein*'s staples has always been its dabbling with Nazi occultist tropes (see chapters 2 and 3). The first cycle of the series did not include much Nazi occultism due to the technological limitations of the computers of the 1980s, which also limited narrative and lore-building potentials. However, the second and third cycles drew heavily on Wolfenstein castle, on mythical organizations like the Golden Dawn and the Thule Society, and on symbols like swastikas and Black Suns. With the exception of *Wolfenstein: The Old Blood*, the fourth cycle turned the Nazi occultism dial back to almost zero in favor of including Jewish mysticism in its place (see chapter 8). In this chapter, we investigate and assess the occultist locations, objects, organizations, persons, and symbols found in the first three cycles.

MYTHICAL LOCATIONS: CASTLE WEWELSBURG

First, we will focus on Castle Wolfenstein, the iconic *Schloss* which gave the series its name. The Castle plays a role in all the game cycles: *Castle Wolfenstein* (1st cycle), *Wolfenstein 3D* (2nd cycle), *Return to Castle Wolfenstein* (3rd cycle), and *Wolfenstein: The Old Blood* (4th cycle). The anonymous Isenstadt castle from *Wolfenstein* (2009) may or may not be the same one. In the first cycle, due to the technical limitations of the time, the in-game castle is almost nothing more than a name, and is depicted by crudely drawn two-dimensional rooms with no more distinguishable features than those necessary at a ludological level. W3D and its prequel *The Spear of Destiny* even feature three more or less interchangeable castles, the original Castle Wolfenstein (German for "Stone of Wolves"), Castle Hollehammer ("Hammer of Hell"), and Castle Nuremberg (a reference to the location of the famous Nazi trials after the war).

In *Return to Castle Wolfenstein*—both a literal return to the castle of that name *and* a figurative homage to its predecessor—the castle receives a lot more historical and geographical detail. It is located in the Harz Mountains of Northern Germany, near the village of Wulfburg (German for "the Wolf's stronghold") and the very real German city of Paderborn. In this iteration of the castle, it is only accessible using a cable-car from the nearby village, a reference to the famous Schloss Adler from the film *Where Eagles Dare* (1968), which itself was based on the historical Hohenwerfen Castle in Austria. In the game, Wolfenstein is owned by Heinrich Himmler, who uses it as a research and prison facility. It also functions as the headquarters of the fictional SS Paranormal Division, led by Marianna Blavatsky (see chapter 2).

In *Wolfenstein: The Old Blood*, the castle with the same name is situated in the Bavarian Alps, near the Austrian border, 400 or so kilometers south of its former location in W3D, SoD, and RtCW. However, Paderborn is still near the castle, even though the former's real-life counterpart is situated in the north of Germany. The cable train returns as a note to its previous iteration. According to the in-game lore, this iteration of Castle Wolfenstein was built by King Otto I in 946. Otto's wife Eadgyth is buried in the catacombs beneath the castle. I will address both characters later in this chapter.

The game series' Castle Wolfenstein is a fictional combination of two historical castles: Werfenstein and—predominantly—Wewelsburg. To start with the first, Werfenstein is a lowland castle in Strudengau in Austria, along the Danube. In 1907, it was bought by Ariosophist Jörg Lanz von Liebenfels (see chapter 2) with the help of some friends from Vienna to use as the headquarters of his Order of the New Templars, or *Ordo Novi Templi*, and as a (newly realized) museum of Aryan anthropology. Famously, Lanz von Liebenfels hoisted the swastika flag on the castle on Christmas Day 1907 (Goodrick-Clarke 2005, 109). In a study, he suggested that the origins of the castle were connected to the "Niblungs" (a Germanic tribe) of the fifth century. During 1908, some festivals were held in Werfenstein, while in 1911 Von Liebenfels spoke of the place as a priory of his order. In poems written by Von Liebenfels and his closest friends, the castle is like a "shining image of the castle-priory against the dark valley of racial chaos; above the sunlit battlements of the 'castle of the Grail' fluttered the swastika flag, while white-cowled brothers performed the holy office in the grove below" (idem, 113).

An even more fundamental prototype for the fictive Castle Wolfenstein was the historical Castle Wewelsburg, a Renaissance castle-now-turned-museum in the village of the same name in the Westphalian *Landkreis* of Paderborn. In January 1933, Himmler traveled through Westphalia, the land of "Hermann and Widukind" (Goodrick-Clarke 2005, 186), respectively Arminius, who vanquished Rome at the Battle of the Teutoburg

Forest in 9 C.E., and Wittekind, the leader of the Saxon independence movement vis-à-vis Charlemagne in 777–785. When confronted with the *Hermannsdenkmal*, a massive statue in commemoration of Arminius (built in 1875, and still standing today), Himmler drew up plans to build a SS location somewhere in the vicinity. In November 1933, Himmler chose Wewelsburg as the location, and it was taken over by the SS in 1934. Starting as an SS museum and educational institute, in Himmler's mind it became more and more an SS order-castle, comparable to the Marienburg of the medieval Teutonic Knights. It was Karl Maria Wiligut a.k.a. Weisthor (see chapter 2), who probably planted and cultivated these plans in Himmler's mind and heart. Weisthor reinterpreted a nineteenth century poem containing an old Westphalian legend, describing a future conflict between Europe and Asia (idem, 168). Wewelsburg was envisaged to be the "bastion" against the "new Hun invasion."

In post-World War II cultural discourse, Castle Wewelsburg has been imbued with a whole range of esoteric or occult characteristics, which—according to historians—are very probably more fictional than factual history (Kingsepp 2012, 4–5):

> There is/was a great dining/banquet hall with a large, round oak table surrounded by (13) (high-back or otherwise large-sized) chairs made of wood/oak tree/pigskin [sic!] (or upholstered with pigskin), each with the name of its "owner knight" engraved (on a silver plate). In this hall/in the castle Himmler and his knights/closest associates would perform occult/mystical/ telepathic/ spiritualistic practices. Beneath the great hall/the castle [sic!] is/was a crypt, in which the coat of arms of deceased SS officers/the deceased officers themselves were/would be burned and the ashes were/would be put in urns, placed on the pedestals in the crypt.

The idea of Castle Wewelsburg being a kind of "SS Vatican," including elaborate (occultic) ceremonies, is the product of post-war enthusiasts who struggled with the differences between what actually happened at Wewelsburg and what Himmler envisaged should happen there in the future. Books like Hein Höhne's *The order of the Death's Head. The story of Hitler's SS* (1966), SS-Brigadeführer Walter Schellenberg's, *The Memoirs of Hitler's Spymaster* (originally written in German and published in 1965, English translation published in 2006), and Austrian journalist Willi Frischauer's *Himmler. The evil genius of the Third Reich* (1953) are examples of such embellishments. These have—nevertheless—had a profound influence on popular and cultural belief, including the Indiana Jones films (discussed in chapter 3) and the *Wolfenstein* series.

In more recent years, scholars have debunked these claims thoroughly. Karl Hüser (1982) and Jan-Erik Schulte (2002, 2009), for example, explicitly assert that there were no ritualistic activities conducted by the SS at Castle Wewelsburg. Nevertheless, they do suggest that Himmler had intentions for using the castle for cultic practices, but his plans never materialized. In 2009, Daniel Siepe asserted that recent research indicates that aside from oath-taking ceremonies, there were no plans for any ritualistic activities by the SS at the Wewelsburg. Consequently, the idea of the castle serving as a place of worship (*Kultstätte*) for the SS has been supplanted by the concept of it being a central gathering place for SS generals (*zentralen Versammlungsort der SS-Gruppenführer*).

MYTHICAL OBJECTS: THE SPEAR OF DESTINY

The *Wolfenstein* series also has its fair share of esoteric objects. The most obvious one is the Spear of Destiny (also known as the Holy Lance, the Lance, or Longinus' Spear), the object that gives one of the games its title. The popularity of the mythology of this holy object is very largely due to Trevor Ravenscroft (1921–1989), a British commando in the North African campaign during World War II, where he was captured and then imprisoned at a German POW camp (1941–1945). In 1972, Ravenscroft published the book that would make him famous: *The Spear of Destiny. The occult power behind the spear which pierced the side of Christ*. The book is a fascinating reinterpretation of the history of the Western world.

After the war, Ravenscroft claimed he met Walter Johannes Stein (1891–1957), a Jew from Vienna, who emigrated from Germany to Britain in 1933. Ravenscroft credited this Stein with telling him the story of Hitler's search for the Holy Lance (Goodrick-Clarke 2002, 118–20). Stein, according to Ravenscroft, had taught at the Waldorf School in Stuttgart before the War. Not incidentally, the Waldorf Schools are based on the anthroposophical principles of Rudolf Steiner, who was once a follower of Madame Blavatsky (see chapter 2), but who later founded his own *Anthroposophische Gesellschaft* in 1912/1913 (Leijenhorst 2006). In 1928, Stein, during his time in Stuttgart, wrote—again according to Ravenscroft—a curious book under the title *Weltgeschichte im Lichte des Heiligen Gral*, a spiritual reinterpretation of world history in the light of the legend of the Holy Grail (Introvigne 2006). Stein especially claimed that the Grail romance *Parzival*, written by Wolfram von Eschenbach (circa 1200) was based on historical events of the ninth century. The novel allegorically spoke about the enduring struggle between the Christian knights and their evil adversaries for possession of the Holy

Lance, the Spear of Longinus that pierced the side of Christ at his crucifixion (John 19, 34).

The anonymous piercing soldier found in John 19:34 is associated by some with the anonymous Roman centurion who, standing beneath the cross, pronounced his belief in Jesus' divine Sonship shortly after Jesus' death (Matthew 27:54 and Mark 15:39). This association can be traced back to the apocryphal Gospel of Nicodemus from the fourth century, also known as the *Acta Pilati*, identifying the unnamed soldier as Longinus (Barber 2004, 188). The character of Longinus is strongly linked to his defining attribute: the spear employed to pierce Jesus' side (Bosman 2019, 203–204). This artifact has made appearances in popular literature and pseudo-scholarly works. It is believed to have passed through the hands of various powerful and often ruthless rulers and dictators throughout history, including Charlemagne, Napoleon Bonaparte, and—according to Ravenscroft—even Adolf Hitler himself (Schrier et al. 2009).

Ravenscroft suggests that in 1912 Stein laid his hands upon a worn-out copy of Eschenbach's *Parzival* in an occult bookshop in Vienna. The copy was full of hand-written annotations concerning oriental religions, alchemy, astrology, and mysticism, including anti-Semitic racial slurs and pan-Germanic political philosophies. According to the name written inside the book its previous owner was Adolf Hitler. The bookshop's owner, Ernst Pretzsche, identified Hitler as a student of the *ars arcana* and gave him the future Führer's address. Stein found Hitler and the two met frequently in 1912 and 1913, discussing the power of the Spear of Destiny. Constantine the Great, Charles Martel, Henry the Fowler, Otto the Great (see below), and the Hohenstauffen emperors Frederick I, Henry VI, and Frederick II were once in the possession of the Lance according to Ravenscroft's version of Stein's version of Hitler. The Spear was supposed to be located in the Treasure House of the Hofburg in Vienna, explaining the "true" reason for Hitler's 1938 Austrian *Anschluss*. Superficially, this sequence of events does not right away seem impossible: *au contraire*. Hitler is well-known for his love of Richard Wagner's operas, especially *Lohengrin* (1850) and *Parsifal* (1882), even though during the war years the latter one was deemed "ideologically unacceptable" and the opera was not performed at Bayreuth during the war years (Magee 2002, 366). The opera *Parsifal* is based on Eschenbach's *Parzival*, but has fused "the original Christian symbolism with the blood mystique of the Aryan racial myth" (Goodrick-Clarke 2002, 119), probably the reason for its later Nazi ban.

Walter Stein did exist, as well as his book on the grail and the history of Europe, but he never knew Hitler personally or spoke with the Führer-to-be personally. Neither did Ravenscroft ever speak directly with Stein or corresponded with him. And the figure of the Vienna bookshop owner Ernst

Pretzsche is a total fabrication by Ravenscroft (Tautz 1990). Through books like *Hitler et la tradition cathare* by Michel Bertrand and Jean Angelini, under the joint pseudonym Jean-Michel Angebert (1971), and Howard Buechner's *Emerald Cup—Ark of Gold* (1991), the myth of Hitler and the Spear of Destiny are still maintained within the popular domain, including *Wolfenstein*'s second cycle.

The *Wolfenstein* series features other—if less well known—esoteric objects, like the Dagger of Warding in *Return to Castle Wolfenstein* and the Thule Medallion in *Wolfenstein* (2009), both connected in-game with the Thule Society, which I will discuss in more detail below.

MYTHICAL ORGANIZATIONS: THE THULE SOCIETY & THE GOLDEN DAWN

The SS Paranormal Division is the most predominant secret organization throughout the game series, appearing in *Return to Castle Wolfenstein*, *Wolfenstein* (2009), and *Wolfenstein: The Old Blood*. But since this fictional Division is actually the in-game variant of the historical SS Ahnenerbe, I will discuss this later in this chapter under the heading of the "crazy scientists." The in-game Kreisau Circle, a German resistance group, featuring in all but the first cycle, and its historical counterpart will be discussed separately too, in chapter 9.

Another important secret organization is the Da'at Yichud, featuring heavily in all installments of the fourth cycle, but this one is distinctly different from the other ones because of its Jewish origins vis-à-vis the Germanic inspiration of the previous organizations discussed in this section. I will return for an in-depth analysis of the Da'at Yichud when discussing the character Set Roth, the principal *Wolfenstein* character associated with this organization (see chapter 8).

After all these considerations we are left with the Thule Society, strongly tied to the plot of *Wolfenstein* (2009). First, we will follow the in-game history and description of the society; second, we will confront the fictional Thule Society with the historical Thule Gesellschaft, including its dependence on the teachings of Helena Blavatsky.

According to the game lore, the Thule Society of the 1930s and 1940s is founded upon the technology of the Thule Civilization. The Thulians, again following *Wolfenstein*, were an ancient and technologically highly advanced people living somewhere in the (near) Arctic regions of the northern hemisphere. For some not entirely disclosed reasons, the Thulian society collapsed in on itself, leaving only its advanced technology behind. In the tenth century, claiming the Germans were the rightful descendants and successors of the Thulians, Henry the Fowler (we will discuss him below in more detail) acquired a part of that technology to secure his military and political successes. He was stopped, however, by a monk, only to be resurrected by Marianna Blavatsky, head of the SS Paranormal Division (in *Return to Castle Wolfenstein*).

In *Wolfenstein* 2009, it becomes clear that the Nazis have acquired yet another piece of the Thulian technology: the existence and manipulation of another dimension, called the Black Sun Dimension, or *Nachtsonne Dimension* (we will discuss the symbol itself more closely elsewhere in this chapter). This other dimension exists parallel to that of Earth, but is unstable. Its sky is dominated by a darkened or eclipsed sun, and its space is occupied with the scattered ruins of (possibly Thulian) human-made structures. According to the game lore, the Thulians—and now the Nazis, or rather the Thule Society of the 1940s—knew how to harness the seemingly unlimited power of this dimension by semi-technological, semi-magical means.

To enter (and use) this dimension, one must pass beyond "the Veil," a barrier between our world and that of the Black Sun. If such a transition is made without protective measures, the individual turns into a physically superior but mentally deranged version of his or her former self. In the game, a device known as the "Thule Medallion" is the primary means by which anyone is allowed to travel safely through "the Veil" and harness the Black Sun's power in the "normal" world. These medallions—apparently there are more than one—are hand-sized devices resembling the face of a clock, equipped with a four-bladed rotor positioned above it. Inside those rotor arms one can place up to four (differently colored) *Nachtsonne* crystals, granting the device and its bearer the ability to manipulate "the Veil." These crystals are exclusively found in the German city of Isenstadt, not accidentally also the location of the Kreisau Circle in that game's installments. Through the manipulation of "the Veil," these devices can enhance the player's avatar's abilities, like distorting space, enhancing speed, perceiving otherwise hidden objects, and passing through solid matter.

The concept of the land of "Thule" is an ancient one. Alongside Hyperborea and Atlantis, it was one of the several *terrae incognitae* of the ancient Greeks and Romans. Thule is mentioned for the first time, in the fourth century B.C.E., by the Greek adventurer Pytheas from present-day Marseille, France (as preserved in Polybius' *Histories* XXXIV, 5). According to him, Thule was located somewhere up north, even further north than Britannia. Other ancient explorers all agreed on this initial location: Geminus of Rhodes (*Introduction to the Phenomena* VI, 9), Strabo (*Geographica* I, 4), and Pliny the Elder (*Natural History* IV, 5). It was a mythical island, land, or even continent, where the sun never set and giant-like people lived. All these descriptions suggest Norway or Greenland with their long midsummer days, while remaining silent about any winter darkness to speak of. The term "Thule Ultima" was coined by the Roman poet Virgil (*Georgics* I, 30) and has been used interchangeably with "Thule" ever since. "Hyperborea" has a similar origin and a similar reception history. Herodotus' *Histories* (IV, 32–36) is credited with its first mention, meaning "beyond Boreas," Boreas being the god of the North Wind. Hyperborea shares many characteristics with Thule: a warm, sunny country beyond the cold of northern Europe.

The "lost continent" of Atlantis is famously mentioned in Plato's *Timaeus* (24e–25a) and *Critias* (108e–121e, 121e–121k), probably not so much being a real-life location, but rather a fictional place the philosopher invented for intellectual purposes. This allegorical origin has not kept travelers and artists from trying to pinpoint its exact location and date. Its name features in novels like Jules Verne's *20,000 Leagues under the sea* (1869/1871), C. S. Lewis's *The Magician's Nephew* (1955), and Ayn Rand's *Altlas Shrugged* (1957); in films like *Atlantis, the lost continent* (1961), and the 2001 Disney film *Atlantis. The lost empire* and its sequel *Atlantis. Milo's return* (2003); and in video games like *Indiana Jones and the fate of Atlantis* (1992) and *Assassin's Creed Odyssey* (2018).

Hyperborea and Atlantis entered Western esoteric lore via the works of Helena Blavatsky (see chapter 2), and their subsequent use is indebted to her interpretations of these *terra incognitae*. In the second volume of *The secret doctrine* (1888), called "Anthropogenesis" or "the birth of humanity," Blavatsky sketches a cyclical understanding of the cosmos in combination with a racial view on humanity's development (Goodrick-Clarke 2005, 20): the rise and fall of seven *Wurzelrassen* ("root races"). The first four races form a sequence of increasing deterioration of spiritual development. Only with the emergence of the fifth one, a new recovery begins, culminating in the seventh, most perfect civilization, yet to come.

Of course, Blavatsky argued that humanity was now at the end of the fourth root race's reign; the Aryans now emerged, ready to take their rightful place in the history of the world, commencing a definite and irreversible rise to greatness. Later, Ariosophists jumped at the opportunity to identify Blavatsky's Aryans with twentieth century German nations, but Blavatsky herself did not do so. The fourth root race, according to the founder of the Theosophical Society, were the Atlanteans, who perished in a cataclysmic flood thousands of years ago; a deluge that submerged their continent and civilization. The Atlanteans possessed incredible psychic powers and superior technology based on the manipulation of a secret energy source, known as "Fohat" – cf. the *Nachtsonne* technology of *Wolfenstein* (2009).

The first root race were the Astrals—endlessly more sophisticated than we could ever imagine, living in an invisible world of eternal light and harmony. The second root race, the Hyberboreans, were only slightly less advanced and lived on a now vanished polar continent. The third race, the Lemurians, faced a similar fate: their continent also sank into what is now known as the Indian Ocean. Lemuria and its fate are not the invention of Blavatsky, but of zoologist Philip Sclater (1829–1913), who theorized about a sunken continent in the Indian Ocean.

As already discussed in chapter 2, Rudolf Sebottendorf founded the historical Thule Society in 1918. He derived the term from Pytheas, but identified it as present-day Iceland, which played an important role in various Aryan-centered theories at the time (Goodrick-Clarke 2005, 145). Under the leadership of Sebottendorf, individuals affiliated with the Germanenorden and the Thule Society, which at times seemed to be closely intertwined, played a significant role during the Bavarian counter-revolution in 1919. This event unfolded as the Munich-based paramilitary Freikorps acted to overthrow the recently established independent Soviet Republic, which had come into existence just a year earlier. In that same year, members of these associations came together to establish the Deutsche Arbeitspartei, or the "German Workers' Party." This party would later undergo a transformation and be renamed the Nationalsozialistische Deutsche Arbeiterpartei, commonly known as the National Socialist German Workers' Party, in 1920. The adoption of the swastika as the symbol of the Nazi party and, subsequently, the Third Reich can be traced back to the influence of individuals such as Von Liebenfels and Von List within the Germanenorden and Thule Society.

Scholarly discussions have arisen regarding the historical authenticity and continuity of the Thule Society. Some scholars debate whether it was a genuine organization or a conceptual construct crafted by enthusiasts of Ariosophy associated with Rudolf von Sebottendorf. Nonetheless, it is historically evident that many individuals who aligned themselves with the ideology of the Thule Society were actively involved in the establishment of the D.A.P. and its evolution into the N.S.D.A.P., as well as connected to their forerunners (Kurlander 2017, 33–61).

After the Second World War, the Thule connection became very popular in the cultural domain. Louis Pauwels and Jacques Bergier argued in their *Le matin des magiciens* ("The morning of the magicians," 1960; see chapter 3), that Hitler was mentored in the early 1920s by two members of the Thule Society, Dietrich Eckhart (1868–1923) and Karl Haushofer (1869–1946). According to Pauwels and Bergier, this Haushofer supposedly founded the Thule Society in 1923, modelling it after similar groups in Tibet, one of the places where the proto-Aryans were supposed to have survived the cataclysmic flooding of the world. The same claims were made in various other semi-historical books like Pierre Mariel's *L'Europe païenne du XXe siècle* (1964), René Alleau's *Hitler et les sociétés secrètes* (1969), Werner Gerson's *Le Nazisme, société secrète* (1969), and Jean-Claude Frère's

Nazisme et sociétés secrètes (1974). Robert Charroux even claimed in his 1964 *Le livre des secret trahis* that the Hyperboreans were aliens from Venus who came to Earth to be its teachers. Ravenscroft (see above) in his *Spear of Destiny*, claimed that the Thule Society, under Eckhart's leadership, performed satanic rituals on Jews and communists, who allegedly mysteriously disappeared from pre-war München (Goodrick-Clarke 2002, 120). He also claimed that seances with naked women were conducted to make contact with dead Thuleans.

Wilhelm Landig (1909–1997) was another important promoter of Thulean Ariosophy after the Second World War. Rooted in the "Aryan-Nordic mythology" of 1950s Vienna (Goodrick-Clarke 2002, 128), former SS volunteer Landig and his comrades dabbled with the ideas of the Italian philosopher and Nazi sympathizer Julius Evola (1898–1974). In his *Erhebung wider die moderne Welt* (1935), Evola argued for the existence of Hyperborea located in the prehistoric Arctic region, occupied with proto-Aryans who reigned over the world during a true Golden Age, "heaven-oriented, solar and heroic-masculine" (Hakl 2006, 348). This ideal world was contaminated and almost destroyed, according to Evola, by a combination of the "earth-oriented, lunar, and matriarchal" (idem) cultures of the southern peoples, the rise of Catholicism in the Middle Ages, the Renaissance, and especially the French Revolution. Over the course of three decades, Landig consolidated his ideas in his Thulean trilogy, *Götzen Gegen Thule* (1971), *Wolfszet um Thule* (1980), and *Rebellen für Thule* (1991). As Goodrick-Clarke summarizes (2002, 137):

Theories of Aryan polar origins and Atlantis are mixed with powerful new nationalist myths of "the last battalion," secret German UFO bases in the Arctic, alchemy, Grail myths and Cathar heresies, and a Nazi-Tibetan connection involving Himalayan masters and an underground kingdom in Mongolia.

A last *Wolfenstein* secret organization in need of discussion here is the Golden Dawn, exclusive to *Wolfenstein* (2009). The Golden Dawn is a group of Russian scholars, mystics, and occultists, formed and led by Dr. Leonid Alexandrov in 1890. At the end of the game, Alexandrov outs himself as secretly working for the Nazis to unlock the secrets of the Black Sun Dimension. Reason for his betrayal were his unsuccessful efforts to be taken seriously by his Russian colleagues, after undergoing a lifetime of academic scorn regarding his Thule theories (which happened to be correct). The Golden Dawn's symbol is a variation of the well-known All-Seeing Eye, or Eye of Providence (Baker 2020), used in Christianity (as a symbol of both the Trinity and God's providence), in Freemasonry (as a symbol of the Great Architect of the Universe seeing all human actions), and in many contemporary conspiracy theories (as a symbol of the World Government).

Wolfenstein's Golden Dawn is a reference to the historical Hermetic Order of the Golden Dawn, a prominent esoteric and occult organization established in 1888 by a trio of notable figures—Samuel Liddell MacGregor Mathers (1854–1918), William Wynn Westcott (1888–1925), and William Robert Woodman (1828–1891). At its core, the Hermetic Order of the Golden Dawn represented a fusion of Blavatskyesque hermeticism (see chapter 2), Christian Kabbala (see chapter 4), alchemy, and a myriad of other mystical influences (Gilbert 2006). This eclectic blend of spiritual wisdom formed the foundation upon which the order's teachings and rituals were constructed. These rituals were meticulously designed to serve as a transformative journey for its members, facilitating personal spiritual growth and unlocking deeper layers of esoteric knowledge.

One of the defining features of the Golden Dawn's teachings was its emphasis on the Tree of Life, a symbolic representation of the cosmos with deep roots in kabbalist thought. Tarot symbolism also played a pivotal role in its practices, providing a visual and symbolic framework for understanding the spiritual journey. Furthermore, the order was known for its efforts in deciphering and interpreting ancient magical texts, contributing to the revival of interest in these esoteric works. The Golden Dawn's enduring significance in scholarly circles is underscored by the association of notable figures like Aleister Crowley (1875–1947) and Arthur Edward Waite (1857–1942), who were members or influenced by the order's teachings. Especially Crowley went on to become a prominent figure in Western occultism, further elevating the order's influence (Pasi 2006).

However, internal disputes and power struggles plagued the Golden Dawn, leading to its eventual fragmentation and decline in the early twentieth century. Despite its tumultuous history, the Hermetic Order of the Golden Dawn remains a focal point of academic study within the realm of Western esotericism, providing valuable insights into the evolution of modern Western magical practices and the broader cultural and theological context of its time. The Hermetic Order of the Golden Dawn was, more than any other esoteric body, responsible for ensuring the survival of much of Western esotericism into the twenty-first century.

There is a possible, if uncertain, connection between the Hermetic Order and Ariosophy in the person of Guido von List (Goodrick-Clarke 2005, 59). In 1902, Theodor Reuss (1855–1923) founded irregular masonic and Rosicrucian lodges in Germany on the authority of Westcott, himself a founding member of the Hermetic Order of the Golden Dawn. Reuss was in regular contact with the German theosophist Franz Hartmann (1838–1912), who in his turn was a promoter of the Guido von List Society (founded in 1908).

GERMANIC HEROES: HEINRICH THE FOWLER AND OTTO THE GREAT

The *Wolfenstein* series features a couple of historical "Germanic" heroes, who were appropriated by Ariosophists and Nazis to construct a collective, mythical past for the struggling German people, especially Henry the Fowler (in *Return to Castle Wolfenstein*) and Otto the Great (in *Wolfenstein: The Old Blood*).

To start with the first one, RtCW introduces "Prince Heinrich" as the prime antagonist of the game. In the game's introduction, explicitly set in 943 C.E., we see Heinrich appear as an iron-clad giant with fiery eyes and an overall gloomy appearance, together with some of his personal knights. A monk, called Simon the Wanderer, whose face is concealed by a large hood, tries to kill Heinrich, but, realizing the ineffectiveness of his efforts, locks him into a magically sealed underground vault. The game seems to suggest that Simon and Blazkowicz are related, being possibly blood relations. When Heinrich I is brought back to life, he says that he senses "the presence of another." At the end of the game, Heinrich is resurrected by Marianna Blavatsky, head of the SS Paranormal Division, who is immediately killed by the angry old prince. The resurrected Heinrich appears to be sub-human, a husk of his former self, incredibly powerful but devoid of many human characteristics. Eventually, Blazkowicz manages to do what Simon could not, and kills Heinrich once and for all.

Historically, Heinrich I, also known as Henry the Fowler (Heinrich der Vogler in German), was a pivotal figure in early medieval European history. Born in 876 C.E. and appointed as the Duke of Saxony in 912 C.E., his leadership was characterized by the unification of the German tribes into a cohesive entity. Through a combination of military conquests and diplomatic prowess, he managed to extend his authority beyond Saxony and assert control over other regions, including Franconia, Bavaria, and Swabia. This unification laid the groundwork for the future Holy Roman Empire. He introduced reforms in governance and taxation, which allowed for more centralized control. Additionally, he encouraged the growth of towns and trade, contributing to economic development and stability within the realm. Heinrich died in July, 936 C.E. (and not 943 as is suggested in RtCW).

Heinrich's unification of "Germany" was inspiring for the Nazi theorists, who appropriated Heinrich's legacy for the unification of all Aryan people into the new Germany, the Third Reich. Himmler himself was a fan (Goodrick-Clarke 2002, 124–25). On July 2, 1936, he organized a special religious ceremony at Heinrich's burial place, Quedlinburg Cathedral, commemorating the thousandth anniversary of the prince's death. Himmler especially praised the German monarch for pushing the Slavic peoples, deemed *Untermenschen* by Nazi ideology, eastward beyond the Elbe. In a mood of profound reverence, Himmler depicted Heinrich as an exemplar of Germanic courage and religious devotion, pledging to carry on his mission in the eastern territories (the so-called doctrine of *Lebensraum*). Later occultist writers, like Brennan (in *Occult Reich*), King (in *Satan and Swastika*), Sklar (in *Gods and Beast*), and Ravenscroft (in *Spear of Destiny*), extensively explored Heinrich Himmler's fascination with spiritualism and his supposed belief that he was the reincarnation of his historical name-bearer, Heinrich. It is telling that in the epilogue of RtCW, just after B.J. has defeated the resurrected Heinrich, we see Himmler standing in the distance looking disappointedly through binoculars.

The RtCW-figure of Simon the Wanderer is also a very interesting figure, even if he only features shortly in the introduction cutscene. He is a (Benedictine) monk, who magically entraps Heinrich in his tomb. Simon could be a reference to Simon Magus, who features shortly in the Acts of the Apostles. Simply called "Simon" there, he asks the Apostles to lay their hands upon him so he can receive the holy Spirit in exchange for money. Peter rebukes him, explaining that God's grace cannot be bought or sold. This short story is expounded upon in apocryphal works like the Acts of Peter, the Acts of Peter and Paul, and Pseudo-Clementine. Traditionally named Simon Magus, Simon the Sorcerer, or Simon the Magician, his name is connected to the forbidden praxis of simony—trading in ecclesiastical blessings (Ferreiro 2021). He is also named "the first of Gnostics" by several Church Fathers, among whom Eusebius of Caesarea, Justin Martyr, Irenaeus of Lyon, Hippolytus of Rome, and Epiphanius of Salamis. It is not a very appropriate interpretation historically, since Gnosticism certainly does not equal or imply simony (see chapter 2).

The name the game gives to Simon, "The Wanderer," is also interesting, especially in regard to the later installments' preoccupation with Jewish mysticism (see chapter 8). Within Western Christianity, the figure of the "Wandering Jew" is a well-known if very anti-Semitic trope (Cohen 2007). At the core of the legend lies the non-biblical encounter between Jesus and a Jewish man in Jerusalem. When Jesus was bearing his cross toward Calvary and wanted to pause briefly, this was at the doorstep of an anonymous man. However, Jesus was met with a harsh demand to hasten his pace, accompanied by the exclamation, "Walk faster!" In response, Jesus stated, "I go, but you will walk until I come again."

From this brief yet confrontational meeting, two primary themes emerge. Firstly, Jesus promises his return at an unspecified future time; until then, the person who encountered him will find no respite. Secondly, the narrative positions "the Jew" vis-à-vis Jesus Christ, neglecting Jesus' own Jewish ethnicity, heritage, and (self-)identity. This positioning is contextualized in a broader Christian historical tendency to contrast Christianity and Judaism, disqualifying the latter for its cruel treatment of and disbelief in Jesus as the Messiah.

The legend in different versions was very popular already in de Middle Ages, for example in the pamphlet *Kurtze Beschreibung und Erzehlung von einem Juden mit Namen Ahasverus* ("Short description and story of a Jew with the name Ahasverus") published in 1602 and *Moses Gorden or the Wandering Jew in the Dress he now wears in Newgate* in 1788. However, the image of the Wandering Jew was not so much part of the anti-Semitic rhetoric of Nazism as one might have expected it to be. For example, the notorious 1937 Nazi exhibition *Der ewige Jude* ("The eternal Jew") does not treat the figure of Ahasverus prominently, but rather "the Jew" as progenitor of capitalism and communism (Tymkiw 2018, 171–220). Intriguingly, the cover of the exhibition brochure does feature the text of the poem "Ahasvers Fröhlich Wanderlied," a satire on Jewish life by—how ironic—the Jewish writer Paul Mayer (Ochse 1999, 27).

Within the fiction literature of the post-War era, there is one instance in which the figure of Ahasverus-cum-The Wandering Jew has been connected to the figure of Longinus and his legendary Spear (see above). In Barry Saddler's novel *Casca* (1979), he introduces the character Casca Rufio Longinus, a Roman legionary, who witnesses Jesus' execution. When piercing Jesus' side to hasten his death, Jesus speaks to him in a phrase reminiscent of the Ahasverus character: "Soldier, you are content with what you are. Then that you shall remain until we meet again. As I go now to My Father, you must one day come to Me." Condemned to walk the face of the earth until Christ's second coming, Casca enlists himself in many historical armies and he meets world-famous people, including Adolf Hitler himself.

The next important historical figure in the *Wolfenstein* canon, is Heinrich's son and successor, Otto I or Otto the Great (912–973). Otto plays an indirect role in *Wolfenstein: The Old Blood*. In contrast to his father, who is defeated by Blazkowicz, Otto remains dead and buried, but his secret diary is at the heart of the installment's dramatic actions. According to letters found in WOB, Helga von Schabbs, head of the SS Paranormal Division, found said diary in a hidden study-chamber at Castle Wolfenstein. Helga expresses not only her pride in her presumed genealogical connection to the ancient German king (as Himmler supposedly did with regard to Heinrich I), but also asserts that following the passing of Otto's wife, Eadgyth, in the year 946 C.E., Otto began to develop a keen interest in what are referred to as "occult sciences." Initially, the implication within the game narrative suggests that this interest may have been rooted in a desire to resurrect his deceased wife. However, as the narrative progresses, it becomes evident that Otto's pursuits evolved, eventually leading to the creation of artificial war drones.

Another letter within the game references a fictional diary or chronicle attributed to one of Otto's scholars. This document mentions the historical Battle of Lechfeld in 955 C.E. (Bowlus 2016), where Otto's army achieved victory over a formidable invading Magyar force numbering 45,000 soldiers. According to the contents of the in-game scholar's letter, Otto's success in this battle was attributed to the use of "secret weapons" that were believed to have been bestowed upon the king by divine intervention, and described as having been given to him "by Almighty God." These clandestine weapons were comprised of an army of artificial war machines, humanoid in appearance, which were seemingly created based on occult knowledge supposedly acquired by Otto during his (fictional) visit to Constantinople.

Regrettably for Otto, these artificial creations proved to be highly unstable. Consequently, the king ordered the immediate termination of the entire operation and commanded his knights to raze Wulfburg, a location mentioned within the narrative. Nonetheless, within one cave at this site, one of these creatures inexplicably survived. The circumstances surrounding its survival and presence in the cave remain uncertain. It is revealed through an in-game letter that the creature is bound within the cave by colossal chains provided by the Iranian scholar and polymath of the tenth–eleventh century C.E., Abu Rayhan al-Biruni, who was a contemporary of King Otto (Ahmed 1984). This monstrous entity remained dormant for centuries until Helga's archaeological excavations inadvertently awakened it.

In WOB, one can find an inscription on a tomb within Castle Wolfenstein reading "EDIT REGINE CINERES HIC SARCOPHAGVS HABET . . . ," or "The ashes of Queen Eadgyth are in this sarcophagus. . . ." The inscription and the name of the buried queen, Eadguyth, are references to Edith of England (910–946), the aforementioned wife of Otto I, who predeceased her husband by 27 years. Initially interred in St. Maurice monastery, Edith's tomb has been situated in Magdeburg Cathedral since the sixteenth century. For a considerable period, it was considered to be a cenotaph. However, during renovations of the cathedral in 2008, archaeologists made a remarkable discovery. They found a lead coffin within a stone sarcophagus, bearing Edith's name. In an intriguing twist, an inscription on this coffin indicated that it contained the remains of Eadgyth, who had been reburied there in 1510.

The condition of the fragmented and incomplete bones discovered in the coffin prompted further investigation in 2009. Subsequently, the bones were transported to Bristol, England, for a series of tests in 2010. The research conducted in Bristol utilized isotope tests on tooth enamel to determine whether Edith had indeed been born and raised in Wessex and Mercia, as historical records suggested. Examination of the bones, particularly the enamel of the teeth in her upper jaw, confirmed that they did indeed belong to Eadgyth (Pitts 2010). Additionally, the analysis of the enamel indicated that the individual entombed in Magdeburg had spent part of her youth in the chalky uplands of Wessex. These findings were particularly significant as the bones represented the oldest remains ever discovered of a member of English royalty. Following these scientific tests, the bones were respectfully re-interred in a new titanium coffin within Edith's tomb at Magdeburg Cathedral on the 22nd of October, 2010.

According to Ravenscroft's *The Spear of Destiny*, both Henry the Fowler *and* Otto the Great were in possession of the holy relic, rationalizing the fact that both "German" rulers were able to unify their kingdoms and to successfully wage war against powerful enemies from the East.

NAZI SYMBOLS: THE SWASTIKA AND THE BLACK SUN

Since its first use in 1920 up until today, the swastika has been undoubtfully the most well-known symbol of Nazism. It features heavily in almost all *Wolfenstein* installments, up to the point that several developers had to organize alternative versions to be released in Germany. The German Criminal Code (*Strafgesetzbuch*), section 86a, forbids the propagation of unconstitutional organizations, including Nazism, through data-storage media like video games. In 2009, *Wolfenstein* (2009) was pulled from German shops after a swastika was discovered in the localized version of the game (Brice 2009). Only with the release of *Wolfenstein: Youngbloods*, was the ban on Nazi symbols in video games lifted altogether in Germany (Vonberg 2018). It is a sign of the powerful associations the swastika still holds over (Western) culture, even if the symbol-bearing Nazis were defeated almost 80 years ago.

Friedrich Krohn, a member of the Thule Society and the Germanenorden since 1913, was the occult and *völkisch* expert of the Deutsche Arbeiterpartei, the precursor of the NSDAP (Goodrick-Clarke 2005, 151). In May 1919, Krohn published an article under the title "Ist das Hakenkreuz als Symbol Nationalsozialistischer Partei geeignet?" or "Is the swastika suitable as the symbol of the National Socialist Party?" Krohn argued in favor of a left-handed (clockwise) swastika in sync with its appearance in theosophical circles and its older Buddhist associations with fortune and health. Hitler, however, liked the right-handed (anti-clockwise) version more—incidentally associated with death and decline, which may or may not be something Hitler knew and acted upon. Krohn was responsible for the aesthetics as they would become internationally known: a black swastika in a white circle on a red background. On May 20, 1920, the swastika-on-a-flag was used for the first time at a rally of the Starnberg NSDAP group, a place of prominence it would never leave until the end of the Nazi regime.

Ariosophists like Jörg Lanz von Liebenfels, Guido von List, and Rudolf Sebottendorf (see chapter 2) followed their common inspirator, Madame Blavatsky, in their appreciation of the swastika. Blavatsky was so enthusiastic about the symbol that she included it in the seal of her Theosophical Society, together with, among others, the Star of David (representing Judaism). From 1892, German translations of Blavatsky's work were published in Franz Hartmann's periodical *Lotusblüten* ("Lotus Blossoms"), featuring the swastika on its front cover, making it the first German publication to do so (Goodrick-Clarke 2005, 25). It was the same Hartmann, who promoted the Guido von List Society, founded by its namesake in 1908.

Von List, in his own turn, was also very much involved in swastika mysticism. He regarded it as an Aryan symbol, "derived from the *Feuerquirl* (fire whisk) with which Mundelfori had initially twirled the cosmos into being" (idem 52). Von List also claimed that the Knights Templar were crushed in 1307 for "their worship of this most sacred Ario-Germanic symbol" (idem 62). Fellow-Ariosophist Lanz von Liebenfels, who tried to imitate the Knights Templar in his own Order of the New Templars (see above), celebrated Christmas Day 1907 by hoisting a swastika flag upon the top of his Castle Werfenstein, which is one of the models for the fictional Castle Wolfenstein (idem 109).

Another Nazi symbol also features in the *Wolfenstein* series, especially in *Wolfenstein* (2009): *die Schwarze Sonne*, or "Black Sun." Its most famous historical design is found in Castle Wewelsburg near Paderborn, acquired by Himmler in 1934. It is found on the white marble floor of the Gruppenführer hall in the northern tower (Goodrick-Clarke 2002, 148; Siepe 2022). It was only after the end of the Second World War that the Black Sun became a symbol synonymous with the swastika as *the* representation of Nazism. Already in the 1950s, the Landig group (see above) used the Black Sun as a "swastika substitute" (idem 3–4), providing for its continuous use in Neo-Nazi groups ever since (idem 128).

The Swiss engineer Erich Halik was the first to establish a connection between the esoteric beliefs of the SS and the circular "Black Sun" emblem carried by German aircraft in the polar regions toward the end of World War II (idem 131). Halik believed, as is evident from a series of articles in *Mensch und Schicksal* between 1951 and 1955, that the Nazis already occupied two "polar empires" in both the Arctic and Antarctic regions. These empires were symbolically associated with the "Golden Sun" and the "Black Sun." The Black Sun myth was taken further by Russel McCloud in his 1991 thriller *Die schwarze Sonne von Tashi Lhunpo* ("The Black Sun of Tashi Lhunpo"). He explicitly links the Black Sun mythology of the Landig Group with the physical wheel found on the floor of Castle Wewelsburg (Goodrick-Clarke 2002, 148).

CRAZY SCIENTISTS: THE SS AHNENERBE

SS Paranormal Division is the most predominant secret organization throughout the game series, appearing in *Return to Castle Wolfenstein*, *Wolfenstein* (2009), and *Wolfenstein: The Old Blood*. According to the in-game lore, the organization was founded by Himmler himself to organize and coordinate research into the history and practice of paranormal powers for the benefit of the Third Reich. In *Return to Castle Wolfenstein*, the Division is headed by Standartenführer Helga von Bulow and Oberführer and "SS High Priestess" Marianna Blavatsky. The first is occupied by finding and using the "Dagger of Warding," a Thulean object used to raise up an ancient Aryan warrior called Olaric. Unfortunately for Helga, Olaric is not a friendly "undead" and dismembers her immediately before B.J. arrives on the scene to finish it off once and for all.

A similar fate awaits Blavatsky: after she successfully resurrects Heinrich I in a magical ritual, she is immediately killed by the German prince before, in his turn, he is killed by B.J. coming to the rescue. Helga von Bulow is also the leader of the Elite Guards, a group within the SS Paranormal Division, exclusively made up of blond, slim women, dressed in very tight, black, leather bodysuits, who form a serious threat to B.J.'s efforts. Helga is initially in the company of Professor A. Zemph, who constantly urges her to take it slowly, scared as he is they will unleash powers they can no longer control. After Helga impatiently kills Zemph—because he threatens to report her to her superiors in the Reich—he is proven correct.

In *Wolfenstein* (2009), the SS Paranormal Division is in charge of the research concerning the Black Sun Dimension, uncovering its Thulean past. Ultimately, also this research is destroyed by B.J.'s interference, closing the portal between the Black Sun Dimension and ours indefinitely.

In *Wolfenstein: The Old Blood*, the SS Paranormal Division returns, now as a subsidiary of the Special Project Division of the Third Reich. This version of the Division is founded and governed by Obersturmbannführer Helga von Schabbs (instead of Himmler as in the previous iterations). Helga von Schabbs is both a reference to Helga von Bulow (from RtCW) and—in appearance and character—to the historical Irma Grese (1923–1945), a notorious female Nazi concentration camp guard at Ravensbrück and Auschwitz. Nicknamed *die Hyäne von Auschwitz* ("the hyena of Auschwitz") Grese was convicted by the Nuremberg trials and executed at the age of 22 (Huber 2011). Castle Wolfenstein is now her ancestral home—she is related to Otto

I, whose grave she hopes to find in order to unlock its secrets. In Istanbul, she discovered Otto's correspondence with Abu Rayhan al-Biruni, who helps the German king with Da'at Yichud technology to secure his military superiority (see chapter 8). Like her namesake from RtCW, this Helga also forces her hand: she tries foolishly to control a monstrosity she awakened from its slumber, only to be (nearly) killed by it.

Helga von Schabbs answers to Oberstgruppenführer Wilhelm "Deathshead" Strasse, a gifted if ruthless researcher himself, and head of the SS Special Project Division. He is B.J.'s primary adversary in *Return to Castle Wolfenstein*, *Wolfenstein* (2009), and *Wolfenstein: The New Order*. Strasse's name is a double reference: firstly, to the historical Wilhelmstrasse ("William Street"), the center of the Prussian and later Nazi government in Berlin; secondly, his nickname is connected to the infamous SS *Totenkopfring* ("Death's Head ring"), worn by SS officers and designed by Willigut at the behest of Himmler himself (Goodrick-Clarke 2005, 187).

Wolfenstein's SS Paranormal Division is the in-game iteration of the historical SS Ahnenerbe, which itself is the incarnation of everything Nazi and pseudo-scientific (Pringle 2006). The Ahnenerbe was a historical organization within the Nazi regime dedicated to researching the historical and cultural heritage of the Aryan race, often delving into pseudo-scientific and esoteric realms. Initially named the Deutsches Ahnenerbe Studiengesellschaft für Geistesurgeschichte ("Society for the Study of the History of Primeval Ideas"), it was established in 1935 by Heinrich Himmler and the Dutch prehistorian Dr. Hermann Wirth. Its primary mission was to prove the superiority of the Aryan race through the study of history, archaeology, and folklore. However, their methods often veered into pseudo-science and the occult.

One of the SS Ahnenerbe's notable expeditions took place in Norway, where they sought the mythical Aryan homeland Thule. This endeavor aimed to establish a historical connection between the Aryan race and the ancient Norse civilization. The expedition was led by Dr. Walter Wüst and Dr. Heinrich Jankuhn. And although both scholars were renowned in their respective fields, their findings were ideologically driven, and were not based on credible academic research. Another expedition was to Tibet, where the SS Ahnenerbe hoped to find ancient relics linked to Aryan origins and the supposed roots of the Nazi ideology. Led by Ernst Schäfer, a renowned ornithologist, the expedition was purportedly scientific, but it was intertwined with esoteric beliefs. They collected various artifacts and documents, but their conclusions were colored by Nazi ideology rather than by academic rigor.

Even though the SS Ahnenerbe and other Nazi research facilities were dissolved at the end of the war, many of their top scientists were able to escape justice and were able to continue their former work in and for the benefit of the United States of America. "Operation Paperclip" was a covert program conducted by the United States after World War II, specifically between 1945 and 1959, to recruit and employ more than 16,000 German scientists, engineers, and technicians, many of whom had been involved in Nazi Germany's military and scientific research (Jacobsen 2014). Among them were famous scientists like Wernher von Braun and Arthur Rudolph. The aim of the operation was to harness the scientific and technological expertise of these individuals for American post-war efforts, particularly in the fields of rocketry, aerospace, and military technology.

According to Heff Stone (2005, 339), "[t]he second most popular American stereotype about Germany after Nazism is the idea that Germany is the home of the world's worst mad scientists." Already starting with the mad Dr. Frankenstein from the 1818 novel by Mary Shelley and its countless Hollywood iterations, films like *They saved Hitler's brain* (1963), *The boys from Brazil* (1978), and *Splash* (1984) show univocally that "the Nazi doctor is a figure of consummate evil who knows what he is doing and does it with disciplined and monomaniacal obsession" (Crawford and Martel 1997, 290). The scientist à la Frankenstein may be mad, but he is not evil in intentions and purposes. The Nazi scientist, however, is knowingly committing evil "and does so cold-bloodedly and brutally" (idem).

Helga von Bulow, Helga von Schabbs, Prof. Zemph, and Wilhelm Strasse all fit the description of mad scientist perfectly. They are methodical, brutal, and highly efficient, with an absolute disregard for any form of morality.

Chapter 7

Don't Pay Any Attention, Please

To Disclaim or Not to Disclaim

From *Wolfenstein: New Order* onwards, all the series' instalments feature a disclaimer. The disclaimer is stated in eight languages, including English, and is shown every time the player starts the game. It is not possible to skip the disclaimer by button-pressing or other game-internal means. The text is white, the background is black. It states:

> *Wolfenstein: The New Order* is a fictional story set in an alternative universe in the 1960s. Names, characters, organizations, locations, and events are either imaginary or depicted in a fictionalized manner. The story and contents of the game are not intended to and should not be construed in any way to condone, glorify, or endorse the beliefs, ideologies, events, actions, persons, or behavior of the Nazi regime or to trivialize its war crimes, genocide, and other crimes against humanity.

The disclaimer was noticed by players and critics. Mike Fahey (2013), for example, from *Kotaku* commented: "I applaud Bethesda for having the strength of character to distance themselves from the Nazi regime in such a public fashion." As discussed earlier, the series as a whole has been criticized for Nazi glorification and neglect of the horrors and victims of the Second World War. Fahey seems to be pleased with the disclaimer addressing this problem directly. Bethesda/MachineGames' decision—it is difficult to distinguish between the publisher and developer with regard to the question who is legally or morally responsible for the inclusion of the text—meets the larger contemporary cultural context, which itself is riddled with disclaimer texts.

Disclaimers are utilized when creators anticipate negative experiences with and negative reactions to (the use of) their products. These act as a pre-emptive defense against libel suits or public outrage (and the accompanying financial backlash caused by both). These negative experiences and reactions may range from physical and mental ones (like seizure disclaimers, wrongful use, and trigger warnings), to moral ones (like accusations of cultural appropriation). Major games and game series other than *Wolfenstein* have adopted such disclaimers at the beginning of their games (Bosman 2015).

The *Assassin's Creed* series, for example, has featured a disclaimer from the earliest instalment in 2007 onwards. It reads:

> Inspired by historical events and characters. This work of fiction was designed, developed, and produced by a multicultural team of various religious faiths and beliefs.

The *Assassin's Creed* series features a complete and total re-imagining of the world's history and its major world religions, including Judaism, Christianity, Buddhism, Hinduism, and Islam (Bosman 2016b, 2016c). What humankind has held to be divine or transcendent is nothing more than the wrongly interpreted remnants of a now extinct, earth-bound super race known as the Isu. Major wars and conflicts in humanity's history are nothing more than veiled disputes regarding the possession of powerful Isu artefacts that can control the course of human history. The game series, especially its earlier instalments, is susceptible to the accusation of being anti-religion, an accusation the developer/publisher wants to avoid by pre-emptively assuring the series' audiences that the games were made by a multicultural and multireligious team of developers. It suggests that the developers could circumvent religious and cultural sensitivities through the diversity of their team.

Interestingly enough, with the release of *Assassin's Creed Syndicate* in 2015, developer/publisher Ubisoft slightly adjusted the series' disclaimer, mirroring new societal sensitivities. It reads:

> Inspired by historical events and characters, this work of fiction was designed, developed and produced by a multicultural team of various beliefs, *sexual orientations and gender identities* [cursive fgb].

The *Tomb Raider* reboot series (since 2015) features a similar disclaimer from the second instalment of *Shadow of the Tomb Raider* (2018) onwards. It reads:

> Shadow of the Tomb Raider was created by a diverse and talented team comprised of multiple genders, backgrounds, ethnicities, religious beliefs, and personalities. Although the game is not based on real life events and represents a work of fiction, it was developed in conjunction with a historian and cultural consultants. This variety and partnership were both instrumental in crafting the world you're about to experience. No matter where you come from or who you are, allow us to be the first to say: Welcome to Shadow of the Tomb Raider.

Shadow takes place in Meso and South America and is heavily influenced by Inca mythology and culture, especially the legendary city of Paititi. Clearly, developer Eidos and publisher Square Enix tried to tackle the series' own colonialist heritage and the cultural appropriation of the Inca culture and history for a "Western" narrative (or at least want to suggest that they have) by the explicit mentioning of historians and cultural advisors (Lacina 2018, Power 2018).

Hinterland Studio's *The Long Dark* (2020) also features a disclaimer, this one apparently warning users not to imitate the game in real life:

> Hinterland Studio Inc. does not condone the wanton destruction of wildlife. As the result of the geomagnetic disaster which serves as part of the fictional foundation of the game, we have taken liberties with the portrayal of wildlife behavior. We are not attempting to create "realistic" wildlife behavior in the game. We know that Wolves do not typically attack people. The Long Dark is a survival experience, and we strive for realism in many areas, but it is NOT a replacement for actual survival training or experience in the wilderness. In the end, our goal is to provide an interesting set of choices for you to play with safely. It is not a wilderness survival training simulation. (. . .) DO NOT ATTEMPT TO USE WHAT YOU LEARN IN THE LONG DARK IN REAL LIFE. DOING SO COULD RESULT IN INJURY, ILLNESS, or even DEATH.

The Long Dark is a first-person survival game, in which the players have to scavenge and hunt for food, while fending off predators, especially wolves. The developer/publisher seems keen to denounce precisely those two things: (1) we made the game as life-like as we can (and we are advertising it as such) but you should not consider it as being such, and (2) even though we portray wolves in the game as vicious human-killers, we want to make sure you understand that wolves do not behave violently toward humans in the wild.

THE PARADOX OF DISCLAIMERS

Disclaimers are all very paradoxical in nature. Disclaimers draw attention to what they want to divert attention from. Producers of disclaimers assume there is a problem that has to be tackled pre-emptively, but one could argue that this tackling itself causes consumers to become aware of a problem that the producer claims is not there. For a moment, let us reconsider the nature of disclaimers and reflect on them from a communication point of view. In his monograph on the legal issues surrounding the depiction of real persons and events in fictional mediums, John Aquino (2022, 50–51) analyses the functions of disclaimers. (1) Legality: explaining filmmakers' intentions in anticipation of, and as pre-emptive protection from a libel suit. (2) Duality: disclaimers tend to argue that the story is simultaneously fictional and factual. (3) Communication: the filmmakers are directly talking to their audiences.

From the point of view of our methodology (the Communication-Oriented Analysis, see introduction), we can comment on these functions and add two extra ones to the list. The use of disclaimers to explain the creators' intentions presupposes a Real Author perspective *and* a one-to-one relation between this Real Author and the Text-Immanent Author. An example of this is the aforementioned *Assassin's Creed* disclaimer. This disclaimer claims that the game series cannot tell a culturally or religiously insensitive story because the developers themselves are from different cultural and religious backgrounds. Later on, this group is augmented by persons of multiple sexual orientations and gender identities. This claim only works if there is no difference between the intentions of the developers (Real Author collective) and those of the Text-Immanent Author telling the actual stories of the game series. This is flawed because players (in the sense of Real Readers) have to trust the disclaimer's claim without any practical possibility of verifying its authenticity. Because the Real Author and the Text-Immanent Author are conceptually not the same communicative instances, the problematic nature of the game instalment can be found either in the developers' intentions or in the game-immanent narrator (the Text-Immanent Author), but not necessarily in both together.

The duality aspect, mentioned by Aquino, is also problematic from a communication point of view. It is problematic because a story cannot be both factual and fictional at the same time (these notions are mutually exclusive) and because it assumes the identification of the Real Author with the Real Reader on the one hand, and of the Text-Immanent Author with the Text-Immanent Reader on the other. It is a kind of literary fundamentalism: the inability to distinguish between the world of the text and the world outside the text, and to understand their mutual relationship. This is the case regarding the *Shadow of the Tomb Raider* and *The Long Dark* disclaimers.

Aquino's third point, that in disclaimers filmmakers communicate directly to their audiences, is also very interesting from a communicative point of view. "Speaking directly to the audience" can take place in two different ways: (1) the Text-Immanent Author can directly address the Text-Immanent Reader or (2) the Text-Immanent Author can do so with the help of a ventriloquizing character that directly addresses the Text-Immanent Reader (also called "breaking of the fourth wall"). In the case of disclaimers, the first option is applicable. This is very visible in *The Long Dark* and *Shadow* disclaimers.

However, in the case of disclaimers, there is another communicative possibility. One could argue that the disclaimer is a separate text vis-à-vis the game text. In that case the disclaimer and the actual game have an intertextual relationship. This means that both texts have the same Real Reader (the actual gamer playing the game, including the disclaimer at the beginning), but not necessarily the same Real Author, Text-Immanent Author, or Text-Immanent Reader. Maybe the game was developed by a specific team, while the disclaimer was written by the juridical department of the developer/publisher. Maybe the disclaimer is narrated by an anonymous narrator, which can or cannot be the same one as the in-game (identifiable) narrator. See for example, the ending of the *Shadow* disclaimer: "No matter where you come from or who you are, allow us to be the first to say: Welcome to Shadow of the Tomb Raider." Are the nameless Text-Immanent Author that invites the Text-Immanent Reader (Player) to *enjoy the game*, and the Text-Immanent Author *of the game* one and the same? I argue that they are not, or not necessarily.

Besides Aquino's three functions of disclaimers, I wish to add two extra ones, again from a communication point of view: the nature of the disclaimer's paradoxical communication, and its relation to cultural appropriation and cancel culture. As argued above, disclaimers tend to inadvertently, and unintentionally (or even counter-intentionally) draw attention to what they want to divert attention from. The Text-Immanent Reader of such a disclaimer will—by its very nature—agree with everything that the Text-Immanent Author is telling it, including the avoidance of cultural and religious sensitivities. However, any Real Reader—again by its nature—has a choice to believe the disclaimer's Text-Immanent Author, or not; or even not to pay any attention to it at all. If the disclaimer of *Assassin's Creed* assures its gamers that there is no problem whatsoever with cultural and religious sensitivities, the disclaimer's Text-Immanent Reader will agree—nothing here to worry about!—but real players of the game may still find its content offensive, impolite, or even blasphemous. If the disclaimer of *Shadow* argues—implicitly—that there is no cultural appropriation to be found in the game, the Text-Immanent Reader will agree—there is none!—but any Real Reader of the game may beg to differ, and may even explicitly be on the lookout now for any sign of appropriation.

Cancel culture is the socio-cultural phenomenon in which persons who have acted or spoken in a way that is deemed unacceptable are ostracized, boycotted, or shunned by (certain groups within) society (Yar and Bromwich 2019, Bromwich 2018). Those who are canceled lose public credibility, and their services and products lose commercial value. Recent examples include the musicians Michael Jackson (Tate et al. 2019) and Kanye West (Hobbs 2022), *Harry Potter* writer J. K. Rowling (Hussein 2018), and the German novelist Karl May (Connolly 2022), just to name a few. Disclaimers are also used to prevent products that they are attached to being canceled by outraged influencers and their audiences.

From a communication perspective, this kind of canceling is the overall disqualification of a given text because of the moral judgment of the text's Real Reader toward the text's Real Author, disregarding the interaction between the Text-Immanent Author and the Text-Immanent Reader. In other words: in the case of cancelation, the disqualification of a song, novel, film, or game is based on the real-life acts and words of their creators. Essentially, again, this is a case of literary fundamentalism: the implicit identification of the Real Author with the Text-Immanent Author.

BACK TO THE WOLVES

Let us return to the *Wolfenstein* disclaimer. It states explicitly that it does not wish to "condone, glorify, or endorse the beliefs, ideologies, events, actions, persons or behavior of the Nazi regime." As we have discussed above, due to the paradoxical nature of disclaimers, individual gamers (the Real Readers of the game) will have to choose whether they want to believe that message or not. The negating of Nazi glorification evokes the possibility of its opposite: if there is no Nazi glorification in the first place, why tell your players so? The net result of the disclaimer could be that more players start searching for indications of *Wolfenstein*'s love of the Nazi era than without the disclaimer.

Publisher Bethesda and developer MachineGames issued another disclaimer, which was part of the promotional material accompanying the launch of the game in 2014. It features the same text as the one at the beginning of the game, but the disclaimer is re-imagined in such a way that it aesthetically and narratively fits within the game's internal lore. The disclaimer itself is printed on a pink-colored note, featuring a stamp with "disclaimer" in capitals and the *Wolfenstein* series' logo, while the actual text is styled using an old-fashioned typewriter's font. The combination suggests that the note was produced by an old typewriter, and issued by a bureaucratic organization, probably the military. This suggested narrative context of military communication is strengthened by two other elements. (1) The disclaimer is accompanied by a larger background in full color, featuring the WNO's aesthetic version of Blazkowicz, holding a shotgun in his left hand and facing multiple Nazi war robots. (2) Above the actual disclaimer's text two sentences are written: "FROM: Bethesda PR High Command. TO: Impressionable Players."

This disclaimer makes things a lot worse for Bethesda/MachineGames. In the *in-game* disclaimer, the communicative roles were clear and simple: Bethesda/MachineGames is the Real Author and individual players are the Real Reader, while the Text-Immanent Author and Text-Immanent Reader remain undisclosed. In the *game-external* disclaimer, the communicative roles of the Text-Immanent Author and the Text-Immanent Reader are filled in, respectively with "Bethesda PR High Command" and "Impressionable Players." The now disclosed Text-Immanent Reader is disqualified by the Text-Immanent Author (PR High Command) as "impressionable." The Text-Immanent Reader will not be offended of course, since it does not have feelings or opinions. Real Readers, on the other hand, who have to identify with the Text-Immanent Reader in order for the communication to function effectively in the first place, will possibly object to this identification: generally speaking, impressionability is not considered to be a positive characteristic, and is associated with children and those with a weaker mental disposition.

The *aesthetics* of the *game-external* disclaimer, including its potential offensive heading regarding the impressionable player, suggests exactly the opposite of what the *text* of the *game-external* disclaimer wishes to achieve: the text suggests that the game (series) is not involved with the glorification of the Nazi era, while the silhouette of Blazkowicz vis-à-vis Nazi killer robots suggests that only "impressionable"—read: weak—players could take offense. The *game-external* disclaimer effectively mocks (from the position of the Text-Immanent Author) any and all allegations made against the *Wolfenstein* series as to Nazi glorification in the past and the present, nullifying the context of the disclaimer's text.

One last point: how can a disclaimer with its grave legal and moral vocabulary be part of the game's promotional material? Promotional material is aimed at entertaining or provoking possible consumers and critics to buy and (positively) review the game in their professional or private circles. A disclaimer neither wants to entertain nor provoke; it wants to do the opposite: to inform and to ease (possible) tension.

In conclusion: if Bethesda/MachineGames—as the disclaimer's Real Author—wanted to counter the previously expressed concerns by players and critics of possible Nazi glorification in the *Wolfenstein* series, and wanted to prevent this from happening again in contemporary instalments like WNO, the *in-game* disclaimer—by virtue of its genre—already communicates two conflicting messages at the same time: it draws attention toward what it wants to divert attention away from. The *game-external* disclaimer, however, effectively destroys this effort by mocking concerned or offended players pre-emptively as "impressionable," disqualifying all earlier critics of the series in an almost pubescent manner.

Chapter 8

Celebrating Streicher's Purim

The Revenge of the Jews

With the release of the fourth cycle, starting with *Wolfenstein: The New Order* in 2014, the series introduced—to quite a great degree—Jewish characters, history, and mysticism into the game lore. Interestingly, the word "Jew" was only introduced in *Wolfenstein II: The New Colossus* in 2017. In chapter 4 ("Roswell, New Mexico"), a note can be found by Nazi researcher Lutz Meier: "Elke discovered that a Jew named Set Roth escaped from Camp Belica with the terrorist William Blazkowicz. This man is rumored to be a living member of the Da'at Yichud." Nevertheless, hints at the Jewish heritage of Blazkowicz and of numerous other characters are found all over the place. Since the series has been criticized for neglecting the Jews as World War II's primary victims (Hayton 2012, 211), and for its omission of the Holocaust (Hayton 2015, 260–65), the abundancy of "Jewishness" in the new cycle seems to be the developers' answer to that criticism. This chapter will be devoted to these Jewish characters, history, and mysticism, while critically relating them to their real-life counterparts, starting with "general" references and continuing with the more "mystical" ones later on.

WILLIAM B.J. BLAZKOWICZ: "MY PEOPLE"

When *Wolfenstein II. The New Colossus* was released in 2017, the critics were keen to point out one very specific theme within the new game: "Yes, B.J. Blazkowicz is Jewish," headlined *Polygon* (Kuchera 2017). "Wolfenstein star revealed to be Jewish," *The Tablet* wrote (Geselowitz 2017). Two years later, *VG247* even stated that "Wolfenstein 2 proves that Jews can be heroes, not just survivors" (Mello-Klein 2019). Already in 2014, with the release of *Wolfenstein: New Order*, Tom Hall (2014), the old lead designer of the older *Wolfenstein 3D* (1992) confirmed internet rumors that Blazkowicz is not only

Polish, but also Jewish: "My intent was: his mother was Jewish, tried to hide that, unsuccessfully."

Nevertheless, already in WNO the writing was clearly on the wall. When B.J. is knocked down by one of Wilhelm Strasse's super soldiers during the failed raid on the general's secret compound, one of Blazkowicz's interior monologues is heard: "My people murdered. So many times. I lost count." The question is, of course, to what "people" is B.J. referring here? There are, I believe, four options: the people of the United States of America, B.J.'s homeland, under whose flag he is serving as a solider; the people of Poland, the land of B.J.'s maternal ancestors; the allied forces, the world-wide coalition trying to bring down the Nazi empire; or the people of Israel.

Even though each of these four can be argued for, in this regard the fourth holds the strongest cards. Not only does WNO (and WOB) continuously hint at B.J.'s Jewish origins, but the very phrase "my people" is a highly religiously-charged one in both Judaism and Christianity. In the Hebrew Bible/Old Testament, the phrase is generally attributed to God, who refers to his "chosen people," the people of Israel (Stulman and Kim 2011). See for example: "I have certainly seen the oppression of My people who are in Egypt, and have heard their outcry because of their taskmasters, for I am aware of their sufferings" (Exodus 3:7); "By the hand of My servant David, I will save My people Israel from the hand of the Philistines, and from the hands of all their enemies" (2 Samuel 3:18). The context of the phrase frequently incorporates a situation in which God promises to guard, save, or rescue his people from foreign oppressors, including the Egyptians and the Philistines. Therefore, "my people" has the association of current oppression and the promise of deliverance from that oppression.

In the Catholic tradition, the phrase "my people" is associated with the *Improperia*, a series of antiphons and responses, traditionally sung on Good Friday (Saliers 2011). The (Latin) refrain is: *Popule meus, quid feci tibi? Aut in quo constristavi te? Responde mihi*. In English translation: "My people, what have I done to you? Or how have I offended you? Answer me." In the *Improperia*, the context of the Exodus is dominant, with phrases like: *Quia eduxi te de terra Ægypti: parasti Crucem Salvatori tuo* ("I led you from the land of Egypt: you brought your saviour to the cross"); and *Ego eduxi te de Ægypto, demerso Pharaone in mare rubrum: et tu me tradidisti principibus sacerdotum* ("I led you out of Egypt, drowning the Pharaoh in the Red Sea: and you handed me to the high priests").

The question is, who is speaking here? There are two options available: Jesus Christ or God. Traditionally, the answer is the former, implying a heavy identification between the God, who led his people from Egypt on the one hand, and Jesus Christ, who is "repaid" for his (repeated) salvation of the same people by a gruesome death on the cross on the other (cf. Bernard

2019). The latter option seems to be more in tune with the content of the verses: God questioning his people for the fact they crucified the one he sent to them in view of their (renewed) liberation.

The identification of the *Improperia*'s addressees is of even more importance. If "my people" is associated with the Jews exclusively, the implicit condemnation heard in the *Improperia*'s phrasing, especially because of its Christian context within the liturgy of Good Friday, can and has been interpreted anti-Semitically. The accusation of deicide—the Jews are responsible for the "murder of God" in Jesus Christ's crucifixion—lurks in the background. Deicide was the traditional Christian argument to persecute the Jews during the last two millennia (Civan 2004). Connecting Blazkowicz, the American soldier with a Jewish background, to the phrase "my people" is a double-edged sword. On the one hand, it strengthens the identification of the Jews as the prime victims of the Nazi regime and of the divine promise of liberation from foreign oppression, but on the other hand it also connects the Jewish people to the old prejudice of deicide, possibly suggesting that their sufferings at the hands of the Nazis hands were, ultimately, brought onto their own heads as a justified retribution for the murder of Jesus Christ.

There are other instances within the *Wolfenstein* series that identify B.J. with "his people." When Blazkowicz captures a Nazi field coordinator (again in WNO) and interrogates him, the latter mocks "I have been known to be just and fair when dealing with people like you." Again, the question is, of course, to which "people" is referred to here. Possible answers include: mentally challenged people, since B.J. has just fled from a psychiatric asylum that was destroyed by Nazi soldiers; people resisting the Nazis, since the officer is taken to Anya's grandparents; and—again—the Jews. The officer himself answers that question a couple of questions later, when he adds: "You are a goddamned mental patient."

After B.J. and Set Roth manage to overcome a Nazi war robot guarding the Belica concentration camp (WNO), in which both were incarcerated, a severely wounded SS-Obersturmbannführer-cum-camp director, Irene Engel threatens the series' protagonist in no uncertain terms:

> You will die like vermin. I will hunt you down. At the end of the Earth, I will find you. Your skin charred and your fats rendered. Your kind exterminated. In the end, I will feed your flesh to the furnace.

Again, the question arises: who lies behind the phrase "your kind." Multiple answers could be given, but one is most likely: again, the Jewish people. Several hints affirm this interpretation, including "vermin," who are "hunt[ed] down" and "exterminated." The equating of Jews with rats was not so much invented by the Third Reich, but was nevertheless immensely popularized by propaganda films like *Der ewige Jude* ("The eternal Jew") by Fritz Hippler from 1940. The film juxtaposes images of Jewish ghettos and images of rats in order to draw an analogy between the migration of Eastern Jews to Western Europe with the migration of rats (Friedländer 2007, 101).

And then there is the imagery of fire and burning: "charred," "fats rendered," "flesh," and "furnace." They all seem like references to the burning ovens of the concentration camps, cremating the mortal remains of millions of gassed Jews and others deemed unworthy of living. However, there is more: in the haggadic literature, a story is told in which Abraham smashes the idols of his father, who is an idol manufacturer. Because of Abraham's refusal to worship the divine fire, King Nimrod throws him into a fiery furnace from which he is saved by the interference of the angel Gabriel (Reissner 2007, 283). According to similar sources, Nimrod also tried to kill Abraham directly after his birth by ordering to kill all male children (Sarna and Hirschberg 2007, 269), a story reminiscent of both the birth of Moses—all male Israelite babies were killed by the Egyptians (Exodus 1:22)—and the birth of Jesus—all young children around Bethlehem were murdered at the order of King Herod (Matthew 2:16–18), known as the Massacre of the Innocents in Christian tradition (Cho 2021).

Another biblical association is that of the "fiery furnace" in Daniel 3. In the story, three Hebrew men are thrown into the furnace by the Babylonian King Nebuchadnezzar II for refusing to bow before the idols he erected (Holm 2008). The three survive the inferno because of a fourth figure, suddenly and inexplicably appearing among the flames (Daniel 3:25). In all cases, B.J. is equated with the Jewish people in general, but specifically with Abraham, Moses, and the three men from Daniel. In all cases, God's intervention guaranteed their survival against overwhelming odds. And vice versa, the Nazi regime is related to ancient rulers the Bible denotes as ruthless and ungodly: Nimrod, the Egyptian Pharoah, and Nebuchadnezzar.

Another strong indication of B.J.'s Jewishness is given when the series' protagonist manages to infiltrate one of the Nazis' primary research facilities, the London Nautica. Blazkowicz finds proof of Nazi scientists reverse-engineering Da'at Yichud technology, something that helped them win the Second World War in 1946. Via radio, B.J. reports to his girlfriend Anya Oliwa, who is back in the resistance's hideout in Berlin:

B.J.: I think I found something.

Anya: What do you see?

BJ: Ancient artifacts. Highly technological in nature. Parchment. Looks like Hebrew. I think the Nazis are trying to reverse engineer all this stuff.

Anya: Are there any identifying marks?

BJ: Da'at Yichud. Dog, Able, apostrophe, Able, Taurus, space, Yoke, Item, Charlie, How, Uncle, Dog.

The documents are identified as written in Hebrew, but B.J. seems to have no problem with either recognizing the Hebrew alphabet or reading them. This is—again—a reference to his Jewish heritage and upbringing. On screen, the two words—*Da'at* and *Yichud*—are shown, spelled in a pseudo-Hebrew font, probably so as to ensure that they can be read by the average gamer, while at the same time retaining an ancient and exotic appearance. B.J. spells the two Hebrew words, not in their original Hebrew spelling, but using the historically appropriate 1943 CCB (US-UK) phonetic (Latin) spelling alphabet.

When B.J. and Set Roth manage to escape by car from the Belica camp, the latter uses the epithet "ape-like" for his liberator: "I hate to make compliments. But I might have underestimated the usefulness of your ape-like physique, Mr. Blazkowicz." This is probably a reference to the distinction between "humans," especially Aryans, and *Untermenschen* or "apes," a pseudo-scientific theory originating from thinkers like the aforementioned Lanz von Liebenfels, but popularized by Nazi theorists. In his *Theozoölogie oder die Kunde von den Sodoms-Äfflingen und dem Götter-Elektron* ("Theozoology or the science of the Sodomite-Apelings and the divine electron") from 1905, Von Liebenfels postulated his theory that the Aryans originated from the sexual procreation between interstellar gods and electricity, while the *Untermenschen*, including Jews, were the result of a pairing between apes and inferior human root races. Therefore, he propagated the mass-castration of these "ape-like creatures." The book also included a plea for the "banning of interracial marriages, selective breeding and polygamy, and advocating the sterilization and elimination of inferior races, from the mentally and physically inferior to the Jews" (Kurlander 2017, 21). It is a rather ominous name spoken from one Jew to another, especially in the context of the Nazi concentration camp.

Roth has, however, also another name for Blazkowicz: Shimshon. When B.J. meets Roth for the first time, the two are not immediately allies, let alone friends. Blazkowicz tries to persuade Roth to spill the beans about the secret Da'at Yichud technology, something Roth—understandably—refuses: "Look at this Shimshon. So much muscle. A physique wrought for combat. (. . .) Get away, Shimshon. Do not waste your time. (. . .) Permit me a moment to consider, Shimshon." Samson, or Simson, is—again—a biblical character, this time from the book of Judges (chapters 13 through 16). In both biblical and later Jewish sources, Samson is both a hero and a villain at the same time: he kills a host of hostile Philistines, but more from a personal motive of revenge than righteous retribution, and he likes to be around foreign, promiscuous women (Crenshaw 1996).

The last of these women cuts his long hair, robbing him of his super-human power, and delivers him over into the hands of his arch-enemies, who want to sacrifice him to their idol. Only at the last moment does God answer Samson's prayer: his powers have returned because his hair has regrown during his imprisonment and he pushes the two pillars he was bound to aside, resulting in his own death but also in that of a thousand Philistine spectators. This association between B.J. and the figure of Samson is a premonition of WNO's ending, in which the series' protagonist sacrifices his own life in order to destroy the Wilhelm Strasse compound, possibly tipping the scales of the war. (Unfortunately, the beginning of WNC negates this sacrifice.) There is no mistaking that Blazkowicz is the cause of many a Nazi's death during the course of the series, just as his biblical counterpart was regarding the Philistines. This association is, however, also a bit problematic, since Samson has a Janus face: he is a hero, but is also inspired by selfish motivations and is a bit of a sexual predator. In the game series, B.J.'s actions are motivated by altruistic intentions and his relationship with Anya is clearly not only sexual in nature, but also romantic and—during the course of WNC—a fruitful one.

Yet another hint is found in WOB. When the German resistance fighter Ludwig Kessler (see below for more details) asks B.J. for an update on Richard Wesley (a deceased OSA agent), the series' protagonist answers with three simple words: "in Abraham's bosom." Within a Christian context, this refers to a well-known parable by Jesus in Luke 16:19–31. Once there was a rich man living in splendor in a large house. At the gate of his house, a beggar called Lazarus lived out his life (not to be confused with another character of the same name from the Gospel of John). Intriguingly, the poor man has a name, while the rich one remains anonymous. The beggar must make do with the crumbs that fall off the rich man's table, and the only treatment his sore wounds receive are the licks of some street dogs. When both Lazarus and the rich man, the one after the other, have died, the first lies in Abraham's bosom, while the latter arrives in Hades' eternal torment. The rich man cries out to Abraham, first to ask for Lazarus' help—which is refused by Abraham—and later to be allowed to warn his five brothers about the fate awaiting them. Abraham rebukes him, pointing out that Moses and the Prophets (= the Hebrew Bible) warns them. But the rich man is not satisfied: only when someone rises "from the dead, they will repent." But again, Abraham rebukes him: "If they do not listen to Moses and the Prophets, they will not be persuaded even if someone rises from the dead."

This parable is traditionally interpreted as a reference to Jesus' death and resurrection—and to the fact that not everybody will be convinced even by this "greatest of all miracles" (Pugh 2014, chapter 10). And indeed, WNC provides a kind of resurrection for B.J. after his apparent self-sacrifice at the end of WNO. However, within the context of *Wolfenstein*, B.J.'s reaction to Kessler is again a hint at his Jewish origins. The expression "Abraham's bosom" is, namely, also found in the extra-canonical book of 4 Maccabees (13:17), where Abraham, Isaac, and Jacob are portrayed as the ones welcoming the souls of the pious deceased (Skolnik 2007). In the haggadic literature, Abraham's bosom is mentioned frequently, signifying a kind of "heaven."

If in WNO, Blazkowicz' Jewish identification was only hinted at, in WNC the identification becomes explicit. In a number of flashbacks, B.J. relives episodes of his very unhappy childhood. His father, Rip, is a stereotypical racist American, hating everything that is not white and Christian, blaming his misfortune on everyone but himself, and physically and mentally abusing his Jewish wife and his son. In one instance, he reflects on his reasons to marry his wife Zofia:

> What is it with you damn Jews? Have all the answers, do you? Smart mouth goddamned Jew. I married you; I figured your father would be an asset but you're just a damn millstone sticking your nose into my business instead of handling your own.

In another flashback, Zofia sings the traditional *Birkat HaGomel* for her young son, a Jewish "blessing or thanksgiving after deliverance from danger" (Berlin 2011, 139). Based on Psalm 107, this benediction must be said after the crossing of a desert, a sea voyage, being freed from imprisonment, or after the recovery from a potentially fatal illness. The blessing is also said by Jewish women at their first synagogue attendance after they have given birth. The timing is significant: both the adult and the young Blazkowicz are in mortal danger, the first because of his Nazi imprisonment, and due to be sentenced to death by beheading, and the latter because of his father Rip's constant violence toward him and his mother.

Later in the installment, it becomes clear that Rip has betrayed his wife to the Nazi occupiers of the United States of America, leaving her to die in a concentration camp. This information is brought to the player by Adolf Hitler himself, who comments on B.J.'s execution, while *en passant* referring to his Jewishness:

> [In German] Raised in Mesquite, Texas. The half-breed child of a salesman and a Polish Jew. His mother was exposed by his father. She died in an extermination camp in Neue Mexico. As an adult his intellectual capacity remained at the level of a child. Indeed, if one cuts him open, as we did after his execution, one finds the innards of a Jew.

Through of all of these references, Blazkowicz is situated in a longer tradition of Jewish "heroes": the arch-father Abraham, the arch-liberator

Moses, Daniel's three men who wouldn't bow to foreign idols, and the Philistine-slayer Samson.

ANNETTE KRAUSE: "STREICHER'S PURIM"

Blazkowicz is not the only Jewish character in the series. Before we tend to Set Roth, without a doubt the most prominent one besides B.J., we focus on two others: Annette Krause, and Anya Oliwa.

To start with the first, when B.J. meets the German resistance fighter Kessler, he also gets acquainted with Annette Krause, a young, orphaned, Jewish woman of German descent. She acts as the assistant of Kessler, who has the role of being her mentor in the small resistance-cell of Paderborn. During the course of WOB, B.J. comes across multiple entries from her diary and a couple of letters, including one to her female love-interest Katrin. If the player decides to save her (instead of Kessler) during the final chapters of the game, Annette and Katrin are seen embracing and kissing each other after the Americans have taken over control of Wulfburg. If the player decides to save Kessler instead of Annette, Katrin is also seen at the end of the game, standing on Wulfburg's quayside, forlornly staring out over the waters in search of her lover.

Annette Krause seems to be moulded after the famous Dutch Jew Anne Frank, well-known for her world-famous diary *Het Achterhuis*, published in English as *The Diary of a Young Girl* in 1947 (Günther 2021). Besides her Diary, Anne Frank also wrote letters to a number of friends and relatives. *Wolfenstein*'s Annette also wrote a diary and letters. Certain passages of Frank's diary were omitted in the published versions for matters of cultural sensitivity, including her romantic and erotic interests in other women in general and her best friend Jacqueline van Maarsen specifically (Jackman 2017).

Halfway through the game, Kessler takes Annette and B.J. from Paderborn to Wulfburg by rowboat through the canals. During this period of relative peace and tranquility, the woman asks Blazkowicz what date it is, to which he replies "the 17th of March; it is a Sunday." Annette replies in a way that acknowledges her Jewish upbringing: "The day of Purim." B.J. confirms this by a simple "yeah." This is, however, more than just another indirect hint at Blazkowicz' Jewishness before the release of WNC. The date March 17th, 1946, the day of Purim, the last day of the Jewish year 5706, is very significant in this context. It is a reference to the Nazi war criminal Julius Streicher's ominous last words on that day in 1946, some moments before his execution.

Julius Streicher (1885–1946) was a member of the Nazi party, the *Gauleiter* of Franconia, and a member of the *Reichstag*. He was also the founder of the fiercely anti-Semitic paper *Der Stürmer*, one of the Nazis' most proliferate propaganda instruments, a job that made him a multimillionaire (Bytwerk 2001). Convicted at the Nuremberg trials, he was sentenced to hang on October 16, 1946—indeed the day of Purim 5706. When he approached the gallows, he shouted "Heil Hitler!" the NSDAP party cry. On the platform, in front of members of the international press covering the trials, he yelled: "Purim Festival 1946!" and after that "The Bolshevists will hang you one day." Usually, Streicher's death cry is interpreted as a reference to the biblical book of Esther, the book associated with the institution of the Purim feast (Bytwerk 2001, 1).

The book of Esther relates the story of the Jewish woman of the same name, who ended up being the wife of King Ashasuerus of the Persian Empire (Block and Marcus 2020). Mordechai, Esther's cousin, uncovers a plot to mass-murder the Jews of the empire by Haman, one of the king's advisors who is offended by Mordecai's refusal to bow before him. At the risk of her own life, Esther exposes the plot to the king, who makes Mordecai a hero, and condemns Haman, his ten sons, and numerous others in several places throughout the empire. Over 75,000 people in total are killed by the Jews. To celebrate this momentous victory, preventing the first "historical" pogrom in Jewish history, the Jews instate the Feast of Purim. In the eyes of anti-Semites, Purim became associated with Jews murdering "innocent" people, usually in a ritualistic manner.

According to Streicher and other Nazi leaders, the Jews were responsible for hideous crimes against Arians, especially in relation to Jewish holidays like Yom Kippur and Purim. In his *Der Stürmer*, he included many stories and drawings of such fictitious ritual murders. One of those stories included a Polish, Christian girl with the name Agnes Hruza, who, on the Feast of Purim, disappeared in the woods and was found with her throat slit open. The illustration showed two Jews holding blond Agnes—meaning "lamb," from the Latin *agnus*—while a third cut her throat, letting her blood flow into a bucket, a scene supposedly intended as a Jewish perversion of the Christian *Agnus Dei* symbolism (Sax 2000, 60).

The Nazis sometimes spent a great deal of effort to mockingly mimic the biblical story. On Purim 1942, for example, the Nazis forced the *Judenrat* ("Jewish Council") of the Polish ghetto of Zdunska Wola to choose ten Jewish men to be hanged "in the revenge of Haman." On the same day, the children of the Jewish Children's Home in Minsk (present-day Belarus) were marched to a freshly-dug ditch where they were buried alive, all while one of the SS officers mockingly threw candy amongst the children (quoted in Sundquist 2018, 122).

Mutatis mutandis, after the defeat of the Third Reich, many Jewish communities instituted a "second Purim," equating Haman and his sons with Hitler *cum sui* (Carrathers 2011). From this perspective, Streicher's reference to Purim is precisely to mock this: the reversal of executioner and victim. Streicher is now hanged on the gallows he intended for the Jews to die on.

But there is more to the Streicher case and the Purim reference in *Wolfenstein*. In 2012, Bernard Benyamin and Yohan Perez published *Le Code d'Esther*, translated into English as *The Esther Code* in 2014 (Benhamou 2012). Both authors claimed a mystical connection between Streicher's execution on October 16, 1946, on the one hand, and the execution of Haman and his ten sons on the other. By numerically interpreting some unusually sized letters in the Hebrew manuscripts of Esther (the *shin*, *tav*, and *zayin* in Esther 9:7–10), the two argue that the book prophesized the execution of Streicher and nine other Nazi war criminals on October 16, 1946, that is on Hoshannah Rabbah, the day of judgment, in the Jewish year 5706.

Unfortunately, the claims in *The Esther Code* do not hold up to scholarly criticism. As scholar Emmanuel Bloch (2020, 145) summarizes: "There is absolutely no relationship between Haman's sons and the Nazis convicted during the Nuremberg trial." Nevertheless, *Wolfenstein*'s mentioning of "Purim 1946" is significant. In the context of the series, it signifies the immanent Jewish revenge regarding the Nazis. And this revenge is executed by Jewish hands, including Annette Krause and the other Jewish members of the resistance (see next chapter), but spearheaded, of course, by the Jewish Blazkowicz himself. Through this, B.J. is yet again equated with a biblical hero, Esther this time, a fearless heroine, who succeeded in saving her entire people from a massive pogrom not unlike the one instigated by the Nazis.

ANYA OLIWA: "MOTHER OF EXILES"

Anya Oliwa, Blazkowicz' nurse at the psychiatric asylum and later his girlfriend and mother of his daughters, shares his Polish but not his Jewish lineage: she is a Christian (probably Roman Catholic), just like her grandparents. This becomes apparent when B.J., Anya, and her grandparents are gathered at the kitchen table sharing a simple meal before they head off to Berlin in an attempt to free several members of the German resistance imprisoned there. She makes the sign of the cross, touching head, chest, and shoulders, in the way Roman Catholics do; the four hold each other's hands to join in prayer. Anya prays:

We ask for your mercy, Lord, as we make to journey across dark waters. Grant us sound feet and silent breath, refuge from the storm, and safe passage 'midst hungry wolves.

At the very end of WNO, Anya is seen holding a lantern up high in her right arm. She shines the light on her fellow resistance fighters, who are helping Strasse's prisoners to escape the compound under constant gunfire from Nazi guards. The mortally wounded Blazkowicz looks out over this scene, but is incapable of reaching out to her. Meanwhile we hear him recite part of a famous poem, clearly applying its content to Anya:

> A mighty woman with a torch, whose flame is the imprisoned lightning, and her name Mother of Exiles: 'Give me your tired, your poor, your huddled masses yearning to breathe free, the wretched refuse of your teeming shore. Send these, the homeless, tempest-tost to me.'

It is the central part of the poem "The New Colossus," a Petrarchan sonnet written in 1883 by American author Emma Lazarus (1849–1887). The poem was written to raise money for the pedestal of the famous New York Statue of Liberty. After the pedestal was realized in 1903, the poem's text was cast onto a bronze plaque and mounted inside the pedestal, where it can still be seen today. The original manuscript is in the possession of the American Jewish Historical Society (Roberts 2011). Lazarus was involved helping Jewish refugees to New York, who came to the United States fleeing from the pogroms in Tsarist Russia and Eastern Europe in general. According to researchers, Lazarus' ancestors were Sephardic Jews, who were among the first Jewish settlers in America (Vogel 1980, 13; Appleby et al. 2015, 370).

The "brazen giant of Greek fame" is a reference to the Colossus of Rhodes, one of the Seven Wonders of the Ancient World (Mason 2013). This "old" Greek statue is compared with the "new" one in New York, the Statue of Liberty. The "sea-washed, sunset gates shall stand" is a reference to the mouths of the Hudson River and the East River, to the west of Brooklyn. The "imprisoned lightning" refers to the electric light in the torch, a novelty when the statue was erected. The "air-bridged harbor that twin cities frame" is a reference to New York's harbor between New York City and Brooklyn.

In the game, a parallel is drawn between the Statue of Liberty and Anya Oliwa, both holding an electric torch in their hands. Anya is the new "Mother of exiles," whom Lazarus wrote about: her exiles are not so much the "huddled masses yearning to breathe free," who came to the United States in search of religious and political freedom and economic prosperity, but rather those who are trying to flee from or fight against the Third Reich, because of its tyranny or because they are deemed "wretched" or "undesirable"

(*Entarteten*) by it. The image of this "New Colossus" even made it into the title of WNO's sequel: *Wolfenstein II: The New Colossus*, the one game of the series that primarily takes place in the United States instead of in Europe.

Of course, it is the same Anya who successfully tried to abort her "Nazi baby" in 1941 (as related in WNO), and who—at the end of WNC—saves her boyfriend B.J. from Nazi soldiers by shooting them with double machine guns, while topless and visibly pregnant by B.J. with twins, and covered in the blood of her enemies (Backe 2018, 18–19).

Now, the name of the author of "The New Colossus" poem, is also significant: Lazarus. We have come across this name before in WOB, may it be implicitly, in the expression "Abraham's bosom." The beggar who—according to the Gospel of Luke—lay in the patriarch's bosom in the afterlife was also called Lazarus. Confusingly enough, the New Testament has two unrelated characters of that same name: the beggar we have discussed before (Luke 16), and the man raised from the dead (John 11). The second Lazarus is a close friend of Jesus. When he dies of some unrevealed illness, Jesus travels to his tomb where he arrives after four days. But after praying to God, Jesus miraculously raises his friend from the dead.

Two links with the *Wolfenstein* narrative can be established. Firstly, Blazkowicz apparently dies at the end of WNO, but is miraculously recovered from the brink of death by his friends. Secondly, halfway through WNC, after B.J. has been captured by the Nazis and executed by beheading, his friends again pull him back from beyond the grave.

SET ROTH AND THE DA'AT YICHUD: "WE DO NOT PRAY"

As mentioned above, over the course of WNO, Blazkowicz infiltrates the Nazi research facility in London, where he stumbles upon ancient technology reverse-engineered by the Nazis. B.J. identifies the technology as "Da'at Yichud" by reading the name from documents lying around. Back in the resistance hideout in Berlin, Anya studies the documents B.J. has brought back home. According to her, the documents describe the creation of "a type of super-concrete" that the Nazis apparently used to create their enormous research, military, and civilian facilities. This *Überconcrete*, as the series calls it, is based on Da'ad Yichud technology. Another document contains an encrypted list of Da'at Yichud members in Poland during the Second World War (which lasted until 1946 according to the allohistorical setting of *Wolfenstein*'s fourth series). By comparing this list with the official German state records on Jewish citizens between 1939 and 1946 Anya finds out that there is—apparently—one person on that list still alive: Set Roth, detained in Camp Belica, in Northern Croatia (the details concerning the camp and its naming will be discussed later on).

As related earlier, B.J. infiltrates the camp to find and rescue Roth. Initially, however, this inmate of the Belica camp is not too keen on B.J.'s proffered assistance. The Da'ad Yichud member has two conditions: if B.J. wants to take him from the camp, he must do so for all the other prisoners too, and even then, Roth is bound to a sworn oath never to betray the Da'ad Yichud secrets to an outsider. B.J. reacts angrily: "Fuck your oath. People are dying. The resistance calls on you." But Roth is not to be easily persuaded, even not by Blazkowicz:

> So, it is a transaction of sorts, right? My personal freedom for the secrets I swore to keep. Sacrifice my honor on the altar of righteousness, well. . . . Permit me a moment to consider, Shimshon.

Eventually Roth is persuaded to accept the "transaction of sorts." And when B.J. destroys the camp and frees all the inmates, he holds the Da'ad Yichud member to his promise. Back in Berlin, Roth gives a first insider's glimpse of what the Da'at Yichud is, "an ancient mystical society," that has operated for "millennia with utmost secrecy, up until now." Caroline Becker is not convinced by the label of "ancient mystical society" and asks him eagerly: "What do you do? Do you pray do you. . . ." Then, Roth sets off on a long description that is paramount for understanding the in-game organization:

> No, no, *mamuhluh* [little mama], we do not pray. We invent things, *mamuhluh*. The technology developed by Da'at Yichud is centuries ahead of anything you have ever seen or imagined and highly dangerous in the wrong hands. The Nazis found our safekeep. They stole our secrets. They used them to win the war. Everything they have accomplished. Everything was built upon our knowledge, but . . . it was not our only safekeep. We have hundreds of them hidden in the secret places of the world. Hundreds. Some small and tentative like the one the Nazis found. Others . . . great halls of knowledge stacked high. Magnificent inventions. Things that to you will seem like magic. Now, I can open for you the gates of such a place. (. . .) The safekeep is hidden deep below the Atlantic Ocean.

The Da'at Yichud seems to be an ancient organization dedicated to the accumulation of scientific knowledge, not for an external purpose, but solely for its own sake. The Nazis apparently found some of the smaller Da'ad Yichud "vaults"—how and when remains unknown—and used the technology found there to increase the power of its military machine to such a degree they won the Second World War and achieved semi-world domination. After a few instances, Caroline is still not sure about the nature of the Da'at Yichud, puzzled about its apparent combination of religion and science.

> Caroline: I am trying to figure out what exactly you were doing in this organization of yours. Was it some kind of supernatural engineering?
>
> Set: We do not believe in things supernatural, *mamuhluh*. We believe in God. The Da'ad Yichud is a philosophy. It is a way of understanding God through knowledge. It is based on pure reason, pure rational thought. Not supernatural *bubkis* [nothing].
>
> Caroline: So, everything you have created, what were you planning on to use it for?
>
> Set: You do not understand, *mamuhluh*. There was never any purpose or intent of use beyond the act of creation. We create to commune with God. Do you see that?
>
> Caroline: You have lost me.
>
> Anya: It is like mathematical equations.
>
> Set: Go on, go on, *meidele* [little girl].
>
> Anya: And each solved equation brings you closer to God.
>
> Caroline: But never intended to be used.
>
> Anya: The act of creation is the intended use.
>
> Set: *Ot azoy, meidele* [so so, little girl]. There is something cooking in that *tshaynik* [tea kettle] of hers. Do you appreciate the distinction, *mamuhluh*? The safekeep I am to reveal to you is not a treasure chamber. It is a deep geological depository protecting some of our most dangerous creations for the safety of the outside world. Their purpose already served. Do you see that?
>
> Caroline: Whatever helps the cause.
>
> Set: *O Gottenyu* [dear God].

Later, Set Roth takes the team to an underwater "vault," on the bottom of the ocean, massive in size (apparently much bigger than the ones the Nazis found) and filled to the brim with Da'ad Yichud technology. Roth opens multiple gates, doors, and other technical devices by singing a song his father taught him. The game identifies the lyrics as "Yiddish," a West Germanic language historically spoken by Ashkenazi Jews (see below for further discussion). The main entrance of the vault is sealed by the Star of David, the hexagram universally associated with Judaism, and in the Second World War the obligatory sign Jews were forced to wear in public to identify them as such. The walls of the vault are decorated with pseudo-Hebrew letters and scribblings. Roth explains to his fellow resistance fighter what they witness:

> Seht gut [very good] How do you *kinderlech* [lit. little children; fig. friends] say? Let us get this show on the road? I tell you, I have waited for this moment. There was [sic] many of us who wanted to even the balance of the war. But things happened fast. Our gatekeepers were murdered, and then some were exiled. We had begun to transfer much knowledge to the governments who fought the Nazis. And there was hope. For a time, there was hope. Until the Nazis dropped the atom bomb. Well, there was no hope then. I remember when the Da'at Yichud would gather in places like this. It was brimming with life and the channels of nature was [sic] opened, but now . . . now I think we may be the last to visit.

The Da'ad Yichud apparently witnessed the unfolding of the Second War without intervening, even though many members were eager to do so, probably in favor of the Allied Forces. When they finally decided to share some of their technological knowledge with the Allied governments, the dropping of the German atomic bomb (again, the fourth series use an allohistorical setting) put a radical stop to the War and the Da'ad Yichud's optimism about being able to tip the scales of war. Roth guides the team to the heart of the vault, using a lot of Yiddish expressions, including *boba maisyas* ("an old wife's tale"), *vos iz pasirt* ("what is happening?"), *nicht shlecht* ("not bad"), and *yingele* ("boy").

When they eventually make it to the center of the vault, where all the old Da'ad Yichud technology is available for the resistance, Roth warns them: "Anything that is useful to you, you may take. Just remember you are in a sacred place." One of B.J.'s companions, Fergus, cannot withhold his enthusiasm and radios the following message back to the resistance headquarters in Berlin:

> Long story short I am now standing inside a secret vault full of things so magical and abnormal in nature the mind has no recourse but to shudder in bewilderment. Of course, I am accompanied by a Nazi-killing lunatic and some kind of genius wizard who claims to be on a first name basis with God Almighty himself.

The connection between religion and science baffled Caroline earlier on, and now also Fergus, who calls Roth "some kind of genius wizard" who is apparently "on a first name basis with God Almighty himself." Nevertheless, the intertwining of science and religion is at the heart of what the Da'ad Yichud seems to be. In an entry to Roth's diary, found in WNC, we read:

> April 5. What a lovely day. People have been asking me all kinds of questions about the Da'at Yichud. They try to understand, I see this, but it is a challenge for them. I must speak like a child to them. Leave out the complex, esoteric stuff.
>
>> The Da'at Yichud is an ancient mystical organization. We existed before the major religions of the world. We think hard, do math and build things to contact God.
>
> That sort of thing. I was sworn in as boychick and I too had a difficult time truly understanding the Da'at Yichud. No, we do not want to control the world. Now, we do not want to destroy the planet with superior technology. Yes, the Da'at Yichud is open to anyone with a curious mind who wants to reach God.
>
>> "But didn't you make clocks, Mr. Set Roth?"
>
> No, yes, sometimes. Watchmaker was my cover long ago, before the war. Ah, well. Maybe they will understand it all, eventually. . . .

Roth claims the Da'ad Yichud existed before the foundation of the "modern" world religions, including Judaism, Christianity, and Islam; that its teachings are of a "complex, esoteric" kind, and that it urges its members to "think hard, do math and build things;" that is philosophy, science, and engineering, with the (as we have seen before) "sole" purpose of communicating with God. Besides that, the Da'ad Yichud appears to be an inclusive, multi-religious, multi-ethnic, and multi-cultural entity, open for everyone with "a curious mind," wanting to "reach God." This is also suggested by one of the *Eva's Hammer*'s crew members from the American resistance, Maya Gilliam. She relates that the Nazis are underway to prepare a shipment containing "ancient Sumerian clay tablets." According to Set Roth, she continues, the Sumerians "were an influence on early Da'at Yichud symbolism." According to Maya, the Nazis intend to use the clay tablets to "decode" Da'at Yichud artefacts currently under research.

In between, there is a curious passage about accusations, by whom remains unknown, that the Da'ad Yichud is aiming at world domination or the destruction of the world. What is the bottom line regarding Set Roth and his Da'at Yichud? To start with, Set Roth is depicted by *Wolfenstein* as a stereotypical, cliché, European Jew from the second part of the twentieth century: bald, skinny, big nose, and tiny, round spectacles (Schiff 1982; Helmreich 1982; Schrank 2007). His speech is littered with Yiddish expressions, a language spoken by Ashkenazi Jews for the past millennium, with more than 11 million speakers worldwide at the beginning of the Second World War (Weinreich 2007).

Roth's name might be a reference to American novelist Philip Milton Roth (1933–2018), who was of Jewish-Ukrainian lineage (Bailey 2021). In 2004, Philip Roth published a novel entitled *The Plot against America*. Just like the *Wolfenstein* series' fourth cycle, it has an allohistorical setting. In *The Plot*, Charles Lindbergh wins the 1940 presidential election instead of Franklin D. Roosevelt. Historically, Charles Lindbergh was not only the first pilot to fly nonstop from New York to Paris (in 1927), but he also held very isolationist political views, impressed as he was by the German war machine in the 1930s. He also supported the isolationist America First Committee and resigned from the army when President Roosevelt publicly rebuked him for this (Olson 2013, 311–12). In the America of *The Plot*, anti-Semitism becomes common in the United States, leaving the American Jews in increasingly worsening circumstances. This premise seems to fit almost one-on-one that of *Wolfenstein 2: The New Colossus*, in which the Nazi occupiers of the States have bonded with the Ku Klux Klan.

Another candidate is Joseph Roth (1894–1939), an Austrian-Jewish journalist and novelist, born like Philip Roth's ancestors, in present-day Ukraine. His wife Friederike Reichler—their marriage was in 1922—became schizophrenic and was admitted to a sanatorium. Later she was murdered in the *Tötungsanstallt Hartheim* (Austria) through the Nazi *Aktion T4*, the mass murder of the mentally disabled by the Third Reich (Connelly 2021). This evokes the scenes from the psychiatric asylum at the beginning of WNO, where Blazkowicz is treated—among other patients—by Anya and her parents, until Nazi soldiers start to kill off all the patients in a raid not unlike those associated with *Aktion T4*.

Another identification of Roth with a historical counterpart is also possible. In his diary we read: "But didn't you make clocks, Mr. Set Roth?" to which he answers: "No, yes, sometimes. Watchmaker was my cover long ago, before the war." This seems to be an allusion to a famous (mis)quotation regarding Albert Einstein. Einstein, who was supposedly feeling guilty about his contribution to the atomic bomb, is supposed to have said: "If I only had known, I should have become a watchmaker." Despite the quote's popularity, Einstein never said this (Keyes 2006, 53). It could also be a reference to the Renaissance watchmaker analogy, associated with Deism. This theology understands God as being an impersonal entity that created the universe and all the laws governing it, but denies it is in any other way actively involved with it (Komonchak, Collins, and Lane 1990, 275). Hence the analogy of God as a watchmaker: the maker created the watch, but now it can and will function without its creator's constant attention; it works autonomously.

Both the names Set Roth and Da'at Yichud are references to the kabbalist lore. The name "Set Roth" is a reference to ten Sephirot, one of the key concepts of almost all kabbalist groups throughout history, even though the significance of these concepts is variable. The same applies to the name of the group of scientists-cum-mystics of which he is apparently the last surviving member. *Yichud* (or *yihud*) means "unification" and is associated with the act of mystical prayer in Lurian and other forms of Kabbala (Sherwin 2006, 109–216). With his prayer, the mystic contributes to the unity of the ten Sephirot, and thus to God's unity, a unity that has been disrupted, according to Lurian Kabbala, by the disharmonizing sephira *din*, affirmed by Adam's fall from paradise. *Da'at* ("knowledge") is a semi-sephira, sometimes appearing between *hokhmah* ("wisdom") and *binah* ("intelligence"), as a way of balancing or synthesizing various forms of human cognitive capacities (Scholem 2007, 631).

Interestingly enough, Set Roth stresses the fact that the Da'at Yichud members "do not pray," which contradicts the *yihud*'s traditional context. Instead of praying, Roth indicates that the members of Da'at Yichud use knowledge, philosophy, mathematics, and science to approach the divine. Roth's diary summarizes this like a kind of Da'at Yichud for dummies: "We think hard, do math and build things to contact God." The mystics' wish to come into contact with God still holds, but the religious figure of the mystic-cum-scholar, whose most important task is to keep praying, is swapped for that of the philosophically inclined scientist, who reasons and invents. This means a paradigm shift from a religious one to an empirical one, as has become dominant since the Enlightenment. The Da'at Yichud seems to be a representative of a kind of Kabbala that is in harmony with the ideals of the *Haskalah*, the Jewish Enlightenment of the eighteenth century. The Jewish thinkers of the *Haskalah* were weary of or even hostile to kabbalist ideas, disqualifying them as heresy or blasphemy on the one hand and as magic or superstition on the other. In the Da'at Yichud we find an "Enlightenment-approved" form of Jewish mysticism combining the modern focus on empirical epistemology with traditional language and concepts from kabbalist traditions.

This does *not* mean that there is no place for God or a transcendent reality *per se*. Roth's ideas are ambiguous: on the one hand he disqualifies "things supernatural" as "supernatural bubkis," exactly as any *Haskalah* scientist would, but on the other hand he claims the members of Da'at Yichud believe in God, who is sought after through "knowledge," based on "pure reasons, pure rational thought." The question is what kind of God is confessed by Da'at Yichud? Even though Roth is sarcastically identified by Fergus Reid as "some kind of genius wizard who claims to be on a first name basis with God Almighty himself," Roth's God more resembles the abstract, non-interventionalist God of the Enlightenment philosophers than the personal God of Judaism and Christianity, who is thought to care deeply for his creation and who intervenes frequently in the workings of the universe. (I will return to the topic of the [non-]interventionist God, when discussing the theme of theodicy, see chapter 10.)

When Roth discusses the nature of the Da'at Yichud research, he clashes with the practical-minded Caroline, who is only interested in the question how and when the Kreisau Circle can use its weapons and technology to defeat the Nazis. Roth argues that the Da'at Yichud's technology was never intended to be used "beyond the act of creation" itself. Anya intervenes by arguing that "each solved equation brings you closer to God," for which Roth applauds her. This discussion refers to two related but distinct "sides" of kabbalist history, known as theoretical (or—quite confusingly—theosophical) and practical (or magical) Kabbala. While there is some discussion between scholars on the question of whether the Kabbala's magical properties are inherent to its core or just a fringe phenomenon, within numerous mystical sources, from the Hekhaloth literature to Eastern European Hasidim, we find practical instructions concerning magical names, amulets, charms, potions, and such (Laenen 2001, 179–82). The creation of a *golem*, for example, is also part of this practical-magical current (see below for more details). *Wolfenstein* equates Caroline Becker's urge to use the Da'at Yichud for the practical purpose of defeating the Nazis with the magical side of Kabbala, and Roth's and Anya Oliwa's more philosophical interpretation—that creation serves no greater or even no other purpose than for humankind to commune with God that is, to understand God in and of itself (*ein sof*)—with the theoretical-theosophical side. And since the Da'at Yichud is clearly presented as a *Haskalah*-esque version of the Kabbala, the series champions the latter over the former.

Interestingly, the theoretical-philosophical view defended by Roth is nevertheless quickly left behind for a more practical application later on in the 4th cycle of the series. Roth actively tinkers with Da'at Yichud technology to aid the resistance and he personally leads a Kreisau-team to a Da'at Yichud underwater vault filled to the brim with war technology used later by B.J. and his team to fight off General "Totenkopf" Strasse. In *Wolfenstein 2: The New Colossus*, Roth is seen in the company of a hybrid creature, consisting of the head of a Siamese cat and the body of a Squirrel monkey, called Shoshanna. The cat-monkey hybrid is a premonition of a scene later in the same game, when Roth performs a very disturbing operation aiming to join B.J.'s decapitated head to the body of a headless German super soldier. The game voices concern about the theoretical-mystical use of Da'at Yichud technology, but rapidly abandons it for a more practical use.

Nevertheless, Roth exhibits both the characteristics of a scientist and a mystic. He is a scientist when he is tinkering with or looking for Da'at Yichud technology. But he is also a mystic, not only when he explains the true nature of his secret organization to the members of the Kreisau Circle, but also when he enters the underwater vault. The vault looks like a palace taken straight from Hekhaloth literature, one of the 49 divine palaces of God through which the Merkavah mystic is supposed to travel to meet God himself. The Da'at Yichud vault's walls are covered with pseudo-Hebrew scribblings, and its numerous fortified doors will only react to Roth's singing and whistling of some mysterious songs, like a Merkavah mystic using the secret names of God to pass through the gates of the places guarded by all kinds of guardians-cum-angels. When in the inner chamber of the vault, it is Fergus Reid who utters the ultimate goal of all mystics: Roth is on first-name basis with God. When the player is instructed by Roth to proceed through a maze-like winding stairway of spheres, apparently made of materialized light, finding the right sequence or rhythm is necessary to reach the central vault, the heart of the "palace." It almost feels like the player is initiated by Roth into the mystery of the Merkavah.

As I have argued before (see chapter 4), the kabbalists usually think of their own doctrines not as new or original, but as ancient and primordial truths they simply relate throughout history. Kabbalists, according to their self-perception, do not invent their wisdom, but discover what has always been there since the beginning of creation. From this follows the idea that—even though the Jewish people is a special and exceptional case within the framework of human history—the divine entity and its wisdom is older than any religion, including Judaism itself. We see this sentiment reflected in Roth's remark that the Da'at Yichud is "a mystical organization," that "existed before the major religions of the world." Maya Gillam does the same when she remarks that the Da'at Yichud influenced ancient Sumerian civilization, usually considered to be the birth place of Western civilization. Therefore, again according to Roth, the Da'at Yichud organization is open "to anyone with a curious mind who wants to reach God," again suggesting that the organization and its secret wisdom is broader and older than any individual world religion.

The question remains what Da'at Yichud actually means in the context of the *Wolfenstein* series. It could mean various things, including "knowledge of unification," "knowledge through unification," or even "knowledge equals unification." In any case, the series produces an "enlightened" version of Kabbala, more concerned with science than with faith (at least theoretically), which has more to do with philosophy than magical practices. The series also "de-Judaizes" the Da'at Yichud, at least theoretically, by claiming it to be older than Judaism and open to all people from all faiths and convictions, even though the organization's language and symbolism *and* Roth's aesthetics and rhetoric is clearly derived from Judaism and kabbalist history.

This is also the more problematic part of *Wolfenstein*'s rendering of mystical Judaism. Not only is Set Roth depicted aesthetically and rhetorically as a stereotypical Jew, including all the negative associations that led to the political climate enabling the Nazis to execute the Holocaust virtually unchallenged by the German population or the Allied Forces (Foxman 2010), but also the whole depiction of the Da'at Yichud is very close to the old idea of a secret, Jewish world government. As suggested in many anti-Semitic texts, including the notorious *Protocols of the Elders of Zion*, a 1930s Russian hoax (Segel and Levy 1995): the Jews—sometimes in collaboration with Templars, Illuminati, Freemasons, or the Vatican—supposedly secretly ruled the world through their direct influence on the world economy and politics. This myth is continued until the present day, for example, in the conspiracy theory concerning the Hungarian-American billionaire businessman and philanthropist of Jewish descent George Soros (Botstein 2022). Not incidentally, the English word for such a secret world government is a "cabal," and it is derived from the word "Kabbala," suggesting an intimate relationship between Judaism and world dominance (Dan 2006, 7).

The Da'at Yichud of the *Wolfenstein* series approaches this idea somewhat closely when suggesting that the organization is ancient, secret, and very powerful. It operates behind the scenes, intervening with the world's affairs only when deemed necessary based on implicit criteria. Even more, Roth suggests that the members of the Da'at Yichud were passive at first when confronted with Hitler, and when they finally wanted to intervene in the Second World War, it was too late since the Nazis had already breached some of the Da'at Yichud's vaults and used the technology found there to tip the scales of war. The series thus suggests that the Jews may not have caused the Second World War or the Holocaust, but that they could have prevented both but did not do so for unclear reasons.

Roth's depiction—as a stand-in for the enlightened scientists of the Da'at Yichud—is even more ambiguous. He tinkers with "forbidden," morally very problematic medical procedures, especially the head-transplants of Shoshanna and Blazkowicz. Roth's actions approximate those of the "mad scientist" trope. This trope is modelled after the infamous SS physician Joseph "Angel of Death" Mengele, who performed deadly experiments on prisoners in Birkenau concentration camp (Hayton 2012, 77–78). The trope conveys how Nazi scientists frequently and unscrupulously involved themselves in ethically highly problematic scientific experiments, often in combination with "dabbling" in "the occult." The *Wolfenstein* series portrays many of them, including Dr. Otto Giftmacher (*Wolfenstein 3D*), Prof. Zempf (*Return to Castle Wolfenstein*), and Wilhelm Strasse himself (*Wolfenstein: The New Order*): they all combine (pseudo)science with occultism to create weapons of mass destruction. Of course, Set Roth is portrayed in the series as one of the "good guys," but at the same time he is involved with techniques and experiments that are commonly not associated with "the good side," but with quite the opposite.

It all leaves the player with an ambiguous attitude toward Roth and the Da'at Yichud. On the one hand Set Roth is portrayed as a peaceful Jewish scientist and philosopher, who ended up as one of the victims of the Holocaust, and who later on provides vital assistance to the Kreisau Circle, tipping the scales of the war in favor of the Allied Forces. The Da'at Yichud is equally portrayed as a benign, pacifist organization more interested in the philosophy of (technological) creation and research than in practical power or political influence. It was even so non-interventionist that it missed its opportunity to end the Second World War in favor of the Allied Forces. If anything, one could blame Roth and the other members for their hesitance and indecisiveness, but not of anything malign.

On the other hand, Set Roth is portrayed as a stereotypical Jew: his appearance (aesthetical), his vocabulary (rhetoric), and his affiliation (political). The combination of these three elements, in combination with Roth's medical experiments, conjures up a darker and more negative image of the Da'at Yichud and—by extension—the Jewish people. Although the Da'at Yichud may appear to be a proto-monotheistic, non-denominational, perhaps even universal religion-cum-philosophy, the only actual Da'at Yichud member the player comes across is Set Roth: the one—the Jew Set Roth—becomes the sole identification of the other—the Jewish organization of Da'at Yichud. This identification is strengthened by the fact that the organization is described, primarily by Set Roth, using words stemming from Jewish mysticism. From the perspective of the player, the Da'at Yichud *is* a Jewish organization.

The identification of Da'at Yichud and Set Roth as Jewish entities, including the former being hesitant to get involved in the war and the latter's medical experiments, creates a new version of the stereotypical Jew and the "Jewish" world government: the Jews appear to rule the world behind the scenes, until the Nazis appear to end this "rule." Ironically enough, a large part of the Da'at Yichud as portrayed in the fourth cycle of the *Wolfenstein* series would fit quite perfectly into the Nazi propaganda effort of the 1930s to discredit Jews and Judaism, in order to prepare the German population for the Holocaust. A last intriguing detail is that the common abbreviation of the "new world order"—NWO—is an anagram of the game *Wolfenstein: New Order*—WNO.

PROBST WYATT III AND THE "SEFER YETZIRAH"

In the beginning of *Wolfenstein: The New Order*, during the raid on General Wilhelm Strasse's secret compound, Blazkowicz and his team of American soldiers are captured by said general. When they are forced to the ground by super soldiers, the general demands that B.J. choose between two of his comrades, Fergus Reid, or Probst Wyatt III: the one chosen will instantly be operated upon by the general, removing the victim's brain from his body; the other one is left to die together with the other prisoners. Based on this choice, either Fergus or Wyatt will accompany B.J. and the resistance over the course of WNO and *Wolfenstein II: The New Colossus*, while the other will serve as the first end boss of WNO.

If Fergus is chosen in WNO (ending in his double demise), a rather interesting subplot unfolds regarding Wyatt in WNC. In the submarine-cum-resistance's base, *Eva's Hammer*, we can see Wyatt roaming through the belongings of "J," a now deceased fellow resistance fighter. Apart from being a very decent guitar player, J was also involved in the production and recreational use of psychedelic drugs. Wyatt himself is psychologically unstable because of the mental stress of the war in general, but specifically so since he was forced to witness the violent decapitation of his mentor Caroline Becker at the hand of SS-Obersturmbannführerin Irene Engel.

Remembering both, Wyatt starts to use J's recreational drugs of unknown substance and quality, leading to several psychedelic trips, traditionally associated with LSD and comparable substances. After one of his trips, Wyatt has a conversation with Set Roth aboard the submarine, discussing the nature of the visions he encountered while on drugs. Initially Roth is not much interested in Wyatt's ramblings. When asked by Wyatt if he has ever spoken to God, Roth replies "many times," adding sarcastically that he is still "waiting for [God] to get back" to him.

Wyatt ignores Roth's sarcasm altogether, because he is much too focused on his own experiences, which he describes as follows:

> I saw highways, you know. (. . .) Light just . . . reaching across galaxies, and it . . . it was like these . . . these symmetrical patterns of, of color and I was just . . . blasting through them at the speed of light. And, and . . . it was like reality warped in on itself and somehow, I was breaking through these dimensional barriers . . . and I could see . . . everything! Except I had ceased to exist. I was but I wasn't I. (. . .) And from my vantage point there were like these, these patterns of light that formed these roots that reached out into this infinitely colossal shape. Like a geometric tree, that was just bigger than the entire universe. And then I heard something. This voice just thundered at the center of my awareness. And this, this being, this shape it spoke and it said just one word. (. . .) Visitor. (. . .) I don't know, it is hard to explain.

At this point, Roth suddenly becomes very interested in Wyatt's visions. He identifies the tree as "a Da'at," part of the "ten Sephirot," and as the "Etz ha Chayim," "the Tree of Life." Roth suggests to Wyatt to "study" the subject, even though he claims that there are "very little books on the subject in English." He sends Wyatt away after making him promise to return to him if he experiences similar visions. Further on, we see Wyatt bowed down over one of Roth's books, probably trying to make sense of both the book itself and how its content could help him understand his visions. We hear him quote: "Enter and pass up through the Gates to attain the Thirty-two Paths of Wisdom."

Even though the game does not specifically reveal which book Wyatt is reading, the quotation gives it away: it is from William Wynn Westcott's (1996, 23) translation of the *Sepher Yetzirah*. Under the heading "the fifty gates of intelligence," the whole quotation is as follows:

> Attached to some editions of the "Sepher Yetzirah" is found this scheme of Kabalistic classification of knowledge emanating from the Second Sephira Binah, Understanding, and descending by stages through the angels, heavens, humanity, animal and vegetable and mineral kingdoms to Hyle and the chaos. The Kabalists said that one must enter and pass up through the Gates to attain to the Thirty-two Paths of Wisdom; and that even Moses only passed through the forty-ninth Gate, and never entered the fiftieth. (See the *Oedipus Aegyptiacus* of Athanasius Kircher, vol. II[b]. [1654] p. 318–319)

William Wynn Westcott (1848–1925) was one of the most prominent occultists of his time (Pasi 2006). Among his many translations is—indeed—an 1887 English translation of the *Sefer Yetzirah*, and among all the things he did in his life, Westcott's name is most prominently associated with the foundation of the Hermetic Order of the Golden Dawn, a late nineteenth century esoteric order, rooted in Freemasonry (Gilbert 2006). The Golden Dawn is also the name of a group of Russian scientists, mystics, and occultists in *Wolfenstein* (2009), headed by Dr. Leonid Alexandrov (Hayton 2015, 258–59). The in-game Golden Dawn has a logo containing the Eye of Providence, commonly associated with Freemasonry (Issitt and Main 2014, 49). Even though Roth mentions that there are not many books in English on the subject, it is strange that he produces this specific one. In the first place, Westcott's translation and commentary on the *Sefer Yetzirah* is much more Christian than Jewish. And in the second place, how did Roth come into possession of that book in the first place: he either already possessed it as part of his private collection, which he apparently had with him while being on the run from the Nazis, *or* the book happened to be on board of a highly-advanced Nazi submarine. Both options seem far-fetched.

When Max Hass, a resistance member with a severe congenital brain injury, limiting his speech to two words only (his own name), distracts Wyatt with a little, walking, battery-operated toy robot, the latter reacts angrily towards the former. Wyatt:

> Look Max, I'm doing like really heavy reading here and your little toy robot is just not compatible with that type of soul journey, man, okay? (. . .) Look, this just is too complicated for you. (. . .) See, I'm trying to find the reference to these gates here, and you just wouldn't understand. (. . .) Maxi, this is really advanced philosophical literature, okay? You can't just start pointing this.

But that is precisely what Max does: he points to an undisclosed passage in Westcott's text, to which Wyatt reacts with "Whoa, Max, that's it." After another psychedelic trip, a suicidal Wyatt talks to B.J. about his own youth, in a distancing way referring to himself as "he" and "the kid." First, he relates how his over-achieving parents were very disappointed when "the kid" joined the military, leading his father to sever all connections with his "ungrateful" son and to his mother taking her life by overdosing on medicine. Secondly, Wyatt—again—describes the content of his drugs-induced visions:

> He saw perfect patterns, swallowing branches of a great tree. The all-knowing space entity at the center, gazing upon him. The kid was approaching the apex of the universe but it all slipped away. And a colossal black trench opened up swallowing the colors and the kid couldn't see anything expect for a transdimensional gaping maw swallowing his soul.

B.J. is forced to knock Wyatt unconscious and bring him to Roth for examination and treatment. While his patient is still unconscious, Roth explains to Blazkowicz what has happened:

> Heavy doses of psychedelics. Now, listen to this. Back in the days of Da'at Yichud, we used similar substances many times. Never, ever, did anyone have the clarity of vision that Wyatt has. It is remarkable.

Wyatt is portrayed by the fourth cycle of the *Wolfenstein* series as an unwilling but very gifted Merkavah mystic. Even though the concept of the Tree of Life is more commonly associated with the later *Zohar*, and the light symbolism is equally commonly associated to Lurian Kabbala, the experience Wyatt describes is one of a mystic ascending into the seven heavens, each with its own seven palaces, until he reaches God himself. "Did you ever speak to God?" Wyatt asks Roth, who answers somewhat sarcastically. But Wyatt has, as he relates in his Merkavah-esque vision: "I heard something. This voice just thundered at the center of my awareness," greeting Wyatt with the word "visitor."

The use of drugs or psychedelia as a means of creating or advancing mystical experiences—a practice apparently common in the history of the Da'at Yichud, according to Roth—is not a large part of kabbalist history, even though some medieval kabbalists wrote, often cryptically, about the use of certain plants, possibly having psycho-active ingredients, in conjunction with ecstatic prayer (Kaplan 2004, 156). However, the association between drugs on the one hand and mystical experiences in general and within kabbalist lore specifically, is more a concoction by modern esoteric writers.

NORMAN CALDWELL: THE GOD KEY

The use of the word "visitor" in combination with the fact that one of the *Wolfenstein 2: The New Colossus'* stages is Roswell, New Mexico, hints at yet another interpretation of religion in general, and of kabbalist lore, presented by the game as older than all other religions, specifically. When Blazkowicz is in Roswell, he is aided by Norman "Super Spesh" Caldwell. In 1947, young Caldwell and his father discovered the remnants of a crashed alien spaceship, leading to Caldwell spending his whole life devoted to conspiracy theories concerning Roswell, Area 51, and UFOs. His hiding place is covered with documents, maps, and pictures that should be able to prove the involvement of the American, and later (in the allohistorical setting of the series) the German governments in the covering up of these alien contacts.

Eventually Caldwell is killed by the Nazis while he is trying to free Blazkowicz from imprisonment and impending execution. When B.J. has returned to the submarine, he fiddles with one of Caldwell's "toys" found in his room on the boat. When Roth sees the hand-sized, pentagonal, golden cylinder, he immediately gets agitated: "Where did you get this? (. . .) It looks like. . . . No, it can't be. Gotte neu. I'm sorry. . . ." And then he walks away talking to himself, leaving B.J. behind in astonishment. Later, Roth confronts B.J. about the artifact:

> What have you done to me, yingele? What have you done? I've been so absorbed with this artifact you brought in to my attention. Absorbed and angry. You see, the Da'at Yichud engineers that made it called it the God Key, a term that only a complete and utter schmuck [idiot] would accept at face value. Because first, it is not a key. (. . .) More important, its actual purpose . . . I don't know what its actual purpose is. Makes me very angry.

After B.J. prevents Wyatt killing himself through a drugs-induced psychosis by knocking him unconscious, the "mystic" awakens on Roth's hospital bed. Still groggy from the drugs, he grabs the "God Key" lying next to him on a small table, while asking Roth: "Is this some kind of doorknob, Set?" Roth, again, is astonished by Wyatt. He takes the object from Wyatt: "What did you say? (. . .) Doorknob he says." In *Wolfenstein Young Blood*, the "doorknob"-cum-"God Key" returns into the hands of B.J. who is trying to manipulate it in order to enter an alternative dimension in which the Nazis have lost the Second World War (that is, "our" dimension). So, Wyatt's identification of the object as a "doorknob" was right on the nose: it literally opens the door to other dimensions.

The series seem to suggest that the origin of the Da'at Yichud's wisdom and technology, and by extension that of the whole of human civilization, including its technology and religion, is grounded in extra-terrestrial life: aliens visiting Earth, bringing technology and wisdom so far advanced that it seems like magic to the uninitiated, and the memory of which has been slowly fading into the fabric of legends, myths, and organized religion. This is actually a variation of Erich von Däniken's classic *Chariots of the Gods?* from 1971 (Feder 2002). The association between Da'ad Yichud and alien technology also has a darker side: in German Nazi propaganda (and in modern anti-Semitic circles), Jews are frequently portrayed as "the other" or the "alien," an entity that does not belong "here," wherever this "here" may be located in terms of space and time (Bonfil 1994).

JEWISH MAGIC: THE FLESH GOLEM

Another reference to Jewish mysticism can be found in the character of the "monstrosity" found at the end of WOB. It functions as the end boss of the game: a mechanical or biological creature, clearly artificial in origin. Green electrical currents are visible inside its mouth, and the being is chained to the walls of an enormous cave under the Bavarian city of Wulfburg, southeast of Castle Wolfenstein and Paderborn village. *Obersturmbannführerin* Helga von Schabbs tries to speak and reason with it: initially her efforts seem to pay off—the monster seems to listen to the sound of her voice—but as soon as she mentions the name of King Otto, the strange entity becomes wild and aggressive, tries to kill Helga and Blazkowicz, but is only successful in the first case.

Over the course of WNO, the identity, origin, and history of the monstrous creature is revealed, if not somewhat vaguely, through letters written by various NPCs (non-playable characters) to one another. In a letter from Helga to her lover Reinhold (found in the Prologue) she mentions she found King Otto's diary in a secret study chamber in Castle Wolfenstein. Not only does Helga express her pride in her (alleged) genealogical connection to the old German king, she also states that after Otto's (historical) wife Eadgyth died in 946, he started to develop an interest in "occult sciences," initially probably—the game implicitly suggests—to find a way to raise her from the dead, but later to construct artificial war drones.

Another in-game letter describes a (fictional) diary or chronicle from one of Otto's scholars (found in chapter 3), who mentions the (historical) battle of Lechfeld (Bowlus 2016) in which Otto's army defeated a 45,000-men-strong army of invading Magyars. According to the in-game scholar's letter, Otto prevailed over his enemies with the help of "secret weapons," given to the king "by Almighty God." The secret weapons consist of an army of artificial war machines, human-like creatures. It is suggested that these were created using information contained in occult documents allegedly found during Otto's (fictional) visit to Constantinople. Unfortunately for Otto, these monsters prove to be unstable. The king orders the whole operation to be terminated and orders his knights to burn Wulfburg to the ground. However, in one cave, one of the creatures remains—why and how is uncertain. The monster is bound there, according to an in-game letter (also in chapter 3), by gigantic chains delivered by the tenth to eleventh century Iranian scholar and polymath Abu Rayhan al-Biruni, a contemporary of Otto (Ahmed 1984). It slumbered for centuries, until Helga's excavations awakened it.

The entity at the end of WOB does not have a proper name within the game itself—it is indicated as "the monster" or "the monstrosity"—but in the game-files the thing is mentioned as "the Flesh Golem" (Hughes 2017). The reference is clear enough: WNO's monstrosity is a golem. The golem is a well-known figure in Western culture (Nocks 1998, 293–97; Barzilai 2020): from the early film *Der Golem, wie er in die Welt kam* (Paul Wegener and Carl Boese 1920) to the "Bear Jew" of Quentin Tarantino's 2009 *Inglorious Basterds*; from the *X-Files* episode "Kaddish" (Kim Manners 1997) and the *Simpsons* episode "Treehouse of Horror XVII" (2006) to the Clayton "Clay" Turner character (Dylan Playfair) in the Netflix series *The Order* (Chad Oakes 2019–2020).

The golem is a "person made of clay by learned and holy men, and brought to life through their expression of mystical formulae," predominantly but not exclusively acting as protectors of the Jewish people (Nocks 1998, 282). Its name is derived from a *hapax legomenon* found in Psalm 139:16. I quote from the New American Standard Version 2020:

> Your eyes have seen my *golem*;
> And in Your book were written
> All the days that were ordained for me,
> When as yet there was not one of them.

The Hebrew word *golem* means "something unformed and imperfect" (Oded and Sperling 2007, 736) and has been translated as *akatergastos* ("what is unrefined") in the Septuagint, *informis* ("formless") in the Vulgate, "substance, yet being unperfect" (King James), "unformed body" (NIV), "inside the womb" (NIT), or "formless substance" (NASB20). Initially the golem appeared in early rabbinic literature and later in subsequent Jewish mystical, magical, and halakhic texts from the third to the eighteen century as "artificial creature[s] in human form but devoid of a human soul, speech, and reproductive capabilities" (Byron 2007, 135–36), created from dust or clay by the manipulations of Hebrew letters, often including the Tetragrammaton, the four-letter name of God. The golem appeared to have been constructed "for no practical purpose other than to demonstrate the mystical skills of their creator" (idem). This last characteristic calls to mind the description Set Roth uses to describe the essence of the Da'at Yichud in WNO:

> We believe in God. The Da'ad Yichud is a philosophy. It is a way of understanding God through knowledge. It is based on pure reason, pure rational thought. Not supernatural *bubkis* [nothing]. (. . .) There was never any purpose or intent of use beyond the act of creation. We create to commune with God. Do you see that?

Applied to the figure of the golem, the same idea can be found in Jewish mysticism, especially in the realm of practical Kabbala (Nocks 1998, 287–90). In the *Sefer Yezirah* ("Book of Creation"), creation is understood as the utterance of the twenty-two consonants of the Hebrew alphabet, especially—again—the letters of the name of God, the Tetragrammaton. When applied to practical use, it is not difficult to see how this kind of cosmology could be translated into the creation of a homunculus, taken from the soil of the earth, like humankind was created according to Genesis 2:7, and brought to life by the utterance of magical letter-combinations or by placing a note with these combinations into the mouth of the golem, like God did with humankind (Idel 1990, 299).

From the beginning of the eighteenth century to the early twentieth century, the golem figure becomes more and more an entity fashioned for practical use rather than for communicating with the divine, and brought into existence to serve its Jewish master and protect the Jewish population in an all too often anti-Semitic, European context (Byron 2007). This golem runs the risk of running amok, endangering what it was supposed to protect. In this aspect it resembles the Western European Frankenstein trope: the creation rebels against its creator (Nielsen 2022, 139–58). Two famous golem stories are attached to this period: the golems of Chelm and Prague.

Elijah bar Aaron Judah Baal Shem was a Polish rabbi from the second half of the sixteenth century living in Chelm. He is credited with creating a golem by placing a parchment with God's name on the golem's forehead to bring it to life. When the golem runs amok, he tears the parchment away, returning the creature to dust (Nocks 1998, 290). Akiva Winik (1954, 179–202), in his description of Jewish life and work in Chelm, relates a legend surrounding Rabbi Elijah:

> Very popular were the legends and the stories about the Rabbi Elijah Ba'al Shem who, it was said, created the golem (an artificial man) in Chelm. I heard the story in the following version: "No one was allowed to enter the attic of the Old Synagogue. No one even knew where the key to the attic could be found. One person whispered to another the secret that in the attic there lies the golem of the famous Rabbi Elijah Ba'al Shem. It was said that Elijah Ba'al Shem created from clay a golem who would stand on market days with an ax in his hand, and as soon as he saw that a peasant was going to beat up a Jew, the golem killed the peasant. An entire week the golem served the Rabbi, the Rabbi's wife, and he performed the manual labor in the Beit Harnidrash. When the local landowner found out about the golem's might, the Ba'al Shem led the golem to the attic, withdrew from him the ineffable name of God, and converted the golem into a heap of clay. The Ba'al Shem locked the door, took with him the key, and since then the attic remained bolted."

The story of Chelm's golem is very similar to that by another sixteenth century rabbi, Judah Löw of Prague. In 1580, a Catholic priest stirred up the Prague masses to rally against their Jewish co-citizens (Nielsen 2022, 139–40). Together with some friends, Judah uses the *Sefer Yetzirah* to create an artificial man, who protects the Jews of Prague for many years. Legend has it that the golem was stored in the Altneuschul synagogue's attic, ready to be brought back to serve its purpose again. According to modern legends, this occasion arose in 1939 when the Nazis wanted to blow up the Altneuschul with all the congregation in it. A Holocaust survivor relates the following story (quoted in Idel 1990, 256):

> The Golem did not disappear and even in the time of the war it went out of his hiding-place in order to safeguard its synagogue. When the Germans occupied Prague, they decided to destroy the Altneuschul. They came to do it; suddenly, in the silence of the synagogue, the steps of a giant walking on the roof, began to be heard. They saw a shadow of a giant hand falling from the window onto the floor. (. . .) The Germans were terrified and they threw away their tools and fled away in panic.

Back to WOB's monstrosity a.k.a. the "flesh golem." On the one hand, King Otto's creature seems to fit perfectly within the larger scheme of the golem legend. It was created and given a life of its own by magical means derived from old manuscripts found in Constantinople. Its purpose was to defend Otto's empire against the advancing Magyars. According to one of Otto's scholars, the golems were a kind of gift from God, a reference to the use of God's name in the entity's vivification process. After having been of use, the flesh golem was hidden away in an underground facility, where it remains dormant until someone awakens it again.

Otto's golem also seems to be rather out of control. But unlike Elijah and Judah, Otto was no longer capable of controlling its rampant power and ordered his knights to burn the whole village of Wulfburg to the ground, effectively burying the monstrosity underground. Originally constructed for the benefit of Otto's "German" empire (an anachronism of course, but nevertheless a popular one in Nazi circles), Helga wants to harness its power again, now for the Nazified, Germanic Third Reich. Instead of being created by a Jew for the protection of the Jewish population, Otto's monstrosity is, although not created for this specific purpose in the first place, an actual danger to the European Jews of the 1940s, since Helga clearly wants to incorporate the golem's "technology" to power the German war machine and for the extermination of the Jews.

Again, the new "Jewishness" of *Wolfenstein*'s fourth cycle bites its own tail. The figure of the golem, originally for the protection of the Jewish people—including against the Nazi threat—is re-appropriated by the series to signify the opposite—the potential destruction of the Jewish people. It resembles the paradox of the Da'at Yichud technology: it originated from Jewish scientists, engineers, and philosophers, but it was used by the Nazis against them. The narrative is susceptible to the interpretation that the Jews were—indirectly and unintentionally—responsible for their own suffering before and during World War II. This narrative is, indirectly, strengthened by the portrayal of Otto's flesh golem.

DEPICTING THE HOLOCAUST: CAMP BELICA

One of the most fascinating and controversial things the *Wolfenstein* reboot has done is the inclusion of the phenomenon of the Nazi concentration camp. It was a bold move regarding two aspects. On the one hand, the Holocaust and the Jews as the primary victims of the Second World War have been neglected by video games using the 1940s as their narrative backdrop (Hayton 2012, 211). WNO clearly corrected this, as discussed above. On the other hand, using a concentration camp as a stage in any video game is risky and problematic in and of itself: can the inherent entertainment characteristic of the video game genre be combined with the atrocities of the Shoah? Nevertheless,

WNO did indeed manage to do so and was praised (Hughes 2017) as well as criticized (McKeand 2018, Widmann 2020) for doing so.

Once the Kreisau Circle has identified Set Roth as the "last surviving member" of the Da'at Yichud and located him as imprisoned in Belica concentration camp (probably portrayed after the Jasenovac concentration camp in erstwhile Croatia), they send B.J. inside for an undercover mission: B.J. is to be taken as a prisoner to the camp to find and extract Roth. The game does not relate any details concerning how B.J. succeeds in getting into the camp; he is one of the Nazis' most wanted persons, but he succeeds in getting into the camp as a prisoner, without being identified as such.

Back in the resistance's hideout, before the mission commences, Caroline asks B.J.: "Are you ready for this?" Then, the camera cuts to B.J. entering the camp as a prisoner, suggesting that his answer will have been "yes!" However, through a *monologue interieur*, Blazkowicz relates that his answer was premature and not the right one: "So stupid. I was arrogant. No one is ever ready for something like this." The camera follows B.J. from an off-shoulder perspective, relating the happenings of the camp from his perspective, without resorting to an actual first person perspective. The doors of a cattle-wagon are opened. Bright light pours in over the inmates, all uniformly dressed in white-red work attire, all (including the women) shaven clean, robbed of their individual characteristics and thus of their identity.

Steel gates are opened, while Frau *Obersturmbannführer* Irene Engel, the camp's commandant, oversees the newcomers' arrival. She takes a weapon-stick in her hands, surrounded by other, anonymous Nazi soldiers. Engel and the others shout: "Get going, scum" and "Quickly, quickly!" In the back we see the sign "Belica" above the entrance, aesthetically resembling the infamous "Arbeit macht frei" sign above the entrance of Auschwitz. Also, in the back we see smoke rising from large chimneys, a reference to the fact that Camp Belica is apparently not only a concentration, but also an extermination camp. One of the women offers her crying infant up to Frau Engel, begging her to have mercy: "Please! Please, good madam. She is dying." Engel reluctantly takes the infant by the leg, dangling it upside down as if she is confronted with vermin that is only to be exterminated. She hits the woman fiercely with her stick: "Get off me!" Then B.J. (and thus the camera) is pushed backward into the wagon, leaving the infant's ultimate fate unclear, although it is arguably a somber one.

In the next scene, we see the captions "Belica, forced labor camp, annexed Croatia" confirming the location. Importantly, at this moment the gamer regains control of its avatar, even though straying from the path is near impossible. Therefore, we have switched from an off-shoulder perspective, back to the familiar first person one. We see B.J. as one of a long row of prisoners walking through a kind of steel ditch within a steel building. On both sides of the "ditch," we see heavily-armed Nazi soldiers, including Frau Engel and her bodyguard-cum-lover Hans "Bubi" Winkle. When looking left and right, B.J. can see numerous other rows of prisoners in the same predicament as he is. When B.J. passes by, Bubi points him out to Frau Engel. She rejects his implicit suggestion to take him out of the row: "Too big. Costly to feed." When Bubi replies he looks familiar, hinting at their earlier meeting on the train, and reiterates his suggestion to put him to work, Frau Engel is persuaded and orders a soldier to extract him from the row. The fate of the other prisoners in B.J.'s row and the other rows is left implicit by the game, but the fact that we do not see them again, suggests that they are sent directly to the gas chambers.

The soldier pushes B.J. to a door to the left, and he then stumbles into a steel and concrete chamber with an ominous apparatus on the right. On the left, behind a window, a Nazi officer orders him through an intercom to put his arm into the machine. When the player activates the machine, we switch back to a third person perspective, frontally now. We see the machine fastening B.J.'s arm in order to print a tattoo with his unique identification number on it, just as happened with the inmates in the historical concentration camps. B.J. endures the painful procedure, while another of his interior monologues is played: "Human beings. Like cattle in this place. Need to stay calm. Remember the mission." The number tattooed on his arm is 04 15 15 13, referring to the corresponding letters in the Latin alphabet: "doom."

After leaving the room, Blazkowicz—back in first person perspective—finds himself in a fabrication plant, where inmates are forced to produce the Super Concrete that the Nazis stole from the Da'at Yichud. One of the inmates has collapsed behind his machine and is now being verbally bullied by Nazi guards goading him to continue with his job. When the player activates the only machine not operated, the perspective again changes to the third person. B.J. talks with his fellow-inmate on his left, Bombate, who will later join him in the Kreisau Circle. "I just try to survive, day by day" he says to B.J, who asks Bombate about Set Roth. Bombate: "I have heard of him. Survived longer than any other." In order to get to where Roth is being held—Roth and B.J. are namely housed in different sections of the camp—Blazkowicz sabotages his machine, distracting the guards, and swaps uniforms with another inmate who longs to see his wife.

When leaving the fabrication room, B.J. is very quickly examined by another Nazi officer, apparently to check for his identity. This officer fails to discover the blatant swap that has just taken place. This is again a reference to the dehumanization of the prisoners: they are interchangeable, dispensable units. Through the door, B.J. enters a courtyard, heavily fenced off, cameras observing the inmates continuously. We hear another interior monologue: "Heard of places like this. Auschwitz. Buchenwald. From East to

West." Through his words, the game places the fictional Camp Belica in the same category as the infamous, historical ones.

Several smaller scenes can be experienced in the courtyard before B.J. meets Roth in one of the barracks. When an anonymous prisoner sitting on the ground, is apparently praying, another inmate warns him: "Hush! None of that! The *Frau* hates everything religious if it isn't Catholicism. No ceremonies. No chanting. No praying." As a kind of "response," Frau Engel is heard over the intercom, speaking in German to the inmates. I provide my own translation:

> I am here to correct God's mistakes. You are impure [*unrein*]. You are degenerate [*Du bist entartet*]. You are human waste [*menschlicher Abfahl*]. Like cancerous growths you must be surgically removed before the cancer spreads to the whole body and everything dies. I am your surgeon. My whip is my instrument.

Engel echoes the Nazi vocabulary used to dehumanize those deemed unworthy of living: "impurity," "degenerated," "waste," and "cancer" (Griech-Polelle 2017). The inevitable fate of all prisoners, sooner or later, is hinted upon by two other inmates, While grey "snowflakes" descend upon the courtyard, upon the inmates, and upon B.J., they say:

> Prisoner #1. Look at all the smoke coming from the chimneys. What are they burning there?
>
> Prisoner #2. What do you think?
>
> Prisoner #1. Well, I don't know. I mean. (. . .) The world needs to know.
>
> Prisoner #2. The world knows. It just doesn't care.

It is quite a shocking scene, truth be told. The flakes descending in the courtyard are almost certainly the mortal remains of murdered and incinerated Nazi prisoners. The dialogue between the prisoners also points out the perhaps even more disturbing historical fact that the Holocaust was certainly not at the top of the Allied Forces' list in their strategic maneuvers against Hitler, to say the least. The Holocaust could proceed virtually unchecked, even though "the world" more or less knew what was happening in the camps, or at least the Allied leadership did (Medoff 2009, Gilbert 2015).

Inside a fly-infested barrack, B.J. meets a group of despondent prisoners. The despair is almost tangible in this scene. Some are lying motionless on their bunk beds, while others whisper softly to one another, ready to silence themselves if necessary and blend in with the crowd. Any attention they draw to themselves is mortally dangerous. They whisper about their favorite stew their mothers made them long ago; they ask questions about the whereabouts of someone's daughter, who arrived on the same train but has since disappeared; they ask B.J. to procure some anti-fever medicine from the Infirmary lest someone who is sick is processed, never to be seen again. But when B.J. returns with the medicine, the husband is already dead, leaving a heart-broken wife next to him.

The prisoners also whisper about one of the guards, nick-named "The Knife," who works in the Infirmary. Officially functioning as the camp's resident doctor, "The Knife" is apparently more interested in sadistically torturing and executing the prisoners left to his care. One of B.J.'s notes reads: "Murderers recruited to guard places like this. Bet The Knife could have hanged from the gallows had the Nazis not found a better use for him." Before B.J. is able to kill him, The Knife captures and tortures him in his "Infirmary," more resembling a slaughterhouse than a hospital: mutilated bodies lie around, incinerators are working constantly, human tissue and blood is splattered all over the place, the sounds of tortured people are continuously heard in the facility.

Set Roth, while trying to attend to a visibly ailing inmate, orders B.J. to disarm the security system and look for a piece of Da'at Yichud equipment in the officers' building he can use to take over one of the camp's massive robots to initiate the liberation of the whole population. However, B.J. is eventually captured by Frau Engel and is brought to the execution square, together with Roth and two other prisoners. A massive Nazi robot, based on appropriated Da'at Yichud technology, crushes the skull of the first, female, prisoner with a dedicated metal device at the end of its arm. Seconds before it is Roth's turn, the scientist manages to overcome and take over the robot, which then destroys the Nazi squad and crushes Frau Engel's head. Engel, however, is not dead but her face is severely mutilated by the device. She pulls herself in front of B.J. cursing him and "his people" (see above). The machine flings her away, after which B.J. takes over the robot's controls and secures an exit for him, Roth, and some other inmates. Even though Roth stated that the liberation of the whole camp was a *conditio sine qua non* for his cooperation with the Kreisau Circle, only a part of the camp's population makes it outside safely, including Bombate, who will then join the resistance for WNO and for WNC.

Depicting the Holocaust, with the semi-fictional Camp Belica as *pars pro toto*, is not an easy thing to do: the horrors of the camp, the gratuitous violence of the guards, the utter worthlessness of a human life, the despair of the inmates, the systemic torture barely disguised as "scientific experiments," and the roaring of the incinerators. The moral judgment of the depiction of the Holocaust in an entertainment medium is ambiguous. On the one hand, one could argue that—*finally*—the horrors of the historical Second World War have found their rightful and previously neglected place in its fictional depiction. Instead of the association between war and entertainment—making violence entertaining—a new one is constructed between war and human suffering. WNO went out of its way to include the "other side" of violent conflict by not only showing the heroic struggle against the morally degraded enemy, but also the consequences of the enemy's regime for "regular" citizens.

On the other hand, one could make a counter-argument: WNO is not only a game depicting the Holocaust *in* a game, but also *as* a game. Just as most war games have established the connection between war and entertainment, WNO constructs a new one between suffering and entertainment. Games are *texts*, so they exist as distinguishable (if not inseparable) from the text-external reality. This characteristic makes it possible for (many, but not all!) texts to be fictional, something a text-external reality cannot afford to be. Games are frequently fiction, subtly "sucking" the Holocaust from the realm of history into the realm of fiction. The Holocaust *becomes* a game, minus its historical significance. The Holocaust's historical perpetrators and its victims become set pieces in a "play," performed for "our" entertainment and leisure.

To add to this argumentation, the Camp Belica level is, quite paradoxically, the easiest and safest one in the whole game, at least from a ludic perspective. The level's lay-out is very linear and even though B.J. can be killed by the guards, they never pose a real threat. B.J.'s life is threatened by The Knife, who stabs him multiple times, but due to the scripted nature of the event, our hero always survives. When Blazkowicz is tied to the execution poles, next to Set Roth, the Nazi killer robot is taken care of before it reaches B.J. The level ends with a power fantasy: B.J. boards the killer robot, now under Roth's control, and shoots himself (and his fellow-inmates) to freedom through the remainder of the camp and the level. While it is technically possible for B.J. to leave the robot or for the robot to be destroyed by concentrated Nazi fire, this is theoretical at the most. The level is designed in such a way that losing is not a realistic option.

The nature of the game's medium makes it necessary for the game's protagonist-cum-player's avatar—Blazkowicz—to survive everything the game throws at the player. The length and complexity of the game makes "permadeath" problematic (Bosman 2018); losing one's progress after just one death is only possible if the player selects one of the higher difficulty levels in the game (called "Mein Leben," a reference to the words the Nazi soldiers gasp when killed in *Wolfenstein 3D*). In normal game mode, the save-system prevents the player from losing too much of their progress. So, on normal mode, even if B.J. dies in the Camp Belica level, the player will only have to replay the previous section of the level, instead of the whole level or the whole game. Needless to say, this was not an option for the inmates of the historical concentration camp: they were all "automatically" on permadeath mode.

Likewise, B.J. is a well-trained, well-fed, emotionally stable, American soldier, who volunteered to be captured by the Nazis and brought to the concentration camp. The other inmates of Camp Belica *and* those of the historical concentration camps were—almost exclusively—the opposite of B.J.: after a relatively short period of time after, or sometimes even before, arrival in the camp, an inmate's physical and psychological strength would weaken very quickly due to malnutrition, abuse, and stress. And entering a historical concentration camp of one's own free choice is theoretically possible, but highly unlikely.

Ludically speaking, Camp Belica bears no real threat to B.J. or the player, while the narrative context suggests the opposite, namely, that Blazkowicz has never been more vulnerable or has been under more dire circumstances, left to the whims of his captors and to the strength of his own wits. This clash between the ludic and narrative dimension of the game is called "ludo-narrative dissonance" and occurs when the gameplay instructs or forces the player to do one thing, while the narrative suggests the player to do another.

As a game avatar under the direction of the text-immanent gamer, B.J. is an atypical phenomenon in the camp: he is voluntarily present, is in perfect shape physically and mentally, and is in no real danger due to the conventions of the game medium in general and game genre specifically. But if we take B.J.'s Jewish identity into account, the perspective changes again. B.J., as a character, is a member of the Jewish people, who—both in-game and historically—is among the largest groups of victims during the Second World War. As a Jewish character, B.J. is part of one of the Nazis' target groups: he is intimately connected to the world of Camp Belica and its inmates. Their suffering is his suffering; their despair his. B.J. is not pretending to be a victim of the Nazis in order to secure an external goal; he *is* a victim of the Nazis, previously as a mental patient in Oliwa's parents' asylum and now as a concentration camp inmate. His professional goal is also his personal goal: to liberate and to be liberated from the Nazis.

B.J. is a Jewish game *character* and a Jewish game *avatar*. This has implications for the text-immanent reader of the game: because of the necessary communicative entanglement between the avatar and the immanent reader, if the former is Jewish, the latter becomes so too. Of course, any real player of the game may or may not be Jewish and may or may not be sympathetic toward either the Nazi regime or the Jewish victims of that regime. The immanent reader, however, does not have that choice: it is entangled with the Jewish character-cum-avatar Blazkowicz. I will deal with the ramifications of this insight in chapter 11.

One last observation regarding Camp Belica: its population is comprised of different ethnicities, specifically including white and black persons of both sexes. It hints at the often-overlooked history of the German persecution, imprisonment, torture, and execution of black people in Germany and the Nazi-occupied territories generally, and in the former German colonies of German South West Africa (now known as Namibia) and occupied North Africa specifically (Lusane 2003). This inclusion aligns with the multi-ethnical composition of the Kreisau Circle resistance group in the fourth *Wolfenstein* cycle (see chapter 9), and prefigures the dominance of the American Ku Klux Klan (McVeigh 2010) in the American street view in *WNC*.

Chapter 9

The Good, the Bad, and the Ugly
The Wrath of the Degenerates

"In the logic of the Nazisploitation film, all Germans are Nazis, all Nazis are members of the SS, and all members of the SS are war criminals, medical experimenters and sexual sadists." That is how Magilow (2012, 2) describes how "low culture" has dealt with Nazi-era Germany: a clear-cut, one-dimensional stereotype. All Germans are exclusively Nazis, and all Nazis are equally evil. And it is not difficult to see how *Wolfenstein* as a series, especially in the older cycles (see chapter 5), fits this description too. In the first two cycles, there are no non-combatants to be seen: everything that moves is a danger to B.J., to be iradicated without any further moral contemplation. In the third cycle, we have some civilians entering into the narrative, but they have no identity other than "non-combatant," with the only consequence that the player is forbidden to shoot these "civilians."

It is only in the fourth cycle, that things get more complicated. Of course, an overwhelming number of non-playable characters are still German soldiers-cum-Nazis whose only purpose is to be defeated by B.J. and (sometimes) by his allies, *but* there are notable exceptions to this "old" dichotomy. On the one hand, the "evil faction" is extended, now including white, American Ku Klux Klan members, wearing their distinct white robes and masks and working together with their new Aryan overlords. On the other hand, the resistance against the Nazi regime is also extended: it is no longer B.J. against the rest of the world; he receives help from an increasing number of odd characters, unified in the in-game version of the historical Kreisau Circle.

Chapter 9

THE *KREISAUER KREIS*: GERMANY'S RESISTANCE MOVEMENT

The Kreisau Circle (*Kreisauer Kreis*) was a Germany-based, intellectual, anti-Nazism resistance group that operated in the years 1940 to 1944 (Dulles 2019; Mommsen 2003, 134–51; Roon 1971). Formed around a nucleus of diverse individuals who shared a common commitment to moral and political principles, the Kreisau Circle sought to envision a new Germany, one that would emerge from the ruins of the Nazi regime. The Kreisau Circle took its name from the Kreisau estate, located in Silesia, where the group initially gathered for meetings. The nucleus of the group consisted of Helmuth James Graf von Moltke (1907–1945), Peter Yorck von Wartenburg (1904–1944), and Adam von Trott zu Solz (1909–1944), each of whom played pivotal roles in shaping the group's ideology and activities. The Circle grew to include theologians, philosophers, legal experts, civil servants, and even military officers. This eclectic mix of members brought diverse perspectives and expertise to the group, enriching its intellectual depth.

At its core, the Kreisau Circle was a forum for intense discussions on the future of Germany after the fall of the Nazi regime. Its ideology was rooted in Christian ethics, liberal humanism, and a commitment to democracy. Central to its members' vision was the belief that Germany needed to undergo a moral and political transformation to ensure lasting peace and reconciliation in Europe. They rejected totalitarianism, racism, and the militaristic aggression of the Nazis. The Circle's members believed in the importance of individual freedom, human dignity, and the rule of law. Their ideas were profoundly influenced by philosophers and theologians such as Thomas Aquinas, Immanuel Kant, and Søren Kierkegaard, as well as by their own experiences and reflections on the atrocities committed by the Nazi regime.

While the Kreisau Circle was primarily an intellectual group, it also engaged in various forms of resistance against the Nazi regime. Members of the Circle used their positions in the government, military, and civil service to undermine Nazi policies whenever possible. For example, Adam von Trott zu Solz, who served in the German Foreign Office, attempted to establish contacts with foreign governments and promote anti-Nazi sentiment abroad. Additionally, the Circle worked to prepare for a post-Nazi Germany by developing plans for political and economic reconstruction. They drafted memoranda and position papers outlining their vision for a democratic and federal Germany, one that would be decentralized and based on the principles of subsidiarity.

The Circle also maintained connections with other resistance groups in Germany, such as the White Rose (*Weiße Rose*) and the Confessing Church

(*Bekennende Kirche*), fostering a network of like-minded individuals committed to resisting the Nazi regime. These connections allowed for the exchange of ideas and information, strengthening the broader anti-Nazi resistance movement. The Kreisau Circle included male and female members from Roman Catholic, protestant, and socialist backgrounds. When Claus von Stauffenberg's assassination attempt on Hitler's life failed on July 20, 1944, the German authorities arrested leading Kreisau-member Peter Yorck. Von Stauffenberg and Yorck were cousins, a connection strong enough for the Nazis to execute the latter too. And since Moltke was also associated directly with Yorck, he too was arrested and executed. The decapitation of the Kreisau's two leaders meant the end of the organization as such.

The in-game version of the Kreisau Circle first appears, very modestly, in *Return to Castle Wolfenstein*. From *Wolfenstein. The New Order* onwards, the resistance group is rapidly expanded by including a very diverse group of "misfits," people who were disqualified by the Nazis for a number of reasons: faith, ethnicity, disability, or political views (see table 9.1).

In the first and second cycle, from *Castle Wolfenstein* to *Spear of Destiny*, there is no mention of any resistance group in-game. In the third cycle, *Return to Castle Wolfenstein* and *Wolfenstein* (2009), the Kreisau Circle is mentioned for the first time. In RtCW, two members of the Circle make their appearance: Kessler (no first name) and Karl Villigut, both assisting B.J. with weapons and intelligence. The name of the second German resistance fighter is somewhat of a mystery: it seems to be a reference to the *SS-Brigadeführer* Karl Maria Wiligut, who designed the *SS Totenkopfring* (see chapter 2). However, the historical Wiligut and the fictional Villigut do not seem to share anything in common but their names. In *Wolfenstein*, the Kreisau's role is enlarged, primarily as the principal mission-giver to Blazkowicz-cum-the player. Especially Caroline Becker, the head and suggested founder of the resistance group, takes on an important role as B.J.'s pre-eminent ally. Kessler and Becker are the only Kreisau members making it into the fourth cycle, although their appearances and backstories are altered to fit the cycle's allohistorical context.

In the fourth cycle, the resistance has grown to its full potential (as of today) in terms of narrative presence and relevance. In the next three sections, we will discuss the various Kreisau members of the fourth cycle, divided by installment, starting with *Wolfenstein: The Old Blood*, since it is the first one of this cycle in the in-series chronology.

Table 9.1. Primary members of the Kreisau Circle in the *Wolfenstein* universe.

Overall	B.J. Blazkowicz	American (cycle 1~3); Physically challenged (paralysed); Jewish (cycle 4)
Return to Castle Wolfenstein	Kessler	German
	Karl Villigut	German
Wolfenstein (2009)	Caroline Becker	German
	Erik Engle	German
	Hans Schmidt	German
	Rachel Herzen	German
Wolfenstein: The Old Blood	Ludwig Kessler	German
	Sophie Kessler	German
	Annette Krause	German, Jewish
Wolfenstein: The New Order	Caroline Becker	German, physically challenged (paralysed)
	Klaus Kreutz	German, ex-Nazi
	Max Hass	German, neurodivergent
	Bombate	Namibia, person of colour
	"J"	American, person of colour
	Tekla	Polish, neurodivergent
	Bobby Bram	Englishman
	Probst Wyatt III	American
	Fergus Reid	Scottish, physically challenged (prosthetic arm)
	Anya Oliwa	Polish
	Set Roth	German, Jewish
Wolfenstein 2: The New Colossus	Sigrun Engel	German, ex-Nazi, obese
	Grace Walker	American, person of colour
	Norman Caldwell	American, conspiracy theorist
	Dimitri Fedorov	Russian, physically challenged (cannot feel pain)
	Horton Boone	American, communist
	Jacques LeRoy	American, person of colour
	Maria Laurent	French
Wolfenstein: Youngbloods	Abby Walker	American, person of colour

If the same resistance member is present in more than one installment within a specific cycle, his or her name is only displayed with the game he or she first appears in.

THE WHITE ROSE: THE KESSLERS

In *Wolfenstein: The Old Blood*, B.J. finds himself—alone and without backup—within hostile territory, e.g., the city of Paderborn in Germany. There he meets a very small, local resistance group—the WOB's version of the Kreisau Circle—consisting of Ludwig Kessler and Annette Krause. As discussed earlier, in chapter 8, Annette Krause is clearly portrayed after the historical Anne Frank. Ludwig and his deceased wife Sophie are, however, also references to historical figures from the 1940s, Sophie and Hans Scholl, both founding members of "The White Rose" (Günther 2021).

The *Weiße Rose* was, not unlike the *Kreisauer Kreis*, a non-violent, intellectual resistance group pitted against the Nazi regime (Newborn and Dumbach 2007), and originating from the University of Munich. The most notable members of the group were the siblings Sophie and Hans Scholl. The group's primary means of resistance was the writing, printing, and distribution of anonymous anti-war pamphlets and accompanying anti-Nazi graffiti. The group continued its activities from June 27, 1942 to February 18, 1943, when its members were arrested by the Gestapo. Four days later, Sophie and Hans were executed, together with their comrade Christoph Probst. The group had been on the brink of establishing contacts with the Kreisau Circle, but this was, of course, cut short by the arrests of the White Rose members.

In the series, a Kreisau Circle member with the name "Kessler" and having no distinguishable background story already appeared in RtCW. In WOB, however, he re-appears with a different and elaborate backstory complete with a first name, "Ludwig." Ludwig Kessler helps B.J. to navigate the canals to travel from Paderborn to Wulfburg. During the boat trip, Blazkowicz has his important if short conversation with the Jewish woman Annette Krause, whom Kessler has lovingly taken into hiding (see chapter 8). Later in the game, the player has to choose to rescue either Annette or Ludwig. If B.J. saves the former, she is seen kissing with her girlfriend at the end of the game; if he saves the latter, Ludwig barges off to continue his resistance work.

As stated earlier, Ludwig and Sophie Kessler are references to Hans and Sophie Scholl, the brother and sister from The White Rose movement. There are a couple of hints to be found. During the game, it becomes clear through notes scattered throughout the game's world that Ludwig Kessler was married to a certain Sophie Kessler. One of these notes is a love letter from Sophie (called "Sophie's Letter") to Ludwig, relating her longing for him and her work as a Nazi-critical journalist in Berlin. A second clue is an in-game newspaper clipping, called "Three Anarchists Hanged for Treason." The clipping relates the execution by hanging of three unnamed "students," who were all "members of a local terrorist group" for "high treason having spread dangerous anarchistic propaganda flyers against the Führer in public squares across Berlin."

Sophie Scholl was arrested in 1943 when she was handing out pamphlets at the Ludwig Maximilian University in Munich. Ludwig is both the name of the game-Kessler and of the university where Sophie was arrested. Yes, the historical Hans and Sophie Scholl were siblings, while the in-game Ludwig and Sophie were married (sharing the same surname). Yes, the historical Hans and Sophie Scholl were executed by guillotine, while the game's Sophie and her fellow "anarchists" were hanged by the Nazis. But the resemblances are too strong to deny. A third hint is found in an in-game flyer called "Rise, German Students!" It is a short pamphlet written and signed by Sophie Kessler, identifying her as a student of philosophy at Berlin University. It calls upon German students to rise against "brutes antagonistic to the free-thinking spirit:"

> German youth—rise up! Defend the name of our nation. Do not let it slip into infamy. Stand up against the fascists of our regime for a new and free Europe, free from the burdening shackles of Adolf Hitler's "ideological education." For a Europe where everyone can live as equals. Rise up now, for soon it may be too late.

As discussed earlier, if B.J. chooses to rescue Ludwig Kessler (leaving Annette to perish), the player overhears the man talking over the radio about hijacking a German zeppelin and flying it off to Berlin in order to drop "flyers" for as long as he can. This is more than a hint at the White Rose's pamphlets prior to February 1943. After the executions, the text of the White Rose's sixth pamphlet was smuggled out of Germany through Scandinavia to the United Kingdom by no other than Helmuth James Graf von Moltke, one of the founding members of the *Kreisauer Kreis*, who was on the brink of contacting the Scholls just before their arrest. In July 1943, numerous copies of the pamphlet were dropped over Germany by Allied planes, entitled "The Manifesto of the Students of Munich."

The White Rose used non-violent means like distributing anti-Nazi leaflets and leaving graffiti in public places to protest the regime's policies, particularly the Holocaust and the war effort. The Kreisau Circle, on the other hand, was a broader and more diverse group of intellectuals, theologians, and political activists, discussing and planning for a post-Nazi Germany, and envisioning a democratic and decentralized state. Their resistance was more focused on long-term political and social change. The White Rose was motivated by moral outrage and a desire to expose the crimes of the Nazi regime, particularly the mass murder of Jews. They aimed to inspire a sense of resistance among ordinary Germans. The Kreisau Circle was motivated by a vision of a different Germany after the fall of the Nazis. They sought to plan for a post-war society that would be based on democratic principles, human rights, and social justice.

Both the inclusion by the series of the real-world Kreisau Circle and of the White Rose diversify the one-dimensional dichotomy of the earlier installments. The fourth cycle clearly demonstrates the historical fact that not all Germans supported the Nazi regime, and that some Germans even had the courage to stand up to Hitler's tyrannical reign, often at the cost of their own life.

THE KREISAU CIRCLE: WOLFENSTEIN'S *ENTARTETEN*

The Kreisau Circle of the fourth cycle (excluding the cycle's prequel WOB, discussed above) consists of an eclectic assembly of individuals, a veritable mosaic of quirky and idiosyncratic men and women, only united by their common hatred of Nazism and by their determination to free the world. Many of them fit more than one category as to why they hate the Nazis and are equally hated by them.

First, there are the soldiers of the Allied Forces, forced from active service into underground resistance because of the Nazis' occupation of their home countries. The "involuntary mystic" Probst Wyatt III (see chapter 8), the guitar playing "J" providing Wyatt with psychedelic drugs, head of the FBI in the newly-liberated USA Grace Walker and her daughter Abby, the conspiracy theorist Norman Caldwell, the communist and self-proclaimed preacher Horton Boone, and the Saxophone-playing Jacques "Paris Jack" LeRoy are Americans. Others include: Bombate from Nazi-occupied Namibia (South West Africa), Bobby Bram from England, Fergus Reid from Scotland, Anya Oliwa and possibly Tekla from Poland, Dimitri Fedorov from Russia, and Maria Laurent from France. Of German origin, there are Caroline Becker, Klaus Kreutz, Max Hass, Seth Roth, and Sigrun Engel.

Next, we find several people disqualified by the Nazi regime for numerous reasons. The physically challenged, like the paralyzed B.J. (at the beginning in WNO) and Becker (both having to use a wheelchair to move around), Fedorov who is incapable of feeling pain, Sigrun Engel, who is bullied by her own mother, Frau Engel, because of her obesity, and Reid with his prosthetic arm. Next, the mentally challenged: the child-like Hass, the psychologically troubled philosopher and mathematician Tekla, and the addicted Wyatt. Then there are the people of color: Bombate, "J," Grace and Abby Walker, and LeRoy; and the Jews Roth and Blazkowicz. Finally, we have two communists (Boone and Fedorov), one conspiracy theorist (Caldwell), and two *entartete Künstler* (Hass as a painter of naive art and LeRoy as a Jazz musician).

The eugenic policies of the Nazis during the Third Reich represent a chilling example of how pseudoscientific ideologies can lead to atrocities when embraced by a totalitarian regime (Kuhl 2002; see also chapter 3). Rooted in notions of racial purity and biological determinism, Nazi eugenics aimed to engineer a racially superior Aryan society while targeting and systematically exterminating those deemed "unfit" or racially inferior. The Nuremberg Laws of 1935 laid the legal foundation for Nazi eugenics, segregating Jews from the Aryan population and instituting a web of discriminatory measures. The T4 program (Connelly 2021), initiated in 1939, marked a significant escalation, as it authorized the systematic murder of disabled individuals, deeming them "life unworthy of life." This program provided a template for the later implementation of the Holocaust.

Central to Nazi eugenic policies was the belief in the hereditary transmission of traits, leading to the forced sterilization of thousands considered genetically "undesirable" (Weiss 2010). Additionally, "racial hygiene" programs promoted the selective breeding of "racially pure" individuals. Primary categories of "undesirables" targeted by the Nazis included: Jews, Romani, disabled individuals, political dissidents (including communists), LGBTQ+ people, Jehovah's Witnesses (because of their collective refusal to be drafted into the German army), individuals of African descent, as well as those who were deemed racially or socially "inferior."

Closely connected to the Nazis' eugenics is the concept of "degenerated art" or *entartete Kunst* (Guenther 1991). It played a central role in the Nazi regime's ideology and policies, particularly in the fields of art and culture. The Nazis used this term to denounce and persecute art forms and cultural expressions that they considered harmful to their vision of a racially pure and ideologically aligned society. The notion was rooted in the Nazis' belief in Aryan racial superiority and in their hostility toward anything they deemed contrary to their ideals. They applied this concept primarily to modern art movements, including Expressionism, Dadaism, Cubism, Surrealism, and abstract art. These artistic forms were seen as a threat to the traditional, idealized representations of beauty and culture that the Nazis sought to promote.

One of the most notorious manifestations of the concept was the 1937 exhibition titled "Entartete Kunst" (Peters 2014). This exhibition, curated by the Nazi regime, featured works of art that were deemed "degenerate" and then confiscated from museums and private collections. The purpose was to ridicule and vilify these artworks, presenting them as morally and aesthetically corrupt. Artists whose works were included in the exhibition, such as Wassily Kandinsky and Marc Chagall, faced persecution and had their art confiscated. It did not stop with the visual arts. Jazz, atonal music, and compositions by Jewish composers were also labelled "Entartet." This led to the suppression of jazz clubs, the banning of certain musical styles, both associated with the emancipation of people of color, and the dismissal of Jewish musicians from prominent positions in orchestras and music institutions.

THE CURIOUS DUO: MAX HASS AND KLAUS KREUTZ

The *Entarteten* of *Wolfenstein*'s Kreisau Circle form a kind of Tarantinoesque "revenge group" (see chapter 1): the victims of the War take revenge on their attackers. Even though not all the members survive the happenings in the games, their collective revenge and subsequential victory is undeniable. A special and illustrative case is that of Max Hass and Klaus Kreutz. Kreutz is in everything a prototypical Aryan, exactly like the Nazis envisioned: blond, muscled, and very strong. In older days, Kreutz was deeply attached to the Nazis' cause; he even decorated his body with Nazi tattoos, including a very large German eagle holding a swastika etched on his breast for everybody to see.

So, when B.J. enters the Berlin hideout for the first time, in WNO, he and Klaus immediately enter into some sort of altercation, since the former holds the latter to be a really dedicated Nazi. Klaus, however, is a trusted member of the Kreisau Circle, soon winning B.J.'s complete trust. His background is revealed to Blazkowicz through Caroline Becker. When B.J. makes a lot of noise cutting some concrete, the gentle giant Max Hass is clearly disturbed by the sound, causing Kreutz to rebuke B.J. and gently take Max somewhere else. Klaus treats the mentally challenged Max as a kind of adopted son. When B.J. wonders about the curious duo, Becker explains:

> Used to be Klaus had a son. Born during the war. A miracle he called it. They had tried for years to have a child. Him and his wife. (. . .) The child was born with a club foot. Klaus knew of course what that meant. He begged the doctors not to report it to the authorities. When Secret Police showed up to take the boy away, Klaus and his wife tried to stop them. The wife died from a bullet in the head. The child too. Klaus . . . could not protect them. (. . .) And he will never forgive the Nazis.

Kreutz' child fell prey to the Nazis' eugenics program. His unnamed son was physically disabled and therefore unworthy of living according to Nazi laws. And even though Kreutz and probably his wife too, were devoted Nazi members, their parental instinct was stronger. They unsuccessfully tried to save their child from a state-sanctioned execution. Only Kreutz survived, apparently changing his political alliance for good. These circumstances made Kreutz take the care for Max Hass upon himself. The in-game description of Hass reads:

> Max Hass was born with a severe brain injury, which forced doctors to surgically remove half his brain. Shunned by his parents, and given that Nazi health policies advocated the euthanizing of anyone with physical deformities and disabilities, Max was raised in secret by his grandmother until she died from a

heart attack. He was found by Klaus Kreutz behind a dumpster, who took him in and raised him as if he was his own son.

Hass is a huge man, towering even over Blazkowicz. The right part of his skull is caved in due to brain surgery in his infancy. Max is generally good-hearted and caring for his friends in the resistance, but is clearly lacking in cognitive capacities, usually behaving in an almost child-like manner. His vocabulary is very limited: he can only utter his own name, using different pitches to communicate different emotions quite effectively. When sleeping in his room, he is seen sucking his thumb, holding a teddy bear in his arms. One time, Hass misplaces his wooden toys, and B.J. is tasked to retrieve them, all to Max' great delight. He walks bare-footed through the hide-out under Berlin and later in the submarine.

Max Hass is apparently suffering from Savant Syndrome, a "rare, but extraordinary, condition in which persons with serious mental disabilities, including autistic disorder, have some 'island of genius' which stands in marked, incongruous contrast to overall handicap" (Treffert 2009). Usually, Max interacts with other people like a very young child, scared of noises and of people arguing. He has had no formal education and generally his mental capacities seem very limited. As said before, he apparently can only speak two words, being his name. But on the other hand, Max is an exceptional chess player, impressing and puzzling the brilliant scientist Set Roth, and a naturally talented billiards player, imitating and quickly surpassing the more experienced Bombate and, being the keen reader that he is, he is able to help Wyatt in solving the philosophical puzzle he is struggling with.

Max seems to be an especially gifted painter. When, at the end of WNO, Kreutz is killed by Nazi soldiers raiding the Berlin hideout, Hass is beside himself with grief, starting a rampage among his father's murderers. In WNC, in the submarine, Hass has apparently created a commemoration room for Kreutz, including a big mural depicting the deceased man. The mural is painted in an Expressionist manner and portrays Kreutz in a way similar to Edvard Munch's famous painting *The Scream* (1893), in 1937 declared by the Nazis as yet another example of *entartete Kunst*.

SIGRUN ENGEL: THE GERMAN VALKYRIE

Another German member of the Kreisau Circle is Sigrun Engel, the daughter of former Camp Belica director Irene Engel. She appears only in *Wolfenstein II: The New Colossus*. Sigrun is one of Engel's five children (as one can deduce from a dialogue between Frau Engel and her younger lover in WNO), and is betrothed to the son of the Berlin Police Commander. Irene Engel has a clear fondness for Nordic mythology. Her daughter is called Sigrun (meaning "victory run"), one of the Valkyries, while various systems on board of her flying command center come from the same source: Odin, the Nordic god of war and wisdom, Hugin and Munin, Odin's raven, and Valhalla, the mythical place of those who have fallen in battle.

At the beginning of WNC, when B.J., Caroline Becker, and Probst Wyatt (or Fergus Reid, depending on the player's choice at the beginning of WNO) are taken prisoners on the *Ausmerzer* ("eradicator"), a large fortified airborne platform used by the Nazis, Irene Engel tries to make her 20-year-old daughter Sigrun decapitate the incapacitated Caroline Becker with an axe. Sigrun is psychologically incapable of doing so, for which she is mocked severely by her own mother in front of the prisoners and a couple of Nazi super soldiers; especially Sigrun's supposed mental weakness and her being physically overweight are targeted.

> Irene Engel: You haven't been doing the exercise we agreed upon. You haven't been following your diet.
>
> Sigrun Engel: Forgive me, mother. I had a small slice of cake yesterday. Only a small slice.
>
> Irene Engel: Stupid cow. You disgrace your race and your family. What will people say when you arrive at an obesity clinic? The daughter of a general. What a disgrace. Show me your cheek, girl. You are even worthy of a slap.

Irene continues to belittle her daughter. She has apparently read her daughter's secret diary, which includes—according to her mother—sexual fantasies.

> Irene Engel: What did my men find when they searched your room? Chocolate, cookies, lemonade, candy. Even besides the crazy things you have written in your diary. (. . .)
>
> Sigrun Engel: You have read my diary?
>
> Irene Engel: But what you can do, is fill a diary full of perversions and words of treason. Some of them even in English. Page after page you pour your dirty mind out, while your body swells up with disgusting blubber like a sea cow. Don't you understand the position you put me in? I am compelled by law to report you.
>
> Sigrun Engels: You had no right to read it. (. . .)
>
> Irene Engel: You want a kiss too? Like you wrote about in your diary. On your thick and fat cheeks? What about here under?

With that last sentence, Irene puts the lips of the decapitated head of Caroline—having executed the woman herself after her daughter had refused—to Sigrun's cheeks as to imitate kisses. She even positions Caroline's severed head into Sigrun's loins, suggesting oral sex between her daughter and the dead woman. It is ironic that Irene Engel should bully Sigrun for her supposedly forbidden fantasies, as she herself seems to have developed a very unhealthy sexual desire for B.J. Later in WNC, during Blazkowicz' decapitation by Frau Engel, she says to her victim: "We would have been . . . so good together. Darling . . . you're breaking my heart." In earlier scenes in WNC, Irene Engel refers to B.J. as "darling." She even puts her gold Handgun 1946 in B.J.'s mouth while he is incapacitated, a scene with clear sexual overtones.

Sigrun struggles to fit into the Kreisau Circle. Klaus Kreutz, the other former-Nazi member, was killed in the Nazi raid on Kreisau's Berlin hideout at the end of WNO. On the captured German submarine, now in use as a new refuge, Sigrun is structurally discriminated against because of her Nazi background in general and because of her mother Irene specifically, especially after Irene executed Blazkowicz publicly. Exceptions to this are B.J. and Probst Wyatt/Fergus Reid, because she saved their lives on board of the *Ausmerzer*. Among the Kreisau crew, Sigrun is predominantly shunned by Anna—for obvious reasons—and by the Afro-American members of the American resistance who join the Kreisau later. At one moment, Sigrun tries to befriend Anya, who refuses, referring to several Nazi atrocities in America witnessed by Sigrun in the company of her mother:

> Anya Oliwa: I've looked through your records. Lists upon lists of atrocities. The Yosemite massacre. Burning of the Baltimore ghetto. Nashville.
>
> Sigrun Engel: Stop. I was just following my mother. I am not responsible. I didn't commit any of those acts myself. If you don't trust me, then why don't you just kill me right now.
>
> Anya Oliwa: But you were there. You stood by and watched it all happen. And you did nothing to stop your mother.
>
> Sigrun Engel: She would have thought me weak. An embarrassment. I just wanted her to be pleased with me.
>
> Anya Oliwa: I am nauseous now. And I don't know if it is the pregnancy or you.

Sigrun defends herself, claiming she is not responsible for the atrocities committed by her mother Irene, but that she was a mere witness *and* that going against her mother's wishes would not have been a reasonable alternative. It is unclear if Sigrun complied with her mother's wishes-cum-orders on the ground of her wanting to be loved by her mother or because she would be punished by her mother for being weak.

In any case, WNC seems to—indirectly—address the issue of *Befehlsnotstand* here with the help of the Sigrun character. *Befehlsnotstand*, a term rooted in the historical context of Nazi Germany, signifies a state of crisis in which individuals within a military or hierarchical structure find themselves torn between moral and legal imperatives (Lewy 2017, 108). It refers to the dilemma faced by those who are ordered to commit actions that contravene their moral principles, such as participating in war crimes or atrocities. The term is emblematic of the ethical challenges that can emerge in rigidly structured organizations. It gained prominence during the Nuremberg Trials when some defendants claimed they were merely following orders. *Befehlsnotstand* prompts discourse on the tension between obedience and individual conscience in extreme circumstances.

Later in WNC, Sigrun is especially rebuked by Grace Walker, the leader of the American resistance. She consistently addresses Sigrun as a Nazi, an identification Sigrun increasingly despises. In one instance, Grace orders Sigrun to find certain information:

Grace Walker: Listen, I am going to need your Nazi eyeballs on this one.

Sigrun Engel: I am not a Nazi.

Grace Walker: Whatever.

Sigrun Engel: (. . .) But please stop calling me a Nazi.

Grace Walker: O, I am sorry. Did I hurt your Nazi feelings? Suck it up, princess.

Later, when Sigrun has performed her job well and reports to the group, she is cruelly dismissed by Grace: "Alright, now fuck off now, Nazi." Initially, Sigrun backs off, but after a short pause she returns, slaps Grace in the face, and grabs her throat showing a remarkable amount of physical strength.

Sigrun Engel: Grace! Don't ever call me a Nazi again. I am not a Nazi. You do not have the right to label me as something I am not. As someone less than yourself. As someone less than human. Say it! Say I am not a Nazi.

Grace Walker: Alright, okay, I get it. You are not a Nazi.

From that moment onward, she has won the respect of Grace and, therefore, of the whole crew. When the Kreisau members go out on their mission to kill Irene Engel, she is excused by notably Grace, saying she has already lived up to expectations.

Another interesting point in Sigrun's character is her fascination for Bombate, notably because of his ethnicity. When she meets Bombate the first time, she asks Anya: "Do you allow blacks on board?" To which Anya replies: "Everyone is allowed on this boat. Except Nazis." This rebuke does not prevent Sigrun from some little personal exploration. Later in WNO, she and Bombate are caught while having sex in the small submarine. Sigrun, probably because of inexperience with real-life sex, mistakes their intercourse for love. And when she expresses her love for Bombate, he shuns her initially and even has sex with another woman later on. Sigrun slaps him in the face, when she finds out, and declares in tears that she will only "use him" for masturbation purposes.

Sigrun's initial remark is both an indication of the racial context she was raised in: Nazi leaders regarded non-white people categorically as *Untermenschen*, not worthy of living in the same world as Aryans. Probably, Bombate is the first "black" person she has ever met, and she notices that he is not just "there," but in a position of equality to the other "white" Kreisau members. This cultural shock is increased later in the game, when Grace and her people join the Kreisau group on board of the submarine, including a number of Afro-Americans. Sigrun's interest in Bombate is culturally, but also sexually, an in-game reference to the old Western narrative claiming that white women are attracted to black men because of their physical and sexual prowess, including the connected ingredients of racial stereotypes and Western orientalism (Hodes 2014). Her sexual intercourse with Bombate signifies her emotional capture by her Nazi past: it stands for everything she wants to be, but was forbidden to be because of her cultural context.

Sigrun is fat-shamed repeatedly by her mother. The Nazi regime promoted a vision of physical fitness as a part of the Aryan ideal. This emphasis on physical fitness, coupled with a desire for racial purity, led to discrimination against those who did not fit the Nazi image of health and beauty: individuals with obesity or disabilities were stigmatized and repressed. Irene Engel indicates multiple times how embarrassed she is that her daughter does not fit the Aryan ideal, neither regarding her physique, nor her psyche. Hitler was appalled by obesity, starting a campaign in August 1940 to combat overweight in Germany, and encouraging the SS members to be "nonsmoking nondrinking vegetarians" (Proctor 1999, 138).

Sigrun is probably named after one of the Edda's Valkyries, winged demi-gods who were responsible for bringing those who fell in battle to Valhalla. Her name could be a reference to an operation with the same name. On July 20, 1944, Claus von Stauffenberg unsuccessfully tried to assassinate Adolf Hitler and seize power for himself in order to broker peace with the advancing allies (Fest 1997). Sigrun does not kill Hitler in any way or capacity, but her information and knowledge of Nazi technology and her mother's plans lead to the start of the Second American Revolution at the end of WNC.

Sigrun's defense against Grace's continuous name-calling is also very interesting, and in two different ways. The first is that Sigrun uses the term "labelling": "You do not have the right to label me as something I am not." Labelling theory, a significant perspective in sociology, delves into how society assigns labels to individuals, often impacting their self-identity and behavior (Moncrieffe 2013). Developed in the mid-twentieth century by theorists like Howard Becker, Edwin Lemert, and Erving Goffman, this theory highlights the social construction of deviance. Central to labelling theory is the notion that individuals' actions are not inherently deviant; rather, they become so through societal reactions. When someone is labelled as a deviant or criminal, it can lead to a self-fulfilling prophecy. They may internalize the label, altering their behavior to conform to society's expectations of them. The process often involves primary and secondary deviance. Primary deviance represents the initial act that leads to a label, while secondary deviance occurs when individuals adopt the labelled identity and engage in further deviant behavior.

Sigrun objects to the labelling she receives from Grace, because it conflicts with her self-perception and self-identity as something else than "Nazi." She also rejects the consequences of such a labeling within the Kreisau group: being identified as a Nazi, she is shunned by the others and is kept out of the decision-making process. She wants the opposite: to be included in the group and its decision making. She wants agency, something she was not given by her mother and her Nazi context. She wants to make her own decisions, unhindered by her Nazi past, which still haunts her.

The second way that Sigrun's reaction to her being labelled is interesting, is the fact that the Nazis effectually did the same. By deeming Jews, communists, Slavs, people of color, Jehova's Witnesses, disabled people, and LGBTQ+ people as *Untermenschen* and "vermin" (like Irene Engel did regarding Blazkowicz in WNO), they could be treated as such. Labelling people as non-humans or sub-humans opens the political, cultural, and moral possibility to eradicate them. If "they" are not people (anymore), you do not have to treat them humanely. Quite paradoxically, it is through Sigrun's protest that this Nazi method of dehumanization is criticized.

TEKLA'S PHILOSOPHY #1: CONSCIOUSNESS

Another important member of *Wolfenstein*'s Kreisau Circle is Tekla, no surname given. She only appears in the Fergus timeline. When B.J. liberated the resistance members, including Fergus, from a German prison and they enter the Berlin hideout, a slender woman of uncertain age approaches the group, shaking her head in disbelief with notes and papers in hand.

> What are you doing here? (. . .) You're supposed to be dead, Fergus Reid. You've been gone for three months. {Stupid anomaly.} People don't come back from Eisenwald. And you, {B.J.}! Long since off the books. I have heard stories about you. I was told you died in 1946. Misinformation. Always. You, {Anya}, I don't even know who you are. Queer variable. Well, none of this has been accounted for. I will have to revise my whole model. Thank you very much.

Tekla seems to be suffering from some kind of neurodivergence: she talks to herself as if with another person (indicated above by "{}"), and she struggles in social situations, having trouble relating emotionally to her fellow-resistance members. She is constantly busy with her notes and calculations, trying to make mathematical-empirical sense of the world around her, usually to no avail. It is difficult to speculate about the exact nature of her condition: it could be autism, schizophrenia, dissociative identity disorder or something else entirely.

In several instances in WNO—she does not survive the end of the game—she discusses her philosophical problems with—among others—B.J. Unfortunately, nobody seems to be able to follow her erratic thoughts. With B.J. and others, she tries to discuss the (dis)continuity of consciousness and the possibility of free will versus a universal determinism. The first of these discussions—or rather lectures—takes place in the middle of the night. Blazkowicz and Anna are sleeping next to one another in the Berlin hideout. Suddenly B.J. is awakened by Tekla sitting next to them on a chair, perhaps already having been there for a long time. Blazkowicz, however, does not rebuke her too strongly, since he appears to be familiar with her eccentricity. When asked if she does not have to sleep, Tekla answers negatively: "I try not to sleep. No telling if I will ever wake up."

Then, Tekla starts to structure and expound upon her first argumentation on the discontinuity of human consciousness. First, she equals the human brain with a "biological computational device running on an electro-chemical process," claiming that the experience of consciousness is an "emergent property" of that process. Humans, according to Tekla, have an understanding of their own consciousness as the continuation of the "self" from past through present to future. She argues, however, against that idea through claiming that, if the brain is temporarily shut down, for example as the result of injury or through the process of sleep, consciousness disappears. When the electro-chemical process is rebooted—waking from unconsciousness or sleep—a "new conscious" emerges from the human brain. Because this new consciousness emerges from the same brain as the previous one, it has immediate and total access to all of its memories. Tekla: "But in actuality, it is just an impostor. Inheriting the body and brain from the previous, now dead, inhabitant."

Blazkowicz takes it all in silently listening to Tekla. When she pauses, he asks her: "What about the soul?" It is not the only time, B.J. uses religious vocabulary, even though we have no specific information on his religious upbringing. The other time is in Camp Belica, when he asks Set Roth if the latter is a believer or not (see chapter 8). Tekla is taken aback by the question:

> Soul. {I knew he was stupid.} There is no such thing as a soul. We are machines of biology. Nothing more, nothing less. {Idiot.} The soul is simply a pointless concept dreamt up by priests and fairy tale men. You are an anomaly you. An outlier. Useless. A laughing anus is what you are.

Tekla confesses a radical materialist approach to metaphysics: only the material, the physical exists, leaving no room for non-material things like the human soul. She disqualifies the concept of the soul as a (conscious or not) invention of "priests and fairy-tale men," in the process equating religion in general with fiction. Nevertheless, there is one entity that escapes Tekla's materialism: B.J. himself, an "anomaly," an "outlier," "useless," and a "laughing anus." During the fourth cycle, Blazkowicz is four times the victim of problematic unconsciousness.

At the beginning of WNO, B.J. remains in a Polish psychiatric asylum for 20 years, slipping in and out consciousness, without being able to move his body or make contact. Secondly, during the transition from WNO to WNC, B.J. is mortally wounded by General Strasse. It is only thanks to Roth's superior medical knowledge and techniques that he survives, if only in a rapidly declining physical state that is only halted after his acquirement of a new body. Again, B.J. is unconscious for a long time. Thirdly, when Blazkowicz is apprehended by the Nazis, halfway through WNC, and then executed by decapitation, his severed head is transported to the Berlin hideout to be placed on life-support and eventually transferred onto the body of a captured German super soldier. During this transportation of his head and during the transplantation operation, B.J. is—luckily for him—unconscious. When B.J. awakens from the operation, Roth asks him if he remembers anything from the last two years, to which the first responds positively. One scene later, Roth approaches B.J. saying: "You are a new man!" And fourthly, it is also possible that Tekla's philosophical ideas on the (dis)continuation of consciousness is connected to the series' continuity throughout the four cycles (as discussed in chapter 5). As discussed, in WNO and WOB (cycle #4) there is a mattress in the Kreisau hideout where B.J. can lie down to sleep *and* dream a part of the older W3D (cycle #2).

Tekla's philosophy seems very much inspired by Derek Parfit's *Reasons and persons* (1984), especially by the first of its four parts on the nature of identity. Parfit challenges traditional assumptions on the nature of human identity and the continuation of said identity as formulated by philosophers like John Locke and Thomas Reid. Personal identity, according to Parfit, is *not* tied to the persistence of an unchanging self over time. Instead, he introduces the concepts of "psychological continuity" and "connectedness" as central to understanding what makes someone the same person over time.

Psychological continuity, according to Parfit, is the thread that connects one's past and future experiences. It involves the continuation of mental attributes such as memories, beliefs, desires, and character traits. Parfit argues that it is the degree of psychological continuity between two distinct points in time that determines personal identity. This means that even if there are disruptions in one's consciousness, as long as there is a strong enough psychological overlap between a past and future self, they can be considered to be the same person. Connectedness, on the other hand, refers to the weaker relationship between successive selves, allowing for the possibility of indirect psychological continuity through a chain of overlapping memories and characteristics. This is exactly what Tekla is arguing with regard to the repeated process of falling asleep and waking up again, something that every human being unavoidably does countless times in his or her life.

B.J.'s classic position of the soul being the *locus* of one's identity and its continuation in time—arguably also over the brink of death as multiple religions claim, including Christianity and (part of) Judaism—is countered by Parfit, who takes a reductionist stance toward the very concept. He argues that the idea of a permanent, unchanging self or soul is unnecessary for understanding personal identity and moral responsibility. His position aligns with a materialist or physicalist perspective, which suggests that everything about a person, including their consciousness and mental attributes, arises from physical processes in the brain and body. Parfit contends that personal identity can be adequately explained by reference to psychological continuity and connectedness, as discussed earlier. In this view, there is no need to invoke the existence of an immortal soul to explain the persistence of personal identity.

TEKLA'S PHILOSOPHY #2: FREE WILL

The next philosophical discussion Tekla raises with Blazkowicz is that of the existence of free will vis-à-vis a kind of universal determinism. In another instance, B.J. walks into her room and finds her sitting on a chair frantically scribbling notes onto a clipboard. The following discussion takes place. This time Tekla does not display any signs of her usual split personality:

Tekla: What to make of you, I do not know. Are you here to help me?

The Good, the Bad, and the Ugly 135

BJ: You seem beyond help. What are you working on?

Tekla: Gathering data. Nazi activity. Behavioral patterns. Ours. Theirs. Doing the math. Developing predictions. Where are they allocating resources? Where will they strike next? And after that? What are the larger trends triggering their actions? Figure out what choices they will make before they make them.

BJ: You talk as if the future is inevitable. As if our choices have already been made.

Tekla: You think there is such a thing as free will. You know so little of the world. You want to be the captain of your faith, do you? This fight you will lose. You cannot go to war against physics.

BJ: My actions are my own. I know that much.

Tekla: All phenomena in the physical world follow the simple rule of cause and effect. Your brain is no exception to the rule. Know the cause, you can predict the effects. The same is true for everything.

When the Nazis overrun the Berlin hideout, Tekla takes temporary refuge in the ventilation system. When B.J. stumbles upon her, she delivers one final monologue to him, which he very briefly interrupts, before running toward her own death, while taking several Nazi soldiers with her to the grave.

Tekla: I heard you arrive. Everything in accordance with the numbers. This day the number of consequence is nineteen. {A prime? Why not?} For the math to square, each and every one on our side must defeat nineteen of theirs. On average. And then we'll win. I have been proficient with what you have taught me. Eleven in the stack. Did I thank you? {I can't remember if I thanked him. Should thank the man that is my friend.} But I have accumulated an additional seven though other means prior to this day.

BJ: (. . .) You should come with me.

Tekla: And violate my model? The model is loyal to universal causality. You ask me to rebel against the laws of nature. Don't you see? The road in front of you is long and so hard I wonder how you will cope. Mine is at its end. On this day. I am glad. To have found a friend.

Tekla initially presents a deterministic perspective by stating, "All phenomena in the physical world follow the simple rule of cause and effect." This statement reflects the idea that every event, including human actions, can be traced back to a series of causes, making them predictable. She argues that understanding the causes allows for predicting the effects, suggesting that human behavior, including choices, can be anticipated based on knowledge of the underlying causes. Tekla implies that the future is predetermined by these causes, saying, "Figure out what choices they will make before they make them." Tekla rubs elbows with philosophers like Pierre-Simon Laplace, Baruch Spinoza, and Thomas Hobbes, who all—in their own fashion—defended some kind of determinism that asserts that all events, including human actions, are determined by prior causes, making them predictable and suggesting a predetermined future. This rules out, at least partially, the idea of individual free will, which is one of the most prominent self-identifications of modern, Western human beings, individually and collectively. B.J. accepts the challenge by asserting the opposite: "My actions are my own." This statement underscores his belief in personal agency and free will, suggesting that he has control over his choices and is not merely a product of deterministic forces as Tekla claims.

The debate between B.J.'s libertarianism and Tekla's determinism has ethical implications, especially in the context of *Wolfenstein*. If one subscribes to determinism, the question arises whether individuals can be held accountable for their actions if those actions are determined by external factors. In the context of *Wolfenstein*, both the violent and bloody enterprises of the Nazis *and* of the Kreisau Circle's members' equally violent uprising are both unavoidable, diminishing or even ruling out the moral responsibility of the participants in either conflict. On the other hand, B.J.'s belief in free will raises questions about personal responsibility and moral agency. He sees himself as the author of his actions, implying that he is morally accountable for them. This implies that not only are the Nazis—individually and collectively—responsible for their violent policies, but that the same applies to the Kreisau Circle collectively, and to Tekla and B.J. individually. The price to pay for having a free will is the necessary acceptance of moral responsibility for one's actions, including ethically dubious ones like the use of violence.

The concept of and the discussion surrounding free will are especially interesting in the context of video games like the *Wolfenstein* series. Video games have specific communicative characteristics, as discussed in the introduction applying the Communication-Oriented Analysis. Player freedom is one of them, or in communication terms, the text-immanent player possesses a certain degree of agency in selecting its path through the narrative crafted by the text-immanent author (Bosman and Van Wieringen 2022, 80–81). However, this agency is subject to constraints at two distinct levels. Firstly, it should be noted that not all games present equal opportunities for player agency. Games categorized as first-person action/adventure, such as *Half-Life 2* (Valve 2004) or *Spec Ops: The Line* (Yager Development 2012), adhere to a linear trajectory akin to a train confined to its tracks.

In such instances, player agency is inherently limited, restricting the player's ability to navigate the unfolding events. Conversely, games often categorized as "sandbox games," with titles like *Fallout 4* (Bethesda Game Studios 2015) or *Mad Max* (Avalanche Studios 2015), offer players a relatively greater degree of freedom to determine their spatial exploration and decision-making processes. Games such as *Dishonored 2* (Arkane Studios 2016) or *Kingdoms of Amalur: Reckoning* (38 Studios/Big Huge Games 2012) extend this freedom, permitting players to tackle in-game challenges through diverse approaches.

However, it is essential to recognize that, notwithstanding variances in player agency, even within the extensive realm of sandbox games, the options available to the text-immanent player remain constrained by the parameters delineated by the text-immanent author. If a game does not afford the text-immanent player the ability to engage in activities such as flight or walking on water, the extent of player agency is delimited by the in-game authorial boundaries. Although the game may appear to endorse absolute player autonomy, the practicality of the medium necessitates the acknowledgment that absolute freedom remains unattainable. Instead, what prevails is relative freedom, circumscribed by the confines of the available technological capabilities and, more crucially, the authorial oversight of the text-immanent author.

The debate between Tekla and B.J. mirrors a philosophical debate about the nature of human agency and freedom. Tekla represents a deterministic perspective, arguing that events, including human actions, are predetermined by external causes. This debate about determinism versus free will is analogous to the discussion in video games about the extent of player agency and freedom. Just as the philosophical debate has ethical implications for individual moral responsibility, the discussion in video games about player agency also has ethical implications. In the context of *Wolfenstein* and similar games, the level of player agency can influence questions of moral responsibility for in-game actions. This parallels the ethical considerations raised in the philosophical debate about determinism.

Even in video games that offer players a degree of freedom, there are constraints imposed by the game's design and authorial boundaries. This concept of relative freedom in video games aligns with the philosophical debate about the relative agency of individuals in the face of external determinants. In both cases, there are limits to autonomy and freedom. The practicality of the medium of video games requires the acknowledgment of the authorial oversight of the game's immanent author. Similarly, the philosophical debate acknowledges external factors that may limit individual agency. In both contexts, there is recognition that freedom or agency is not absolute but exists within certain constraints.

In summary, the discussion between Tekla and B.J. regarding freedom and agency in the philosophical context parallels the discussion about player agency and freedom in video games. Both discussions involve questions of autonomy, constraints, and the ethical implications of the level of freedom individuals or players have in making choices and taking responsibility for their actions.

Chapter 10

Failing Gloriously
Wolfenstein's *Theodicy*

At the beginning of *Wolfenstein: The New Order*, set in a fictional version of 1946, Blazkowicz and a team of British and American soldiers try to invade the secret compound of SS general and scientist Wilhelm Strasse to turn the tide of the war the allies are rapidly losing. During a short period, the soldiers enjoy a moment of relative peace while they try to find their way through the outer limits of the compound. At one moment, a soldier nicknamed "Blondie" asks one of his comrades—somewhat out of the blue—if he is a believer. The other soldier, identified as Prendergast (no first name), replies approvingly: "Southern Baptist." The Southern Baptist Convention is the world's largest Baptist organization and the second-largest Christian (Protestant) denomination in the United States of America. It has gained a somewhat infamous reputation for its past support for and theological defense of racial segregation and its adherence to the "Lost Cause," the pseudo-historical myth that the Confederate ("southern") States of the American Civil War (1861–1865) were on the "right" side of history (Roach 2021, Newman 2001). The Convention apologized in recent times for its behavior and views regarding the theological consequences of ethnicity (Carter 1995).

Blondie continues his little inquiry. He asks Prendergast if he goes to church "every Sunday." Prendergast answers with "Yeah" and formulates his own question to Blondie: "What, you ain't got churches in England? You ain't got no priests there?" Blondie replies: "Yeah. Well, the Nazis sort of are bombing them all at the moment, so it's a bit of a problem." In retrospect, this almost nonsensical little dialogue between Blondie and Prendergast gets a sinister undertone a little later in the game. When Blazkowicz, Blondie, Prendergast, Furgus Reid, and Probst Wyatt (see chapter 8) have infiltrated the base, they are captured by Strasse and locked away in an incinerator room. Prendergast has a severe injury to one of his eyes and both of his legs are broken from an earlier fall. While Blazkowicz and Fergus/Probst (depending on the choice the player makes) try to find a way out, the incapacitated Prendergast screams out his own monologue, somewhere between a prayer and a curse.

> Sweet heavenly father, help me. Help me, God! Why are you doing this to me? Why? You hate me. God. Oh, why do you hate me? Every day I read my Bible. I haven't even French kissed my fucking fiancé. I am saving it for my wedding night. God damn you, what's the point, Jesus? Please, Jesus. Jesus, save me! Save me, you fucking asshole. I have been through hell already; can't you see that? I have been shot, stabbed, and I was almost rapped in the head, for fuck's sake. Broke my fingers, broke my hand, broke both my feet. Shot in the arm, lost my fucking eye, for God's sake! Don't I deserve one night with my girlfriend?

Prendergast is a devout Christian and not only in his own eyes. The game goes out of its way to establish that fact: he is a member of the Southern Baptists, he goes to church every Sunday, he reads the Bible every day, and he abstains from kissing his fiancée (let alone having sexual intercourse with her) "saving himself" for the wedding night. Prendergast is "righteous" in the Christian sense of the word and worthy of God's help and protection. But instead of receiving divine assistance, Prendergast argues that God has forsaken him: he was shot, stabbed, and raped, he broke his fingers, hand, and both of his feet, and lost his eye.

Prendergast even voices his dissatisfaction with God's policy: "What are you doing to me? Why? You hate me. God. Oh, why do you hate me?" He curses God: "God damn you, what's the point Jesus? (. . .) Save me, you fucking asshole. I have been through hell already; can't you see that?" Prendergast still seems to believe that God could help him, "Sweet heavenly father, help me. Help me, God! (. . .) Please, Jesus. Jesus, save me." But apparently God has other plans with the poor soldier, because He does not intervene. Eventually, Prendergast is saved by Blazkowicz. He joins the Kreisau Circle during Blazkowicz's period of paralysis. Before B.J. manages to reach the Berlin hideout, Prendergast has been sent on an unspecified mission he never returns from.

THEODICY, OR THE PROBLEM OF EVIL

Prendergast's religiously-charged incinerator speech appears to be one of Jens Matthies' favorite ones. Matthies, MachineGames' creative director, declares in a 2014 interview (Wolfe):

> The scene also features one of my favorite speeches in the game, namely Private Prendergast's nervous breakdown. Most players are too pre-occupied with not dying to listen to Prendergast, but if you do, he has interesting things to say.

Why Matthies is so intrigued by this section remains unknown: the interviewee does not go into details and the interviewer refrains from asking any. Maybe because of the contrast between Prendergast's belief in his Christian God vis-à-vis his experiences of evil and suffering. *Si Deus est, unde mala?* as the Roman and Christian philosopher Boethius so eloquently phrased in his *De Consolatione Philosophiae* ("On the consolation of philosophy," I.IV, 105–106) written in 524: "if God is, where does evil come from?" Rabbi Harold Kushner phrased it in more modern words in his well-known 1981 book with the fitting title *When bad things happen to good people*. The rabbi relates how he reacted when his then three-year-old son Aaron was diagnosed with progeria, or "rapid aging," an uncurable disease (1983, xx).

> How does one handle news like that? (. . .) [W]hat I mostly felt that day was a deep, aching sense of unfairness. It didn't make sense. I had been a good person. I had tried to do what was right in the sight of God. More than that, I was living a more religiously committed life than most people I knew, people who had large, healthy families. I believed that I was following God's way and doing His work. How could this be happening to my family? If God existed, if He was minimally fair, let alone loving and forgiving, how could He do this to me?

Prendergast and Kushner both struggle with the problem of the actual and practical human experience of evil and suffering vis-à-vis the belief in the existence of a benevolent and all-powerful God. Dubbed "theodicy" (from the Greek *theos*, "God," and *dikè*, "justice," hence the "justification of God") by Godfried Leibniz in his 1710 *Essais de Théodicée sur la bonté de Dieu, la liberté de l'homme et l'origine du mal*, this problem is inherent to all monotheistic religions. As Hume summarized in part 10 of his 1779 *Dialogues concerning Natural Religion*:

> [I]s [God] willing to prevent evil, but not able? Then is he impotent. Is he able, but not willing? Then is he malevolent. Is he both able and willing? Whence then is evil?

Historically, the Christian tradition has two different "defences" (Hick 1966). One group of theodicies, named after the Greek bishop Irenaeus of Lyon (circa 140–202), tries to "excuse" the nature of evil, suggesting that "behind" or "beyond" lies a greater good to be gained. God allows evil to exist and to cause human suffering because it is "useful" in one way or another: it is a test of faith, a proof that one really believes in God; it is a righteous punishment for our own sins; an opportunity to gain spiritual fruits; and a "blessing in disguise" since humans are too limited to understand the grand scheme of creation. Theologians like Origen (Scott 2022) and philosophers like Gottfried

Leibniz (Jorgensen and Newlands 2014), Friedrich Schleiermacher (Badham 1998), and Richard Swinburne (1998) fall into this category.

Prendergast's case illustrates how difficult this kind of reasoning is in the face of actual, individual suffering, like Rabbi Harold Kushner argued in his aforementioned book *When bad things happen to good people* (1981). It is very hard to reason that anything good comes from Prendergast's suffering by Strasse's Nazis. Neither is he—as far as the narrative provides us—punished for his evil deeds: he is (self) portrayed as righteous. And even though one could argue that self-righteousness is a sin in and of itself, the game does not seem to make that specific point. Neither is it a test of faith: Prendergast was already a devout believer, and he continues to profess his faith even in the face of annihilation.

The second group of theodicies, named after the African bishop Augustine of Hippo (354–430), tries to "excuse" God himself, suggesting that at the core of suffering and evil lies human free will. God allows evil to exist, not because it is in any shape or form "useful," but because it is the ultimate consequence of the human will. If humans are truly free, this means at least the possibility of people choosing against God. God is not to blame for human suffering, people are. Theologians like Thomas Aquinas (Davies 2011) and John Calvin (Helm 2004: 93–128) fall into this second category.

This excuse also falls flat in the case of Prendergast. One could argue that his suffering is the result of other peoples' expression of their free will to, voluntarily and explicitly, cause him harm, e.g., the Nazi soldiers. Without people choosing Nazism, there would not have been a Second World War, and without the war Prendergast and his fellow-soldiers would not have stormed Strasse's compound. True as this may seem, it still puts tremendous strain on God for at least allowing such atrocities, in combination with His apparent reluctance to mitigate Prendergast's righteousness versus his tortures. If behaving or being righteous does not extend beyond its own reward, from a practical point it loses quite some of its appeal.

THEODICY AFTER AUSCHWITZ: CHRISTIAN REACTIONS

The twentieth and twenty-first centuries, especially after the Second World War, have seen the rise of new categories of theodicies. In his 2015 book *Pathways in theodicy*, Mark Scott discusses the three most prominent ones: process theodicies, cruciform theodicies, and anti-theodicies. Process theodicy (for example Griffin 2004 [1976] and 1991), in principle dismissing Aristotelian metaphysics, argues in favor of God's infinite "conceptual realization of the absolute wealth of potentiality" (Whitehead 1978

[1929], 343), "a bottomless well of cosmic possibilities from which all creation flows" (Scott 2015, 126).

In this view, God has lost his traditional omnipotence in exchange for his continuous and potentially risky involvement in a Jobesque *Chaoskampf* (Watson 1971, 265–368). God does not exist, He is happening. However, notwithstanding its personalistic vocabulary, process theology and theodicy do not provide a personal God with whom devotees can have a personal relationship. And, even more important, leaving the divine entity out of the theodicy question does not solve the problem of evil and suffering since they still very much keep on existing, continuously posing an existential problem for all humankind collectively and individually.

Cruciform theodicies focus on God's co-suffering with humanity in and through Jesus Christ's suffering on the cross—hence the name. This theodicy finds it origin in the theological reception of precisely the Holocaust, when theologians like Jürgen Moltmann (1993), Johann Baptist Metz (2007), and Dorothee Sölle (1975)—all Germans themselves—pondered over the question where God was during the Shoah. In this view, God—in Jesus Christ's passion on the cross (*passio*, meaning "suffering")—experiences the whole of humanity's suffering, "including economic exploitation, political disenfranchisement, social ostracism, rejection and betrayal by friends, and even alienation from his own family" (Scott 2015, 147).

The third theodicy is its own antagonist: the denial of the necessity or possibility of defending God against the accusation of bearing responsibility for human suffering and evil. Again, the immeasurable evil of the Holocaust forms the historical décor of many of these theodicies, both theistic and atheistic ones. In his famous book *(God) After Auschwitz*, Zacahry Braiterman (1998) coined the term "antitheodicy" defining it as: "any religious response to the problem of evil whose proponents refuse to justify, explain, or accept as somehow meaningful the relationship between God and suffering" (363).

Anti-theodicies reject any attempt to defend God, "often with the underlying critique that theodicy trivializes suffering and silences the voice of the victim" (Scott 2015, 174). Atheistic anti-theodicies ground their rejection of such a defense in the larger framework of their rejection of the notion of any transcendent reality in the first place or as an argument against the existence of a divine being (see for example Mackie 1955). Theistic anti-theodicies deny the necessity or possibility for such a defense without rejecting the concept of God, arguing that any theoretical theodicy cannot do justice to the historical, practical suffering of individuals (see for example Surin 2004, Phillips 2001).

Chapter 10

GOD AFTER AUSCHWITZ: JEWISH REACTIONS

The theological consequences for Jewish theology were even more severe than for their Christian counterpart, since the Shoah was explicitly targeted at the Jewish people. Daniel Garner 2014, 3) talks about this specific part of Jewish theology even as "Holocaust theology" or "as the dimension of modern Jewish thought which attempts to face the theological problems created for Judaism by the catastrophe of the Holocaust." He distinguishes three phases in this attempt. (1) During or immediate after the Shoah, Ultra-Orthodox and Chasidic rabbis—often victims of the Nazi regime themselves—tried to make sense of what had (just) happened (see for example compilation by Schindler [1990], Schweid [1994], and Katz e.t. [2006]). (2) The period from the 1906s to the 1990s was characterized by often controversial responses to the Shoah-theodicy (see for example Fackenheim [1968], Greenberg [1977], Levinas [1988], and Blumenthal [1993]). (3) Since the 1990s, the third phase focusses on compiling, analyzing, and criticizing existing theodicies. The aforementioned Braiterman (1998) is one of those critics, but also Michael Morgan (2001) and Katz (2005) are among them.

Richard Rubenstein, in his famous book *After Auschwitz* (1966), voices a antitheodic stance: by the Shoah the covenant between Israel and God has been broken, and event though he never went full-on atheistic, his theological concept of God was no longer that of an omnipotent deity but more akin to paganism. Eliezer Berkovits, in his *Faith After the Holocaust* (1973), argues for a variant in Augustinian theodicy. He used the notion *hester panim*, the "hiding of the divine face," to argue in favor of God's withdrawal from humanity's fate in an ultimate attempt to safe-guard human free will. And Emil Fackenheim proclaimed continuous defiance toward Hitler and his genocidal policy by a collective refusal to seize Jewish existence all together, the so-called "614th commandment" (1968).

Jewish responses also arose from kabbalist thinkers, even though these have been less scrutinized than the more mainstream ones, using notions like *ayn sof* ("the infinite"), *tsimtsum* ("self-contraction"), the ten *sephirot*, *shekhinah* ("presence"), and *tikkun* ("resoration") to contemplate the theological consequences of the Holocaust (see also chapter 4). The Chasidic rabbi Kalonymous Kalmish Shapira (1889–1943), for instance, tried to understand the earthly sufferings of God's Chose People as a consequence of the *Din* ("power") obscuring *Chesed* ("mercy") within God himself (1940 [2004]), in combination with the idea that Israel's suffering in the camps were directed by external evil forces (*Kelipot*). The casualties of the Shoah were not victims, let alone sinners, but martyrs in a global war against Israel, God, and Torah.

The aforementioned German scholar Fackenheim used the notion of *tikkun* to think about the possibility or restoring Jewish life after the Holocaust. This "restauration" of the divine/human world in their mutual relationship is not a reality, but a slim possibility: it offers a kind of hope, that is, of and in itself, partial. The world remains broken by the Nazi atrocities, but it posses, at the same time, the possibility of reparation remains, at least to prevent and total implosion of Jews culture and religion all together (1982); hence his 614th commandment to never surrender to Hitler's goals, not even and especially not posthumously.

The American novelist and amateur theologian Arthur Cohen (1928–1987)—famous from his "pamphlet" "Why I Choose To Be A Jew" from 1959—uses the concepts *ein sof* and *tsimtsum* to construct a kind of Jewish deism in which God has "replaced" itself to make room for creation. In this "void" humanity has been given its change to live, prosper, and choose its own path, either in accordance with the divine will or against it. Cohen argues that Jews have a special vocation in the world after the Shoah (1962): because of their spiritual and religious traditions and their special covenantal relation with God, they have the possibility—duty even—to redeem all of human history, making every Jew a "messianic being."

Feminist Jewish scholar Melissa Raphael (*1960) focusses on *shekhinah*, one of the ten *sephirot*, the female attribute of the divine, to think theologically about the Shoah. She sees God as

> an accompanying God whose face or presence, as Shekhinah, 'She-Who-Dwells-Amongst-Us,' [who] goes with Israel, in mourning, into her deepest exile, even if Israel cannot see her in the terrible crush. (2003, 6)

She identifies immediate salvation and interruptive action as "male," while the power to suffer and to console as "female." The male, patriarchal God has been weighed in Auschwitz and found incapable of preventing the Holocaust. Instead, the actions of individual women in the concentration camps are acts of restauration, or *tikkun*, which helps to mend both God and humanity. God-as-She co-suffers with Her people in the camps, not by ending it, but by exactly suffering it until completion.

WOLFENSTEIN'S THEODICY

If we return to *Wolfenstein* again, the concept of theodicy does not only appear in *Wolfenstein* in the case of Prendergast—an individual player can easily miss his theologically charged rantings if he or she is occupied with finding an exit to escape from the incinerator room, but also later in WNO, in Camp

Belica, when the game makes all the effort it can to focus the player's attention onto the theological charge against God. Narrated in a flashback later in the game, Roth and Blazkowicz are shown in the Belica camp, witnessing a Nazi robot abusing a—probably Jewish—fellow-inmate for no clear reason. She appears lifeless, suggesting the machine has killed her. Frau Engel kicks the corpse with her boot and strikes it with her stick multiple times. When no sign of life is seen, she orders a Nazi robot to bluntly remove the corpse by lifting it up by its head.

> Roth: This woman, I knew her well. Resilient. A will of iron. Her family all gone. All of them, yet. . . . Faith. Faith kept her going. I . . . I . . . I cannot believe with such certainty. For me, in everything there must be doubt. Otherwise, there is no room to question. To learn. This place. This is the fruit of unquestioned, ferocious conviction. This is where absolute certainly leads.
>
> B.J.: Yet you are a believer.
>
> Roth: I often wonder what kind of god would sanction suffering such as this. And I question myself whether my faith is misplaced.
>
> B.J.: Maybe he is testing us?
>
> Roth: Well, Shimshon. If he is testing us, we are failing gloriously.

There is a lot to unpack in this most unnerving and quite brutal scene, even if we leave aside the fact that a video game depicts an execution of a Jewish inmate in a fictional Nazi concentration camp (see chapter 8 for a detailed discussion). The dialogue between B.J. and Roth takes place in a Nazi concentration camp, the most graphic incarnation of the Holocaust and the Nazis' crimes against humanity. It is precisely in this context that the question of theodicy is challenged to its limits. As Sarah Pinnock states: "After Auschwitz, theodicy is exposed as perpetrating amoral justifications of evil and rationalistic caricatures of practical faith struggles" (2002, xi).

The woman, tortured and possibly killed by the Nazi robot and Frau Engel remains anonymous. The fact that she remains without a proper name is indicative of the dehumanizing praxis of the Nazi concentration camp system: inmates were reduced to objects with a registration number, tattooed on their body like cattle. B.J. experienced the same at the beginning of the level, reduced to an object to be freely manipulated by all others. Even though Roth and Blazkowicz know each other's name (and before that Roth called B.J. not by his number but by using an ironical nickname: Shimshon), they do not know the name of the woman in question, or at least they do not use it.

Despite her anonymity, she is praised sincerely by Roth for the strength of her will, her resilience, and especially her faith. The first is indicative of the fact that she was apparently strong enough to do some small deed of resistance triggering her predicament, the second of the fact that she was able to endure so much before giving in, and the third of the firmness of her faith. We do not know which faith the anonymous woman adhered to, but because of the context of the concentration camp *and* because the Jew Roth just uses the word "faith" without any further qualification, it may be interpreted that she is also Jewish.

Roth is measuring the strength of his own faith against the woman's, and, in his own judgment, he falls short, using the word "doubt." But for Roth this is not only a negative thing: he appreciates the fact that one doubts. "Otherwise, there is no room for questions." This is not a disqualification of the woman's faith, but criticizes the Nazi regime, which they all are victims of. Roth qualifies "this place," a *pars pro toto* for everything that is wrong about the Nazi regime, as "the fruit of unquestioned, ferocious conviction (. . .) where absolute certainty leads." Through this phrasing, Roth characterizes Nazism as a false religion, the primary theological error of which is the refusal or impossibility to question ideas and to doubt truth claims, an interpretation posited in the academic debate (for example Babik 2006).

B.J. objects: "yet you are a believer," implying that the combination of Roth's Jewishness and Roth's words on the necessity of doubting in relation to faith is problematic. Roth answers this unspoken question with an implicit reference to the theodicy, wondering what kind of a God would "sanction suffering like this" *and* if the fact that God seems to act arbitrarily could be a reason to stop believing in God altogether. B.J. reacts to this classic question—why does God allow evil and suffering if He is all-good and all-mighty?—with the just as classic answer that God is, maybe, testing our faith. Blazkowicz's response to Roth's question is of the Irenaean type: evil is excused because it serves a higher and better goal, in this case the testing of one's faith.

Roth tanks B.J.'s classic theodicy by replying that "if he is testing us, we are failing gloriously," thereby refuting the theological possibility that God permits (if not worse) the Holocaust in general, and their personal predicament in the concentration camp specifically, and by taking the defense very seriously. If evil and suffering are allowed by God to test the strength and resilience of our faith, humanity is repeatedly failing to pass this test. Ironically, the anonymous woman passes the apparent "test," even though this goes unnoticed by both Roth and Blazkowicz. Roth claims he is not as strong as she is, through which the game suggests that Roth may not pass the same test.

If we zoom out to the entirety of the fourth cycle, especially to WNO and WNC, can we establish a theodicy of the series of its own? In other words, does the series answer its character's question on the existence of evil vis-à-vis that of God? Roth is clearly wrestling with his faith in a Supreme

Being who is, nevertheless, very closely connected to the philosophy and theology of Da'at Yichud. This wrestling is not only visible in the scene discussed above, but later, in WNC, when Probst Wyatt (see p. 100–104) asks him if he has ever talked to God. "Yes, many times," Roth answers, only to continue with "I am still waiting for him to get back to me." It is a small but telling example of the theological struggle taking place within the character of Roth, who is confronted with an apparent paradox between his belief in God and his (own) experience of evil and suffering in the world.

One possible answer is that of violent retaliation: a kind of divine wrath being executed by the righteous ones—the combined, surviving members of the Da'at Yichud and the Kreisau Circle—on God's authority. Redemptive violence is a concept rooted in the realm of social and cultural studies, often explored within the context of conflict resolution and the role of violence in achieving transformative or redemptive outcomes. This concept posits that violence can be perceived as a means to achieve redemption or salvation, both on a personal and societal level. In his influential work *The Powers That Be* (1998), Walter Wink delves into this notion of the "myth of redemptive violence," arguing that it is a prevalent narrative in human history where violence is justified as a means to bring about positive change or salvation. Wink's analysis emphasizes the danger of perpetuating a cycle of violence through this myth: for him "myth" stands for a delusional fantasy, rather than a foundational origin story. Johan Galtung, a prominent figure in peace research, contrasts the concept of "positive peace" with a mere "negative peace" that entails the absence of overt violence, challenging the idea that violence can be redemptive in any form (1996).

In the context of popular culture and media, scholars like Jack Nelson-Pallmeyer (2001) have examined how the portrayal of violence in movies and television often reinforces the myth of redemptive violence, perpetuating such narratives and normalizing aggressive solutions to conflicts. This myth is also quite prevalent in the *Wolfenstein* series, including the fourth cycle of WNO, WOB, and WNC. The only solution the games provide—individually and collectively—to overcome the violent Nazi empire is by using the same means just a little bit more efficiently. Fight fire with fire. Fight Nazis super soldiers who are loaded with advanced weapons with an American one-man-army equipped with even better technology. Blazkowicz kills Hitler (twice), evil scientists, sadistic SS generals, paranormal all-female divisions, undead Nazi zombies, and countless regular troops. And out of all this violence, salvation is reached at the end of each story-arc. Violence does seem to be to do the trick.

The theme of redemptive violence is also connected to Judaism and Christianity. In the Hebrew Bible/Old Testament, the theme is of high importance, especially in the context of the Exodus, where the Israelites' liberation from slavery in Egypt is marked by the ten plagues, the parting of the Red Sea, and the utter destruction of Pharaoh's army, and in the context of the conquest of the Promised Land by the Israelites, depicted as a violent campaign, where God's chosen people engage in battles to secure their inheritance. A larger number of theologians and exegetes have questioned and criticized this, at least viewed through our twentieth and twenty-first century eyes, problematic phenomenon (Bergmann, Murray, and Rea 2011; Brueggemann 2009; Copan 2011; Seibert 2009; Wright 2008).

This myth and its occurrence in the Hebrew Bible/Old Testament are explicitly voiced by the character of Horton Boone, a Marxist-Leninist communist, leader of the New Orleans resistance cell in the United States, and self-appointed preacher wearing a spiced-up version of a Catholic clergyman. His anti-capitalist ideas made him advocate against the involvement of the US in the European War, but after the Nazis also occupied his own homeland, his opinion changed dramatically. When Boone's group, together with Blazkowicz, tries to break the Nazis' control over the New Orleans ghetto (in WNC), the player can hear him "preaching" over the loudspeakers:

> Don't you Nazi sonsabitches know what the Bible says? Love thy neighbor and so forth! Well, I'm a servant of God and I can tell you our Lord is almighty pissed at you violating the commandments.
>
> And God said unto the gathered folks: Ye shall smite the Nazi swine directly to death for they is the scourge of the earth.
>
> An lo, he said, ye shall throw them Nazis into the fire pits of hell where they be a-roasted upon spits and a thousand demons shall a-feast upon their Nazi flesh for all eternity.

Horton's preaching is a combination of (well known) biblical verses and spiced-up, foul-mouthed delivery. "Love thy neighbor" is a reference to Mathew 22:37–39, which is—on its turn—a reference to Leviticus 19:17. "Servant of the Lord" is a title given by the Hebrew Bible/Old Testament to numerous righteous people, serving God with their deeds (Harmon 2020), for example Abraham (Genesis 26:24), Moses (Exodus 14:31; 34:5), David (2 Samuel 7:5.8), and Isaiah (20:3). The criticism of violating God's commandments is also a recurring theme, especially in the prophetic literature, like Isaiah 25:5, Jeremiah 9:13 or Amos 2:4 (Ortlund 1996). And the "fire pits of hell" is a reference to several New Testament texts on life after death where there "will be weeping and gnashing of teeth" (Mathew 13:50; cf. Mark 9:43 and Revelations 20:15) (Fudge 2011).

Originally, in these texts both the text-external author as well as the text-immanent reader were of the same religious-ethnic group, the Israelites. So, the rebuking of the prophets is primarily self-criticism: the Israelite prophet informs his fellow-Israelites that they have done wrong and that they should repent if they want to prevent God smiting them for their disloyalty (Brueggeman 2001). The concept of prophetic self-criticism in the Old Testament has sometimes given rise to anti-Judaism and anti-Semitism within the Christian theological tradition: Jewish self-criticism turns into Christians criticizing Jews with the help of prophetic texts from the Hebrew Bible/Old Testament (Cohn-Sherbok 1992). In the case of Horton in *Wolfenstein* (WNC) the roles are changed again. Horton is a Christian preacher and the Nazis were predominantly Christian, while Blazkowicz is both Jewish (through his mother) and Christian (through his father). Now, a Christian is rebuking Nazi Christians with the help of a Jewish text, positioning a half Jewish-half Christian character as the instrument of God's wrath.

This constellation is somewhat reminiscent of the plot of the film *Inglorious Basterds*. This 2009 film, directed by Quentin Tarantino, revolves around a group of Jewish-American soldiers—the "basterds" from the title—who take part in a covert operation behind enemy lines to (successfully) eliminate Adolf Hitler, thereby ending the Second World War earlier. The Basterds kill Hitler in a theatre during the premiere of the film *Stolz der Nation* ("Nation's Pride"), just like Blazkowicz can do on the Venus film-set in WNC, while auditioning for the lead role of B.J. in a German film about the capture and death of "Terror Billy." While the player can decide to kill Hitler right away, the screen fades to black reading "game over," suggesting this is not the canonical ending of the game. In W3D, B.J. is also seen killing Hitler, who is one of the level's end bosses. (The problems of the continuity between the cycles are discussed in chapter 5).

Another possible answer to *Wolfenstein*'s theodicy is deism. As already discussed briefly above in chapter 8, deism understands God as an impersonal entity that created the universe and all the laws governing it, but denies he is in any other way actively involved with it (Komonchak, Collins, and Lane 1990, 275). Set Roth and his Da'at Yichud seem to fit this description, as has become clear in the many instances we have already discussed: "We do not pray, we invent," is his short characterization of the Da'at Yichud theology; when confronted with the question whether he has ever spoken to God, Roth sarcastically answers "Yes, many times. I am still waiting for him to get back to me."; his self-identification as a watchmaker in his diary; etc.

This last statement is probably a reference to the concept of *Le Dieu Horloger*, or "The Watchmaker God." As Alister McGrath observed (2017, 191), the eighteenth century philosophers regarded the world as a watch and God as the watchmaker. God endowed the world with a certain self-sustaining design, such that it could subsequently function without the need for continual intervention.

The non-interventionist quality of eighteenth century deism is exactly what is at stake here. The Da'at Yichud seems to uphold an image of God as the great architect of the universe, responsible for "programming" said universe with the eternal laws of physics and causality, enabling it to continue to function without external interference or manipulation by any outside force, *in casu* a divinity, a creational entity. On the upside, this image of God allows for a high integration of the natural sciences within a theological framework. A *Dieu Horloger*, who created the universal laws of the cosmos, is easily combined with theoretical physics, general relativity, quantum mechanics, and so forth.

From the point of view of theodicy, deism can be attractive. God does not concern himself with individual cases, only with the grand design. Evil and suffering—both natural and moral in nature—are part of the overall design of the cosmos, either because of humanity's free will or because the complex harmony of the wider universal system does not prevent disharmony at a smaller level. Deism keeps God all-powerful, allowing for both the Irenaean and Augustinian theodicies, that is, natural evil is a necessary side-effect or precondition of goodness, while moral evil is just the effect of people making the wrong choices.

However, deism sacrifices one very important characteristic of God, at least as He is thought of in the monotheistic religions in general. As a human being, it is quite impossible to have a personal relationship with the immutable and sovereign God of deism, ruling over the top-level laws of the universe. God might still be considered to be a loving and caring God, but only at the most macro of levels. This is not a God that can be prayed to, as Roth explained to Caroline. One can calculate that such a God exists by probing into the fabric of the universe. To invent is to pray. To understand is to believe.

Historically *and* in *Wolfenstein*'s case, this deism is associated with the concept of natural theology, the "branch of philosophy which investigates what human reason unaided by revelation can tell us concerning God" (Joyce 1992, 1). It is "an attempt to demonstrate the existence or determine the characteristics of God without recourse to divine revelation" (McGrath 2017, 18). Natural theology, because it is not based on any given revelation, is supra-confessional and is quite useful in modern, secular discourse, as for example in the *Wolfenstein* series (Bosman 2019, 15–36). As discussed above (chapter 8), Roth's diary clearly states that the Da'at Yichud is an "ancient mystical organization," existing "before the major religions of the world."

The Da'at Yichud, therefore, can include many features and characteristics of multiple world religions and spiritualities, giving membership to people from all faiths and denominations without discriminating.

The God of Roth and Da'at Yichud is not a personal one with whom one can have an intimate relationship, rather it is a Prime Cause one can only "meet" by approaching its effects through space and time. The God of *Wolfenstein* does not interfere with the war in any way or capacity, including the Holocaust and the concentration camps. You can pray to him, but to no avail. Even though God's existence in itself is not questioned, in the *Wolfenstein*'s universe there is little to no difference between a deist God and no God at all. This, ultimately, invalidates any possible answer to the theodicy question: there is no one to blame or to demand justice from. Here the myth of redemptive violence and *Wolfenstein*'s deism coincide: the only way to deal with evil and suffering is to kill the cause of these using any force necessary. Humanity is on its own, while God is watching in the far distance, untouched by anything it sees or hears.

PART III
Evaluation

Chapter 11

Playing the Jew

Consequences for the Player

The Jewish identity of William "B.J." Blazkowicz is a creation by the later installments, which all contain the possibility of re-interpreting the older ones in this new light. Even though the developers of *Wolfenstein: The New Order* (Hall 2014) argue that B.J. was always intended to be a Jewish character, this only becomes apparent in the fourth cycle. In all installments of the previous three cycles—from *Castle Wolfenstein* (1981) and *Beyond Castle Wolfenstein* (1984), through *Wolfenstein 3D* (1992) and *The Spear of Destiny* (1992), to *Return to Castle Wolfenstein* (2001) and *Wolfenstein* (2009)—B.J. is first and foremost the stereotypical white, male, American super soldier-cum-one man army without any religious affinity or ethnic complexity whatsoever. Intriguingly enough, B.J. inhabits the exact physique that the Nazis were so fond of; the same Nazis whom Blazkowicz is so committed to killing. There is a reason Irene Engel gets sexually aroused by B.J.'s physical prowess in *Wolfenstein II: The New Colossus*; the same reason why Set Roth mockingly refers to him as having "an ape-like physique" in *Wolfenstein: The New Order*.

In *Wolfenstein: The Old Blood*, however, the first hints at B.J.'s being a Jew are dropped in the form of interactions between B.J. and two of his allies, Annette Krause and Ludwig Kessler, as discussed above. B.J. reacts to the death of his fellow-soldier as the latter being "in Abraham's bosom," while identifying March 17th, 1946, as "the day of Purim," two things a non-Jew would not generally say. In *Wolfenstein: The New Order*, B.J.'s Jewish identity is elaborated, but still implicit: his constant use of the phrase "my people" during his interior dialogues; Roth calling him "Shimshon," his invocation of Lazarus' poem "The New Colossus"; B.J.'s association with other biblical "heroes" like Esther, Abraham, Moses, and Daniel's three men in the furnace vis-à-vis biblical "monsters" like Haman, Nimrod, the Egyptian Pharaoh, and

Nebuchadnezzar; B.J.'s matter-of-fact mastering of the Hebrew alphabet and language. They all point in one direction.

All this implicitness ends in *Wolfenstein II: The New Colossus* with the introduction of Zofia, B.J.'s mother. Through flashbacks, we see young Blazkowicz protected by his Jewish mother against his father's violence. Zofia comforts her son by singing the traditional Jewish prayer *Birkat HaGomel*. Eventually, it is revealed that Rip, B.J.'s father, handed over his Jewish wife to the Nazis as soon as the United States was conquered. In several delusional dreams, we see B.J. meeting his—then deceased—mother who continues to comfort her—now grown-up—son.

With the start of the 4th cycle, the *Wolfenstein* series also introduced many more references to the Jewish people, their history, and religion than are just connected to the figure of Blazkowicz. Set Roth and Probst Wyatt form an interesting duo representing Jewish mysticism, both in—respectively—its "genuine" Jewish *and* Christian-appropriated forms. Roth also stands for the more deistic, rationalist, supra-denominational, "scientific" part of the Jewish mystical tradition, especially in its self-image of the *Haskalah*, the Jewish Enlightenment of the eighteenth century, while Wyatt represents the more rapture-centered, ecstatic, experiential side of the kabbalist traditions (the latter implicitly acknowledged as such by the former in WNC).

Wolfenstein: The New Order made the—undeniably—strongest "move" toward Jewish history in connection to the Second World War by including a level taking place in a fictional, allohistorical Nazi concentration camp. It places B.J.—both as a character and as the player's avatar—as an inmate in said camp, including his being transported in train waggons and standing in prison queues, surrounded by merciless and faceless camp wardens, witnessing various atrocities toward fellow-inmates, being tattooed on the underarm like a piece of meat, and almost ending up in an incinerator after some serious torture. In the end, B.J.—of course, following the "logic" of shooter games like the *Wolfenstein* series—changes into an unstoppable murder-machine decimating the camp's guards and freeing a considerable number of its inmates. The last bit is—unfortunately—less historical than the start of the level.

It is also within the context of this camp—if presented in the form of a later flashback by Blazkowicz—that the question of theodicy is raised *and* kept unanswered. Roth doubts his traditional convictions concerning the Jewish (and Christian) God, who is both all-loving and all-powerful, in the face of the Nazis' atrocities in and outside Camp Belica. B.J. seeks refuge in one of the traditional "defenses" of God, in the vein of Irenaeus of Lyon: "Maybe God is testing us." To which Roth answers that if He is, "we are failing gloriously." Both deism and divine wrath executed by the righteous ones—being

B.J. and his comrades from the Kreisau Circle—are suggested by the game as possible solutions for God's apparent lack of interference.

Several characters from the 4th cycle are imbued with a religious identity. Roth and Blazkowicz are Jews, the former more explicitly (and stereotypically) than the latter. Roth's religious identity is only made explicit in WNC and strictly speaking B.J.'s religious identity is never explicitly stated as such. Two other characters are identified as Roman Catholic, one implicitly, one explicitly. Anya Oliwa can be identified as a Catholic because of her Polish heritage and the fact she prays with B.J. and her grandparents invoking "your mercy, Lord," in a typical fashion. While Anya's Catholicism is kept implicit, that of Irene Engel is made explicit by one of the inmates urging his comrade to shut up about religious matters: "The *Frau* hates everything religious if it isn't Catholicism." Two other characters are (Protestant) Christians, again one implicit and one explicit. Prendergast proclaims his faith in God in the incinerator chamber and—earlier—his allegiance to the Southern Baptist Convention. Horton Boone, the communist preacher from New Orleans, can also be identified as a Protestant, albeit from an unspecified denomination, based on the collar he is wearing and his pseudo-biblical rants against the Nazis.

There has been, is still, and probably will continue to be in the foreseeable future discussions about *Wolfenstein*'s incorporation of these Jewish elements, in particular the character of Set Roth, the identification of B.J. as Jewish, the use of kabbalist notions, and—especially—the appearance of a Nazi concentration camp as the backdrop of a game level, even though— quite paradoxically—the series up to and including the 3rd cycle has been criticized for its consistent lack of attention for the primary victims of the Second World War, that is, the Jews, and—to a lesser degree—the automatic identification of all Germans as Nazis, thereby neglecting the historical and moral differences between combatants and non-combatants, between Nazis and their sympathizers and the German resistance, and the overall "glorification" of the Nazi era.

To put it methodologically, this discussion takes place at the level of the text-external real reader, judging the ethical ramifications of the relationship between the textual world—the game—and the world outside the text—our shared, lived reality. The accusations against the series—the neglect of the Jewish victims, the glorification of the Nazi era, and the one-dimensional depiction of Germans—are positioned in the tension between the *Wolfenstein* series and the historical reality it takes as its primary example—the Second World War. These external, real readers are (exclusively) qualified and (methodologically) situated to pass such moral judgment on any text. And the questions those text-external critics ask are genuine and important: Can one gamify the Second World War? Can one use a Nazi concentration camp for entertainment purposes?

But for the moment, I want to pause and focus on the communication within the game itself. In the *Wolfenstein* series, with the exception of *Wolfenstein: The New Order* and possibly *Wolfenstein II: The New Colossus*, all individual installments feature a non-descript text-immanent author. This text-immanent author communicates through the various characters—Blazkowicz, Helga von Bulow, Ludwig Kessler, and so forth—with an equally non-descript text-immanent reader, and through these characters and immanent reader to the text-external readers, asking these real readers to identify with the text-immanent reader. These real readers may or may not be inclined to identify with the text-immanent reader of the text, resulting in positive or negative attitudes toward the text. If a real reader of a *Wolfenstein* installment does not identify with its immanent reader, he or she will dislike or criticize the game. And this has indeed been done historically in the real world: he or she rejects the game's narrative and its communication by the text-immanent author.

In this sense, video games like the *Wolfenstein* series are no different to other texts, like novels or films. But because *Wolfenstein* is a video game series, that is, comprised of digital-interactive ludo-narrative texts, the communication necessarily becomes more complex. In video games, the text-immanent reader is necessarily "entangled" with its in-game player character-cum-player's avatar (as I have discussed in the introduction of this monograph). This means that the game's story is told *to* the text-immanent reader (as is usually done in any given text), *about* the text-immanent reader (as far as the avatar is subjected to and guided by the directorship of the immanent author), and *by* the text-immanent reader (as far as this is allowed by the immanent author).

In most games in the *Wolfenstein* series, the player's avatar is B.J. Notable exceptions are *Wolfenstein: Youngblood* and *Wolfenstein: Cyberpilot*. In the second one, the player controls a nameless hacker; in the first one, the player controls either Jessie or Zofia, Anya and B.J.'s twin daughters. This means that in the majority of games, the immanent player is necessarily entangled with B.J. (or with one of his daughters or a nameless hacker): everything that happens to B.J. also happens to the immanent reader (and vice versa). Even though the *Wolfenstein* games are not very "freestyling" in nature from a ludological perspective—the games are more or less "on rails" as any narrative-focused first person shooter tends to be—from a narratological perspective B.J.-cum-the-player is suggested as being free to venture through the game's adventures at his/its own leisure and whims.

This means, at least for three games of the fourth cycle—*Wolfenstein: The New Order*, *Wolfenstein: The Old Blood*, and *Wolfenstein II: The*

New Colossus—that the immanent player is entangled with not only the character-avatar Blazkowicz (as is also the case in most of the other games), but with the *Jewish* character-avatar Blazkowicz. To a certain extent, the text-immanent reader of these three games also *becomes* a Jewish reader because of the entanglement. (This leaves aside the fact whether any individual real player acknowledges this or not; I will return to this topic later.) This is *not* the case in *Wolfenstein: Cyberpilot* or in *Wolfenstein: Youngblood*. The hacker of the former does not have any religious or ethnic identity whatsoever, and the Blazkowicz twins are—at least ethnically—not Jewish, since their mother Anya is not (orthodox Jews adhere to the idea of matrilineality).

The question is, of course, if this identification of the Blazkowicz-entangled immanent reader as Jewish is applicable to only the above mentioned three games in which this identification of B.J. as Jewish is made (in more or less implicit ways), or that it can be extended—retrospectively—to all other, previous games with B.J. as the main protagonist-character-cum-player's-avatar? In other words, are B.J. and the immanent player of the games prior to *Wolfenstein: The New Order* also Jewish entities? From the position of these earlier, individual games, the answer is negative: they simply do not suggest B.J.'s Jewish identity, so the immanent-reader cannot be Jewish either.

From an intertextual perspective, the answer is positive: the character of B.J. is a continuum across all the installments, and so is his Jewish identity, even though this is only revealed much later in the series. On the other hand, within the *Wolfenstein* series there are multiple "cycles" which may or may not be within the same (narrative) continuum (see chapter 5 for a discussion about this topic). If the B.J. of one cycle is not the same character in another cycle, the question of retrospectively identifying B.J. as Jewish becomes more problematic.

However, leaving this discussion of retrospectivity aside, does it matter that the Blazkovicz—player entanglement has a Jewish identity? I would argue "yes," but in a different way for the text-immanent reader than for the text-external real readers. The text-immanent player receives a (shared) Jewish identity in its entanglement with an almost explicitly Jewish character, *in casu* B.J. If we take the Camp Belica level as a *pars pro toto* for the whole of *Wolfenstein: The New Order* and the same game also as a *pars pro toto* for the whole series, the shared Jewish identity of both B.J. and the entangled immanent reader means that the atrocities of the camp are not appropriated for entertainment purposes (even though this can still be the case from the perspectives of the text-external real author and real reader), but are rather reflections on and interpretations of how historical Jews were imprisoned, tortured, and murdered in Nazi concentration camps.

Even more, Blazkowicz-cum-immanent player is imbued with various degrees of agency, something that the historical inmates of the concentration camps were robbed of entirely. In the beginning of the game, Blazkowicz-cum-player is given very limited agency: Blazkowicz is confined to very circumscribed spaces and to very concrete, specified actions; the player is unable to exercise any more freedom than given to the entangled B.J. character. The immanent player is "captured" within the confines of the player's character's movement possibilities. It is only after a certain amount of time that the Blazkowicz-cum-player regains a larger part of its agency, with which it tries to escape the camp, something that is only successful after many more difficulties have been overcome.

Of course, at the level of the text-external real player, things are different. Real players, behind the safety and comfort of their pcs or consoles, are not imprisoned in a camp, do not have to fear for their lives, and perfectly know they will live to see another day. However, the text-immanent player-cum-avatar does not have the same luxury. From its perspective, the situation is dire indeed. A real reader of *Wolfenstein: The New Order*—probably informed by some experience regarding the principal rules of modern-day first person shooters—will deduce that the restriction in agency of the player's avatar is only temporary, and that the previous, full control will be given back at one point or another. Another real player will also probably deduce that B.J. will find a way out of the prison one way or the other. The text-immanent reader—again—does not have that luxury.

By not only introducing more than one Jewish character into the new installments, but also by molding the player's avatar as an almost explicitly Jewish character, the game series succeeds in using the Second World War generally and the Holocaust specifically within a video game text without reducing any of these to mere set pieces in an entertainment story. However, this infusion of the game's narrative with Judaism is not without problems of its own. I will address these problems in the next chapter.

Chapter 12

Playing the War
Wolfenstein's *Esotericisms*

The *Wolfenstein* series is a strange mixture of apparently contradictory religious-philosophical currents: Ariosophy (and its post-War appropriation in the form of Nazi occultism) on the one hand, and Jewish mysticism (or Kabbala) on the other. Both seem to be absolute and mutually exclusive opposites: the former is fundamentally a radical, racial appropriation of Blavatsky's hermetic esotericism, while the latter is mainly a container concept used in Judaism and Christianity to denote a large range of historical, Jewish groups and individuals searching to attain spiritual enlightenment. Ariosophy provided a philosophical-spiritual reasonableness to the political endeavor of constructing a collective, glorious Aryan past for the Germans of the first part of the twentieth century, including its rabid anti-Semitism.

Nevertheless, the *Wolfenstein* series has succeeded in incorporating both in the four cycles of its series, if not both in one and the same installment (see table 12.1), with the notable exception of *Wolfenstein: The Old Blood* and *Wolfenstein: Cyberpilot*.

The first three cycles were exclusively involved with Nazi occultism, that is, the post-Second World War cultural processing of the Nazi era, usually in the form that is expressive of the incomprehensibility of the Holocaust by any other means than the suggestion of diabolic or occult powers involved. This includes, in the case of the *Wolfenstein* series, in references to Schloss Wewelsburg and Werfenstein in the form of the titular "Castle Wolfenstein," fictional objects and secret organizations associated with the historical Thule Society and the SS Ahnenerbe, historical German kings like Henry I and Otto I appropriated as Aryan "supermen," symbols like Swastikas and Black Suns, and so forth.

With the introduction of the fourth cycle, the series more or less dropped its characteristic featuring of Nazi occultism in favor of Jewish mysticism, with the exception—as already observed above—of *Wolfenstein: The Old*

Table 12.1. The relative occurrence of Nazi occultism and Judaism/Kabbala throughout the *Wolfenstein* series.

Abbr.	Title	Nazi occultism	Judaism/Kabbala
CW	Castle Wolfenstein	+	-
BCW	Beyond Castle Wolfenstein	+	-
W3D	Wolfenstein 3D	++	-
SoD	Spear of Destiny	++	-
RtCW	Return to Castle Wolfenstein	+++	-
W09	Wolfenstein	+++	-
WNO	Wolfenstein: The New Order	-	+++
WOB	Wolfenstein: The Old Blood	+++	+
WNC	Wolfenstein II: The New Colossus	-	++
WYB	Wolfenstein: Youngblood	-	+
WCB	Wolfenstein: Cyberpilot	-	-

Blood. In WOB, both worlds merge: it features a Nazi occultist interpretation of King Otto I, Wewelsburg-cum-Wolfenstein, and zombie Nazi soldiers on the one hand, and references to "Abraham's bosom," Anna Frank, and the White Rose on the other, and the inclusion of an Aryan golem. Of all the installments of the fourth cycle, *Wolfenstein: The New Order* has the most references to Kabbala, followed closely by *Wolfenstein II: The New Colossus*, while in WOB and *Wolfenstein: Youngblood* the Jewish mysticism is tuned down significantly (but without a return to the series' former preferences). *Wolfenstein: Cyberpilot* has no reference to either Nazi occultism or Jewish mysticism.

Even though Nazi occultism-cum-Ariosophy and Jewish mysticism-cum-Kabbala seem to be at odds with one another, they are both part of the esoteric part of the Western world. As discussed at the beginning of this monograph, "esotericism" is defined as what (1) deviated or deviates from dominant or "orthodox" religious beliefs in the Western world, (2) focusses on individual spiritual enlightenment, (3) and does so often by initiation into otherwise secret knowledge (Hanegraaff 2006a). Both are also part of the "hermetic" branch of esotericism (vis-à-vis the Gnostic one), meaning that both profess a principle, cosmological unity of the universe instead of a fundamentally dualistic one.

Both Ariosophy and Kabbala fall within the boundaries of this definition of esotericism. Ariosophy, indebted to the equally hermetic esoteric movement of Blavatsky's Theosophy, deviates from mainstream Western philosophy and institutionalized Christianity of any denomination. Its adherents—Jörg Lanz von Liebenfels, Guido von List, and Rudolf Sebottendorf—preached to and were member-cum-founders of various secret societies in which secret knowledge was shared among initiates, unattainable by and incomprehensible to outsiders. Kabbala, in all of its various, historical iterations throughout the ages, also falls within the definition. Jewish mysticism was and still is at odds with mainstream (orthodox) Judaism. Its rabbis and visionaries were indiscriminately searching for a personal experience of the divine; this enlightenment was only attainable by those initiated and experienced in the practice.

It is self-explanatory, but also necessary to say here and now that Ariosophy and Kabbala, even though they share certain characteristics, are also very different from one another, maybe even more so than in what they have in common. Kabbalists of all ages never strived much for political influence or early domination. They rather strived for personal enlightenment in the presence of the Divine, helping others to do the same and to heal the broken world by doing good deeds and through contemplation. The Ariosophists had a marked political intention, a racist and an anti-Semitic world-view, striving for the submission of the world to the Aryan *Übermensch* at any and all cost.

As already discussed shortly in the previous chapter, the inclusion of Jewish mysticism specifically, and Jewish characters in general in the fourth cycle is not unproblematic. Connecting the American soldier Blazkowicz, who has a Jewish background, to the phrase "my people" introduces a complex and multifaceted dynamic. On the one hand, this association serves to emphasize the Jewish community as the primary victim of the Nazi regime, highlighting its historical connection to the divine promise of liberation from foreign oppression. However, on the other hand, it also evokes a connection between the Jewish people and an old Christian prejudice known as "deicide," potentially implying that the sufferings inflicted by the Nazis were, in some distorted sense, a justified retribution for the crucifixion of Jesus Christ.

A similar dilemma arises in the portrayal of the Da'at Yichud. The series portrays this organization as ancient, secretive, and extraordinarily powerful, operating discreetly in the background and intervening in world affairs only when certain implicit criteria are met. Furthermore, the narrative suggests that the members of the Da'at Yichud initially remained passive when confronted with Hitler and the impending Second World War. When they finally decided to intervene, it was too late, as the Nazis had already breached some of the Da'at Yichud's vaults and harnessed the technology found within to tip the scales of the war. This narrative implies that while the Jews may not have caused the Second World War or the Holocaust, they potentially had the means to prevent both, but for reasons left ambiguous, they did not.

A similar thematic pattern emerges in the figure of the golem, as depicted in *Wolfenstein: The Old Blood*. The golem, originally created for the protection of the Jewish people, particularly against the Nazi threat, is re-appropriated by the series to symbolize the potential destruction of the Jewish community. This parallels the paradox of the Da'at Yichud technology, which also was created by Jewish scientists, engineers, and philosophers, but was used against them by the Nazis. The narrative can be interpreted as suggesting that, indirectly and unintentionally, the Jews may have contributed to their own demise prior to and during World War II. This interpretation is indirectly reinforced by the portrayal of Otto's flesh golem.

Roth's portrayal in the game is notably enigmatic, serving as a representation of the enlightened scientists associated with the Da'at Yichud. He engages in what could be considered "forbidden" and ethically highly problematic medical procedures, particularly exemplified by the head-transplants performed on Shoshanna and Blazkowicz. Roth's actions evoke the archetype of the "mad scientist," a trope fashioned after the infamous SS physician Joseph "Angel of Death" Mengele. This trope outlines the tendency of Nazi scientists to recklessly delve into morally questionable scientific ventures, often intertwined with dabbling in the occult. While Set Roth is portrayed as a protagonist in the series, his involvement in these ethically dubious experiments seems at odds with the typical depiction of a "hero."

This narrative ambiguity leaves players with mixed feelings toward Roth and the Da'at Yichud. On the one hand, Set Roth is presented as a peaceful Jewish scientist and philosopher, a Holocaust survivor who later plays a pivotal role in supporting the Kreisau Circle, ultimately tilting the scales of the war in favor of the Allied Forces. The Da'at Yichud is similarly depicted as a benevolent, pacifist organization more interested in philosophical and technological exploration than in wielding political power. Their non-interventionist stance even led them to miss an opportunity to influence the outcome of the Second World War in favor of the Allies. While one could criticize Roth and his peers for their hesitancy and indecisiveness, their intentions appear far from malevolent.

On the other hand, Set Roth's portrayal aligns with stereotypical depictions of Jews in terms of appearance, language, and political affiliation. This convergence of elements, in conjunction with Roth's medical experiments, constructs a darker and more negative image of the Da'at Yichud and, by extension, the Jewish community. The Da'at Yichud, although initially presented as a proto-monotheistic, non-denominational, or even universal religion-cum-philosophy, is personified solely by Set Roth, a Jewish character. This conflation is further accentuated by the vocabulary used by Roth, derived from Jewish mysticism, and solidifying the Da'at Yichud as being a Jewish organization from the player's perspective.

The association of the Da'at Yichud and Set Roth as Jewish entities, coupled with the organization's reluctance to become embroiled in the war and Roth's controversial medical experiments, constructs a version of the stereotypical Jewish conspiracy theory, portraying Jews as secretly controlling world affairs until the Nazis emerged to disrupt this supposed "rule." Ironically, a substantial portion of the Da'at Yichud's portrayal in the fourth cycle of the *Wolfenstein* series could thus be likened to the 1930s Nazi propaganda campaign, which sought to discredit Jews and Judaism, laying the groundwork for the Holocaust.

This does not "prove" that *Wolfenstein* as a series or that individual installments of the series are "bad" in a moral sense of the word, even though the incorporation of a disclaimer in the installments of the fourth cycle are at least communicating that (someone at) MachineGames was well aware of the possible morally problematic interpretations of the series by some of its individual players. If anything, it "proves" how difficult it is to "work" with the Second World War in general and with the Holocaust specifically, something Adorno already knew when he, in 1951, famously said that "nach Auschwitz ein Gedicht zu schreiben, ist barbarisch."

Nevertheless, it has been done, frequently and with various results, both by Hollywood and Silicon Valley; Adorno's hesitance has not become canonical. The adjustments found in the fourth cycle—the inclusion of Jews and other victims of the Nazis and the differentiation between Germans and Nazis—were very welcome to counter the one-dimensional use of Nazi occultist tropes in the previous installments. The choice to identify the main protagonist/player's avatar as a Jew was another narratively very interesting and—up to a certain point—successful method of enabling the series to incorporate a part of the Holocaust in an entertainment game without reducing the Shoa to just another set piece in an otherwise very stereotypical American hero story.

But all this does not mean the problems are over: *Wolfenstein* runs the continuous risk of falling onto the sword of its own solution. By portraying the Da'at Yichud as a shadowy, worldwide, secret, Jewish organization that once had the opportunity to stop the Nazis pre-emptively, but refrained from doing so, thereby enabling the Nazis to take advantage of the Da'ad Yichud technology, the series suggests Jewish responsibility for the Jews' persecution, as well as the historical existence of such an organization, while this was only a malicious fiction spread by the Nazis to rationalize the Holocaust in the first place.

Bibliography

Ahmed, Akbar. 1984. "Al-Beruni. The first anthropologist." *Royal Anthropological Institute of Great Britain and Ireland* 60, 9–10.
Alsen, Eberhard. 2000. "A Definition of Romanticism, Light and Dark." In *The New Romanticism. A Collection of Critical Essays*, edited by Eberhard Alsen. New York: Garland Publishing.
Apel, Dora. 2012. *War culture and the contest of images*. Ithaca: Rutgers University Press.
Appleby, Joyce, Eileen Cheng, and Joanne Goodwin (ed.). 2015. *Encyclopedia of women in American history*. London: Routledge.
Aquino, John. 2022. *Truth and lives on film. The legal problems of depicting real persons and events in a fictional medium*. Jefferson: McFarland & Company.
Babik, Milan. 2006. "Nazism as a secular religion," *History and theory* 45(3), 375–96.
Backe, Hans-Joachim. 2018. "A redneck head on a Nazi body. Subversive ludo-narrative strategies in Wolfenstein II: The New Colossus." *Arts* 7(76).
Badham, Roger. 1998. "Redeeming the Fall. Hick's Schleiermacher versus Niebuhr's Kierkegaard." *The Journal of Religion* 78(4), 547–70.
Bailey, Blake. 2021. *Philip Roth. The biography*. New York: Skyhorse Publishing.
Baker, David. 2020. "Optical connections. The all-seeing eye." *Optician*, February 2020. Accessed October 1, 2023. https://www.opticianonline.net/content/features/optical-connections-the-all-seeing-eye.
Bannister, Robert. 2010. *Social Darwinism. Science and myth in Anglo-American social thought*. Philadelphia: Temple University Press.
Barber, R. 2004. *The holy grail. Imagination and belief*. Cambridge: Harvard University Press.
Barrowclough, David. 2016. *Digging for Hitler. The Nazi Archaeologists search for the Aryan past*. Oxford: Fonthill.
Barzilai, Maya. 2020. *Golem. Modern wars and their monster*. New York: New York University Press.
Benhamou, Rebecca. 2012. "French bestseller unravels Nazi propagandist's cryptic last words about Purim." *The Times of Israel*, December 28. Accessed April 17, 2023. https://www.timesofisrael.com/french-best-seller-unravels-nazis-cryptic-last-words-about-purim.

Bergmann, Michael; Murray, Michael; Rea, Michael. 2011. *Divine evil? The moral character of the God of Abraham*. Oxford: Oxford University Press.
Berkovits, Eliezer. 1973. *Faith after the Holocaust*. New York: KTAV.
Berlin, Adele. 2011. "Birkat, Ha-Gomel." In *The Oxford Dictionary of the Jewish religion*, edited by Adele Berlin, 139. Oxford: Oxford University Press.
Berlin, Isaiah. 1999. *The Roots of Romanticism*. Oxford: Princeton University Press.
Bernard, David. 2019. *The glory of God in the face of Jesus Christ. Deification of Jesus in early Christian discourse*. Leiden: Brill.
Black, Monica. 2015. "A messiah after Hitler, and his miracles. Bruno Gröning and post-war popular apocalypticism." In *Revisiting the "Nazi Occult." Histories, Realities, Legacies*, edited by Monica Black and Eric Kurlander, 205–22. Rochester: Camden House.
Bleich, Olaf, Plass-Flessenkämper, Benedikt and Schmid, Lukas. 2022. "30 Jahre Wolfenstein 3D: Skandalspiel und Shooter-Wegbereiter." *PC Games*, April 23. Accessed June 6, 2022. https://www.pcgames.de/Wolfenstein-2-The-New-Colossus-Spiel-61046/Specials/Wolfenstein-3D-Rueckblick-Retro-EGo-Shooter-doom-id-Software-1393527.
Bloch, Emmanuel. 2020. "The Code of Esther. A counter-investigation." *Hakirah* 28, 129–45.
Block, Eli and Marcus, Yosef. 2020. *Megillat Esther. The Book of Esther. With commentary from the Talmud, Midrash, classic rabbinic commentators, and the Chabad Rebbes*. New York: Kehot Publication Society.
Blumenthal, David. 1993. *Facing the Abusing God*. Louisville Kentucky: Westminster/John Knox Press.
Brennan, J. H. 1974. *Occult Reich*. London: Futura.
Brice, Kath. 2009. "Wolfenstein recalled in Germany due to swastika use." *Games Industry*, September 23. Accessed October 4, 2023. https://www.gamesindustry.biz/wolfenstein-recalled-in-germany-due-to-swastika-use.
Brueggemann, Walter. 2001. *The prophetic imagination*. Minneapolis: Fortress Press.
Brueggemann, Walter. 2009. *Divine presence amid violence: Contextualizing the Book of Joshua*. Eugene: Cascade.
Bonfil, Robert. 1994. "Aliens within. The Jews and Anti Judaism." In *Handbook of European History 1400-1600. Late Middle Ages, Renaissance and Reformation*, edited by Thomas Bradly and James Tracy, 263–302. Leiden: Brill.
Bosman, Frank and Van Wieringen, Archibald. 2022. *Video Games as Art. A Communication-Oriented Perspective on the Relationship between Gaming and the Art*. Berlin: De Gruyter.
Bosman, Frank. 2019. *Gaming and the divine. A new systematic theology of video games*. London: Routledge.
Bosman, Frank. 2018. "Death Narratives: A Typology of Narratological Embeddings of Player's Death in Digital Games." *Gamenvironments* 9, 12–52.
Bosman, Frank and Mock, Leo. 2016a. "We do not pray, we invent. Judaism and Jewish mysticism in the video game *Wolfenstein. The New Order*." In *Religious stories in transformation. Conflict, revision and reception*, edited by Albertina Houtman, Tamar Kadari, Marcel Poorthuis, and Vered Tohar, 376–98. Leiden: Brill.

Bosman, Frank. 2016b. "The poor carpenter. Reinterpreting Christian Mythology in the Assassin's Creed Game Series." *Gamevironments* 4, 61–87.

Bosman, Frank. 2016c. "Nothing is true, everything is permitted. The portrayal of the Nizari Isma'ilis in the Assassin's Creed game series." *Online* 10, 6–26.

Bosman, Frank. 2015. "Assassin's Creed changing disclaimer." *Frankgbosman*, December 2. Accessed April 5, 2023. https://frankgbosman.wordpress.com/2015/12/02/assassins-creed-changing-disclaimer.

Botstein, Leon. 2022. "The challenge and legacy of being a Jew from Hungary." In *George Soros. A life in full*, edited by Peter Osnos, [ebook]. Boston: Harvard Business Review Press.

Bowlus, Charles. 2016. *The Battle of Lechfeld and its aftermath. August 995. The end of the age of migrations in the Latin West*. New York: Taylor & Francis.

Bozoky, Edina. 2006. "Catharism." In *Dictionary of Gnosis & Western Esotericism*, edited by Wouter Hanegraaff, 242–47. Leiden: Brill.

Braiterman, Zachary. 1998. *(God) After Auschwitz. Tradition and change in Post-Holocaust Jewish Thought*. New York: Princeton University Press.

Broek, Roelof van de. 2006a. "Hermetic literature I: Antiquity." In *Dictionary of Gnosis & Western Esotericism*, edited by Wouter Hanegraaff, 487–99. Leiden: Brill.

Broek, Roelof van de. 2006b. "Gnosticism II: Gnostic literature." In *Dictionary of Gnosis & Western Esotericism*, edited by Wouter Hanegraaff, 417–32. Leiden: Brill.

Broek, Roelof van de. 2006c. "Gnosticism I: Gnostic religion." In *Dictionary of Gnosis & Western Esotericism*, edited by Wouter Hanegraaff, 403–16. Leiden: Brill.

Bromwich, Jonah. 2018. "Everyone is cancelled." *The New York Times*, June 28. Accessed April 5, 2023. https://www.nytimes.com/2018/06/28/style/is-it-canceled.html.

Bytwerk, Randall. 2001. *Julius Streicher. Nazi editor of the notorious anti-Semitic newspaper Der Stürmer*. New York: Cooper Square Press.

Carmody, D. L. and Carmody, J. T. 1996. *Mysticism. Holiness East and West*. Oxford: Oxford University Press.

Carruthers, Jo. 2011. "Esther and Hitler. A second triumphant Purim." In *The Oxford Handbook of the reception history of the Bible*, edited by Michael Lieb, 515–28. Oxford: Oxford University Press.

Carter, Gary. 1995. "An apology for racism." *The Washington Post*, June 21. Accessed July 2023. https://www.washingtonpost.com/archive/politics/1995/06/21/an-apology-for-racism/25ce442e-8733-47de-85b1-0dd7c7fd62ec.

Chan, M. 2003. "Homo geneticus or imago Dei? Beyond genetic reductionism." In *Beyond determinism and reductionism. Genetic science and the person*, edited by M. Chan and R. Chia. Adelaide: ATF Press.

Chapman, Adam. 2020. "Playing the historical fantastic. Zombies, mecha-Nazis and making meaning about the past through metaphor." In *War games. Memory, militarism and the subject of play*, edited by Philip Hammond and Holger Pötzsch, 91–110. New York: Bloomsbury.

Cho, Sung. 2021. *Matthew's account of the Massacre of the Innocents in the light of its reception history.* London: Bloomsbury.
Civan, Judith. 2004. *Abraham's knife. The mythology of the deicide in antisemitism.* USA: Xlibris.
Crawford, Beverly and Martel, James. 1997. "Representations of Germans and what Germans represent. American film images and public perceptions in the Postwar Era." In *Transatlantic images and perceptions. Germany and America since 1776*, edited by David E. Barclay and Elisabeth Glaser-Schmidt, 285–308. New York: Cambridge University Press.
Crenshaw, James. 1996. "Samson." In *HarperCollins Bible Dictionary*, edited by Paul Achtermeier, 966–67. New York: HarperCollins.
Cohen, Arthur. 1962. *The Natural and the Supernatural Jew.* New York: McGraw-Hill.
Cohen, Arthur. 1959. "Why I Choose to be A Jew." *Harper's Magazine* 218, 63–66.
Cohen, Richard I. 2007. "The 'Wandering Jew' from Medieval Legend to Modern Metaphor." In *The art of being Jewish in modern times*, edited by Barbara Kirshenblatt-Gimblett and Jonathan Karp, 147–75. Philadelphia: University of Pennsylvania Press.
Cohn-Sherbok, Dan. 1992. *The crucified Jew. Twenty centuries of Christian anti-semitism.* New York: HarperCollins.
Connolly, Kate. 2022. "German publisher pulls Winnetou books amid racial stereotyping row." *The Guardian.* August 23. Accessed April 5, 2023. https://www.theguardian.com/world/2022/aug/23/german-publisher-ravensburger-verlag-pulls-winnetou-books-racial-stereotyping-row.
Connolly, Charlie. 2021. "The man who chronicles the loss of Old Europe." *The New European*, June 2. Accessed April 21, 2023. https://www.theneweuropean.co.uk/brexit-news-europe-news-the-life-of-joseph-roth-7986706.
Copan, Paul. 2011. *Is God a moral monster? Making sense of the Old Testament God.* Grand Rapids: Baker.
Cullinane, James. 2009. "Review. Wolfenstein." *Stuff*, September 1. Accessed May 6, 2022. https://www.stuff.co.nz/technology/2812534/Review-Wolfenstein.
Deveney, John. 2006. "Spiritualism." In *Dictionary of Gnosis & Western Esotericism*, edited by Wouter Hanegraaff, 1074–82. Leiden: Brill.
Dan, Joseph. 2006. *Kabbalah. A very short introduction.* Oxford: Oxford University Press.
Dan, Joseph. 2006. "Jewish Influences III. 'Christian Kabbalah' in the Renaissance." In *Dictionary of Gnosis & Western Esotericism*, edited by Wouter Hanegraaff, 638–43. Leiden: Brill.
Davies, Brian. 2011. *Thomas Aquinas on God and evil.* Oxford: Oxford University Press.
Elliott, Andrew. 2017. *Medievalism, politics and mass media. Appropriating the Middle Ages in the twenty-first century.* Woodbridge: D.C. Brewer.
Ensslin, Astrid. *The language of gaming.* Basingstoke: Palgrave Macmillan.
Everett, William. 2020. "Walt Disney, Dr. Benjamin Spock, and the Gospel of ideal childrearing. Creating superlative nuclear families in Mary Poppins, Chitty Chitty

Bang Bang, and Bedknobs and Broomsticks," in *Children, childhood, and musical theater*, edited by Donelle Ruwe and James Leven, 39–58. London: Routledge.

Fackenheim, Emil. 1994. *To Mend the World*. Bloomington and Indianapolis: Indiana University Press.

Fackenheim, Emil. 1968. *Quest for past and future. Essays in Jewish theology*. Bloomington: Indiana University Press.

Faivre, Antoine. 2006. "Hermetic Literature IV: Renaissance – Present." In *Dictionary of Gnosis & Western Esotericism*, edited by Wouter Hanegraaff, 533–44. Leiden: Brill.

Falk, David. 2020. *The Ark of the Covenant. In its Egyptian context. An illustrated journey*. Peabody: Hendrikson Academic.

Faulkner, Jason and Nicol, Haru. 2022. "When will Wolfenstein 3 get a release date?" *Game Revolution*, January 25. Accessed May 11, 2022. https://www.gamerevolution.com/guides/431933-wolfenstein-3-release-date-pc-ps4-ps5-xbox-switch.

Feder, Kenneth. 2002. "Ancient astronauts." In *The Skeptic Encyclopedia of Pseudoscience*, edited by Michael Schermer, volume 1, 17–22. Santa Barbara: ABC-CLIO.

Fahey, Mike. 2013. "Wolfenstein Publisher bravely adopts anti-Nazi stance." *Kotaku*, May 8. Accessed April 5, 2023. https://www.kotaku.com.au/2013/05/wolfenstein-publisher-bravely-adopts-anti-nazi-stance.

Ferreiro, Alberto. 2021. *Simon Magus in patristic, medieval and early modern traditions*. Leiden: Brill.

Fest, Joachim. 1997. *Plotting Hitler's death. The German resistance to Hitler. 1933-1945*. Translated to English by Bruce Little. New York: H. Holt.

Fine, Steven. 2016. *The Menorah. From the Bible to modern Israel*. Cambridge: Harvard University Press.

FitzGerald, Michael. 2021. *Nazis and the supernatural. The occult secrets of Hitler's evil empire*. S.l.: Sirius international.

FitzGerald, Michael. 2013. *The Nazi occult war. Hitler's compact with the forces of evil*. London: Arcturus Publishing.

Friedländer, Saul. 2007. *The years of extermination. Nazi Germany and the Jews, 1939-1945*. London: HarperCollins.

Fox, Matt. 2013. *The video game guide. 1,000+ Arcade, console and computer games, 1962-2012*. Second edition. Jefferson: McFarland.

Foxman, Abraham. 2010. *Jews and money. The story of a stereotype*. New York: Palgrave Macmilllan.

Frischauer, Willi. 1953. *Himmler. The evil genius of the Third Reich*. New York: Belmont Books.

Fuchs, Michael. 2012. "Of Blitzkriege and Hardcore BDSM. Revisiting Nazi sexploitation camps." In *Nazisploitation! The Nazi image in low-brow cinema and culture*, edited by Daniel Magilow, Elizabeth Bridges and Kirstin Vander Lugt, 279–94. New York: Continuum.

Fudge, Edward. 2011. *The fire that consumes. A biblical and historical study of the doctrine of final punishment*. Eugene: Cascade books.

Galtung, Johan. 1996. *Peace by peaceful means. Peace and conflict, development and civilization*. Londo: Sage.

Garner, Daniel. 2014. *Antitheodicy, atheodicy and Jewish mysticism in Holocaust Theology*. Piscataway: Gorgia Press.

Gasman, Daniel. 2017 [1971]. *The scientific origins of national socialism*. New York: Routledge.

Gilbert, Robert. 2006. "The Hermetic Order of the Golden Dawn" In *Dictionary of Gnosis & Western Esotericism*, edited by Wouter Hanegraaff, 544–50. Leiden: Brill.

Geselowitz, Gabriela. 2017. "Wolfenstein star revealed to be Jewish." *Tablet*, October 26. Accessed April 8, 2023. https://www.tabletmag.com/sections/news/articles/wolfenstein-star-revealed-to-be-jewish.

Greenberg, Irvin. 1977. "Cloud of Smoke, Pillar of Fire" In *Auschwitz: Beginning Of A New Era? Reflections on the Holocaust*, edited by E. Fleischner, 7–55. New York: KTAV.

Griffin, David. 2004 [1976]. *God, power, and evil. A process theodicy*. Philadelphia: Westminster.

Griffin, David. 1991. *Evil revisited. Responses and reconsiderations*. Albany: State University of New York Press.

Gilbert, Martin. 2001. *Auschwitz and the Allies. A devastating account of how the allies responded to the news of Hitler's mass murder*. London: Pimlicon.

Gilbert, Robert. 2006. "Hermetic Order of the Golden Dawn." In *Dictionary of Gnosis & Western Esotericism*, edited by Wouter Hanegraaff, 544–50. Leiden: Brill.

Godofwarlover. 2018. "A certain subject ruined me liking Wolfenstein . . ." *Deviant Art*, January 15. Accessed May 6, 2022. https://www.deviantart.com/godofwarlover/journal/A-certain-subject-ruined-me-liking-Wolfenstein-725680953.

Goodrick-Clarke, Nicholas. 2006a. "Lanz von Liebenfels, Jörg." In *Dictionary of Gnosis & Western Esotericism*, edited by Wouter Hanegraaff, 673–75. Leiden: Brill.

Goodrick-Clarke, Nicholas. 2006b. "List, Guido Karl Anton (von)." In *Dictionary of Gnosis & Western Esotericism*, edited by Wouter Hanegraaff, 693–94. Leiden: Brill.

Goodridge-Clarke, Nicholas. 2005. *The occult roots of Nazism. Secret Aryan cults and their influence on Nazi ideology*. London: Tauris.

Goodrick-Clarke, Nicholas. 2002. *Black Sun. Aryan cults, esoteric Nazism and the politics of identity*. New York: New York University Press.

Grieb, Margit. 2009. "Fragging Fascism," in *After the digital divide? German aesthetic theory in the age of new media*, edited by Lutz Koepnick and Erin McGlothlin, 186–204. Rochester: Camden House.

Griech-Polelle, Beth. 2017. *Anti-Semitism and the Holocaust: Language, Rhetoric, and the Traditions of Hatred*. New York: Bloomsbury.

Guenther, Peter. 1991. *Degenerate art. The fate of the Avant-garde in Nazi Germany*. Chicago: Los Angelos County Museum of Art.

Günther, Christian. 2021. "Wolfenstein: The Old Blood." *Stiftung Digitale Spiele Kultur*, December 15. Accessed April 16, 2023. https://www.stiftung-digitale-spielekultur.de/spiele-erinnerungskultur/wolfenstein-the-old-blood.

Hakl, Hans Thomas. 2006. "Evola, Julius." In *Dictionary of Gnosis & Western Esotericism*, edited by Wouter Hanegraaff, 345–50. Leiden: Brill.

Halter, Ed. 2006. *From Sun Tzu to Xbox. War and Video Games*. New York: Thunder's Mouth Press.

Hanegraaff, Wouter. 2006a. "Esotericism." In *Dictionary of Gnosis & Western Esotericism*, edited by Wouter Hanegraaff, 336–40. Leiden: Brill.

Hanegraaff, Wouter. 2006b. "Jewish Influences V: Occultist Kabbalah." In *Dictionary of Gnosis & Western Esotericism*, edited by Wouter Hanegraaff, 644–47. Leiden: Brill.

Harmon, Matthew. 2020. *The servant of the Lord and his servant people. Tracing a biblical theme through the canon*. Westmont: InterVarsity Press.

Hayton, Jeff. 2015. "Beyond good and evil. Nazis and the supernatural in video games." In *Revisiting the "Nazi Occult." Histories, Realities, Legacies*, edited by Monica Black and Eric Kurlander, 248–69. Rochester: Camden House.

Hayton, Jeff. 2012. "Digital Nazis. Genre, history and the displacement of evil in first-person shooters." In *Nazisploitation! The Nazi image in low-brow cinema and culture*, edited by Daniel Magilow, Elizabeth Bridges and Kirstin Vander Lugt, 199–218. New York: Continuum.

Hall, Tom. 2014. *Twitter*, March 2. Accessed April 8, 2023. https://twitter.com/ThatTomHall/status/440012925067988992.

Helm, Paul. 2004. *John Calvins' ideas*. Oxford: Oxford University Press.

Helmreich, W. 1982. *The things they say behind your back. Stereotypes and the myths behind them*. New Brunswick: Transaction Books.

Hick, John. 1966. *Evil and the God of love*. London: Macmillan.

Hite, Kenneth. 2013. *The Nazi occult*. Oxford: Osprey Publishing.

Hobbes, Jack. 2022. "Kanye West documentary cancelled, rapper dropped by agent amid anti-Semitic remarks." *New York Post*. October 23. Accessed April 5, 2023. https://nypost.com/2022/10/24/kanye-west-doc-canceled-dropped-by-agent-amid-anti-semitic-remarks.

Hocking, C. 2007. "Ludonarrative Dissonance in Bioshock: The problem of what game is about." *Click Nothing*. October 7. Accessed May 22, 2023. https://clicknothing.typepad.com/click_nothing/2007/10/ludonarrative-d.html.

Hodes, Martha. 2014. *White women, Black men*. New Haven: Yale University Press.

Hoffmann, Peter. 1997. *Stauffenberg. A family history. 1905-1944*. New York: Cambridge University Press.

Höhne, Heinz. 1966. *The order of the Death's Head: The story of Hitler's SS*. London: Penguin.

Holm, Tawny. 2008. "The fiery furnace in the book of Daniel and the Ancient Near East." *Journal of the American Oriental Society* 128(1): 85–104.

Holzenhausen, Jens. 2006. "Valentinus and Valentinians." In *Dictionary of Gnosis & Western Esotericism*, edited by Wouter Hanegraaff, 1144–57. Leiden: Brill.

Huber, Axel. 2011. *Grausamer als die Norm des Grauens. Die SS-Aufseherin Irma Grese*. Munich: GRIN Verlag.

Hughes, William. 2017. "Wolfenstein. The New Order dared to play games with the Holocaust." *AVclub*. January 26. Accessed May 6, 2022. https://www.avclub.com/wolfenstein-the-new-order-dared-to-play-games-with-the-1798256804.

Hüser, Karl. 1982. *Wewelsburg 1933 bis 1945, Kult- und Terrorstätte der SS. Eine Dokumentation*. Paderborn: Verlag Bonifatius-Druckerei.
Hussein, Samir. 2018. "J.K. Rowling faces backlash after tweeting support for 'transphobic' researcher." *NBC News*. November 13. Accessed April 5, 2023. https://www.nbcnews.com/feature/nbc-out/j-k-rowling-faces-backlash-after-tweeting-support-transphobic-researcher-n1104971.
Idel, Moshe. 1990. *Golem. Jewish magical and mystical traditions on the artificial anthropoid*. New York: State University of New York Press.
Introvigne, Massimo. 2006. "Grail traditions." In *Dictionary of Gnosis & Western Esotericism*, edited by Wouter Hanegraaff, 436–38. Leiden: Brill.
Issitt, Micah and Main, Carlyn. 2014. *Hidden religion. The greatest mysteries and symbols of the world's religious beliefs*. Santa Barbara: ABC-CLIO.
Jackman, Josh. 2017. "Anne Frank was attracted to girls." *Pink News*, September 7. Accessed April 16, 2023. https://www.thepinknews.com/2017/09/07/anne-frank-was-attracted-to-girls.
Jacobsen, Annie. 2014. *Operation Paperclip. The secret intelligence program that brought Nazi scientists to America*. New York: Little Brown.
Jorgensen, Larry and Newlands, Samuel (eds). 2014. *New essays of Leibniz's Theodicy*. Oxford: Oxford University Press.
Joyce, George Hayward. 1922. *Principles of natural theology*. London: Longmans.
Kaplan, Aryeh. 2004. *Meditation and Kabbalah*. Lanham: Rowman and Littlefield.
Karthaus, Ulrich. 2007. *Sturm and Drang. Epoche – Werke – Wirkung*. 2nd edition. München: C.H. Beck.
Katz, Steven, Biderman, Shlomo, and Greenberg, Gershon (ed.). 2006. *Wrestling with God. Jewish responses during and after the Holocaust*. New York: Oxford University Press.
Katz, Steven (ed.). 2005. *The Impact of the Holocaust on Jewish Theology*. New York: New York University Press.
Kearney, Richard. 2002. *On stories*. London: Routledge.
Kershaw, Ian. 1999. *Hitler, 1889-1936. Hubris*. New York: W.W. Norton.
Keyes, Ralph. 2006. *The quote verifier. Who said what, where, and when*. New York: St. Martin's Griffin.
King, Francis. 1976. *Satan and swastika*. St. Albans: Mayflower.
Kingsepp, Eva. 2012. "The Power of the Black Sun. (oc)cultural perspectives on Nazi/SS esotericism," paper presented at 1st International Conference on Contemporary Esotericism, Stockholm University, Sweden, August 27–29, 2012; https://contern.org/cyberproceedings/papers-from-the-1st-international-conference-on-contemporary-esotericism/eva-kingsepp-the-power-of-the-black-sun-occultural-perspectives-on-naziss-esotericism.
Kircher, Athanasius. 1654. *Oedipus Aegyptiacus*, volume IIb. Rome.
Kirkpatrick, Sidney. 2010. *Hitler's holy relics. A true story of Nazi plunder and the race to recover the crown jewels of the Holy Roman Empire*. London: Simon & Schuster.
Komonchak, Joseph, Collins, Mary and Lane, Ermot. 1990. "Deism." In *The new dictionary of theology*, edited by idem, 275. Dublin: Gill and Macmillan.

Konda, Milan. 2019. *Conspiracies of conspiracies. How delusions have overrun America*. Chicago: University of Chicago Press.

Kourie, Caelia. 2015. "Weaving colourful threads: A tapestry of spirituality and mysticism." *Herv. teol. stud.* 71, 1–9.

Kuchera, Ben. 2017. "Yes, B.J. Blazkowicz is Jewish." *Polygon*, October 26. Accessed April 8, 2023. https://www.polygon.com/2017/10/26/16553486/wolfenstein-bj-blazkowicz-jewish.

Kuhl, Stefan. 2002. *The Nazi Connection: Eugenics, American Racism, and German National Socialism*. Oxford: Oxford University Press.

Kurlander, Eric. 2017. *Hitler's monsters. A supernatural history of the Third Reich*. London: Yale University Press.

Kurtz, Andrew. 2002. "Ideology and interpretation in the first-person shooter." In *Growing up postmodern. Neoliberalism and the war on the young*, edited by Ronald Strickland, 107–22. Oxford: Rowman & Littelfield.

Kushner, Harold. 1981. *When bad things happen to good people*. New York: Schocken.

Lacina, Dia. 2018. "Shadow of the Tomb Raider tries, but fails, to tackle its own colonialism." *Vice*. September 20. Accessed April 5, 2023. https://www.vice.com/en/article/d3jgeq/shadow-of-the-tomb-raider-review-tries-but-fails-to-tackle-its-own-colonialism.

Laenen, Sjef. 2001. *Jewish mysticism. An introduction*. London: Westminster John Knox Press.

Lawrie, Douglas. 2005. *Speaking to good effect. An introduction to the theory and practice of rhetoric*. Stellenbosch: Sun Press.

Lehrer, Steven. 2006. *The Reich Chancellery and Führerbunker complex. An illustrated history of the seat of the Nazi regime*. Jefferson: McFarland & Company.

Leijenhorst, Cees. 2006a. "Neoplatonism II: Middle Ages." In *Dictionary of Gnosis & Western Esotericism*, edited by Wouter Hanegraaff, 837–41. Leiden: Brill.

Leijenhorst, Cees. 2006b. "Neoplatonism III: Since the Renaissance." In *Dictionary of Gnosis & Western Esotericism*, edited by Wouter Hanegraaff, 841–46. Leiden: Brill.

Leijenhorst, Cees. 2006c. "Anthroposophy." In *Dictionary of Gnosis & Western Esotericism*, edited by Wouter Hanegraaff, 82–89. Leiden: Brill.

Leijenhorst, Cees. 2006c. "Steiner, Rudolf." In *Dictionary of Gnosis & Western Esotericism*, edited by Wouter Hanegraaff, 1084–91. Leiden: Brill.

Levinas, Emmanuel. 1988. "Useless Suffering" In *The Provocation of Levinas: Rethinking the Other*, edited by R. Bernasconi and D. Wood, 156–67. London: Routledge.

Lewy, Guenter. 2017. *Perpetrators. The world of the Holocaust killers*. Oxford: Oxford University Press.

Long, Rebecca. 2021. "The anti-fascist 'Bedknobs and broomsticks' deserves its golden jubilee," *Observer*, August 8. September 9, 2023. https://observer.com/2021/08/bedknobs-and-broomsticks-angela-lansbury-anniversary.

Lowood, Henry. 2006. "A Brief Biography of Computer Games." In *Playing video Games. Motives, responses and consequences*, edited by Peter Vorderer and Jennings Bryant, 25–28. Mahwah: Lawrence Erlbaum Associates.

Lübke, Wilhelm. 1878. *History of sculpture form the earliest ages to the present time.* Translated by F. E. Bunnètt. London: Smith, Elder & Co.

Lucentini, Paolo and Compagni, Vittoria. 2006. "Hermetic literature II: Latin Middle Ages." In *Dictionary of Gnosis & Western Esotericism*, edited by Wouter Hanegraaff, 499–529. Leiden: Brill.

Lusane, Clarence. 2003. *Hitler's black victims. The historical experiences of Afro-Germans, European Blacks, Africans, and African Americans in the Nazi Era.* London: Routledge.

Mackie, J. L. 1995. "Evil and omnipotence," *Mind* 64(254), 200–13.

Magee, Bryan. 2002. *The Tristan Chord*, New York: Owl Books.

Magilow, Daniel. 2012. "Introduction," in *Nazisploitation! The Nazi image in low-brow cinema and culture*, edited by Daniel Magilow, Kristin Vander Lugt, and Elizabeth Bridges, 2–20. London: Continuum.

Mason, Peter. 2013. *The colossal. From Ancient Greece to Giacometti.* London: Reaktion Books.

May, Gerhard. 2006. "Marcion." In *Dictionary of Gnosis & Western Esotericism*, edited by Wouter Hanegraaff, 765–68. Leiden: Brill.

McGinn, B. 2008. "Mystical consciousness: A modest proposal." *Spiritus: A Journal of Christian Spirituality* 8(1), 44–63.

McGowan, Todd. 2020. *Universality and identity politics.* New York: Columbia University Press.

McKeand, Kirk. 2018. "Videogames' portrayal of the Holocaust does a disservice to both players and victims." January 18. Accessed May 6, 2022. https://www.pcgamesn.com/jewish-opinions-on-nazis-in-videogames.

McVeigh, Rory. 2010. *The rise of the Ku Klux Klan. Right-wing movements and national politics.* Minneapolis: University of Minnesota.

McGrath, Alister. 2017. *Christian theology. An introduction.* 6th edition. Chichester: John Wiley & Sons.

McGrath, Alister. 2017. *Re-imagining nature. The promise of a Christian natural theology.* Chichester: John Wiley.

Medoff, Rafael. 2009. *Blowing the whistle on genocide. Josiah E. DuBois, Jr., and the struggle for a U.S. response to the Holocaust.* West Lafayette: Purdue University Press.

Mees, Bernard. 2008. *The science of the Swastika.* New York: Central European University Press.

Meija, Robert, Banks, Jaime, and Adams, Aubrie. 2017. *100 Greatest video game franchises.* Blue Ridge Summit: Rowman & Littlefield.

Mello-Klein, Cody. 2019. "Wolfenstein 2 proves that Jews can be heroes, not just survivors." *VG247*, February 15. Accessed April 8, 2023. https://www.vg247.com/wolfenstein-2-proves-jews-can-heroes-not-just-survivors.

Metz, Johann Baptist. 2007. *Faith in history and society. Toward a practical fundamental theology.* New York: Crossroad.

Millet, Kitty. 2017. *The Victims of slavery. Colonization and the Holocaust. A comparative history of persecution.* London: Bloomsbury.

Moltmann, Jürgen. 1993. *The crucified God. The cross of Christ as the foundation and criticism of Christian theology*. Minneapolis: Fortress Press.
Mommsen, Hans. 2003. *Alternatives to Hitler. German resistance under the Third Reich*. London: I.B. Tauris.
Moncrieffe, Joy. 2013. "Labelling, power and accountability. How and why 'our' categories matter." In *The power of labelling. How people are categorized and why it matters*, edited by Joy Moncrieffe and Rosalind Eyben, 1–16. New York: Taylor & Francis.
Morgan, Morgan. 2001. *Beyond Auschwitz*. New York: Oxford University Press.
Morris, Nigel. 2007. *The cinema of Steven Spielberg. Empire of light*. London: Wallflower.
Neiberg, Michael. 2017. *The Treaty of Versailles. A concise history*. Oxford: Oxford University Press.
Nelson-Pallmeyer, Jack. 2001. *Jesus against Christianity. Reclaiming the missing Jesus*. Harrisburg: Trinity Press International.
Newborn, Jud and Dumbach, Annette. 2007. *Sophie Scholl and the White Rose*. Oxford: One World.
Newman, Mark. 2001. *Getting right with God. Southern Baptists and Desegregation. 1945-1995*. Tuscaloosa: University of Alabama Press.
Nielsen, Wendy. 2022. *Motherless creations. Fictions of artificial life, 1650-1890*. London: Routledge.
Nocks, Lisa. 1998. "The Golem. Between the technological and the divine." *Journal of Social and Evolutionary Systems* 21(3), 281–303.
Ochse, Katharina. 1999. *Joseph Roths Auseinandersetzung mit dem Antisemitismus*. Würzburg: Königshausen & Neumann.
Oded, Bustanay and Sperling, David. 2007 "Golem." In *Encyclopaedia Judaica*, edited by Fred Skolnik, volume 7, 2nd edition, 735–38. Detroit: Thomson Gale.
Olson, Lynne. 2013. *Those angry days. Rossevelt Lindbergh, and America's fight over World War II, 1939-1941*. New York: Random House.
Oort, Johannes van. 2006. "Manicheism." In *Dictionary of Gnosis & Western Esotericism*, edited by Wouter Hanegraaff, 757–65. Leiden: Brill.
Ortlund, Raymond. 1996. *Whoredom. God's unfaithful wife in biblical theology*. Westmont: InterVarsity Press.
Parfit, Derek. 1984. *Reasons and persons*. Oxford: Oxford University Press.
Pasi, Marco. 2006. "Crowley, Aleister." In *Dictionary of Gnosis & Western Esotericism*, edited by Wouter Hanegraaff, 281–87. Leiden: Brill.
Peaple, Simon. 2002. *European Diplomacy. 1870-1939*. Oxford: Heinemann.
Perrin, D. 2005. "Mysticism." In *The Blackwell companion to Christian spirituality*, edited by A. Holder, 442–57. Oxford: Oxford University Press.
Peters, Olaf. 2014. *Degenerate art. The attack on modern art in Nazi Germany, 1937*. New York: Prestel.
Phillips, D. Z. 2001. "Theism without Theodicy." In *Encountering evil. Live options in theodicy*, edited by Stephen T. Davis, 145–61. Louisville: Westminster John Knox.
Pinnock, Sarah Katherine. 2002. *Beyond theodicy. Jewish and Christian continental thinkers respond to the Holocaust*. Albany: State University of New York Press.

Pitts, Mike. 2010. "How the study of teeth is revealing our history." *The Guardian*. June 17. Accessed October 4, 2023. https://www.theguardian.com/science/2010/jun/17/study-teeth-revealing-history.

Powers, Tom. 2018. "Is Shadow of the Tomb Raider exploitation?" *The Escapist*. September 18. Accessed April 5, 2023. https://www.escapistmagazine.com/opinion-is-shadow-of-the-tomb-raiders-mesoamerica-an-homage-or-an-exploitation.

Principe, Lawrence. 2006. "Alchemy I: Introduction." In *Dictionary of Gnosis & Western Esotericism*, edited by Wouter Hanegraaff, 12–16. Leiden: Brill.

Pringle, Heather. 2006. *The master plan. Himmler's scholars and the Holocaust*. London: Harper Perennial.

Proctor, Robert. 1999. *The Nazi war on cancer*. Princeton: Princeton University Press.

Pugh, Ben. 2014. *Atonement theories. A way through the maze*. Eugene: Wipf and Stock.

Raphael, Melissa. 2003. *The female face of God in Auschwitz*. New York: Routledge.

Reissner, Hanns. 2007. "Abraham." In *Encyclopaedia Judaica*, edited by Fred Skolnik, volume 1, 2nd edition, 280–88. Detroit: Thomson Gale.

Roberts, Sam. 2011. "How a sonnet made a statue the 'Mother of Exiles.'" *The New York Times*, October 26. Accessed April 17, 2023. https://archive.nytimes.com/cityroom.blogs.nytimes.com/2011/10/26/how-a-sonnet-made-a-statue-the-mother-of-exiles.

Roach, David. 2021. *The Southern Baptist Convention & Civil Rights, 1954-1995. Conservative theology, segregation, and change*. Eugene: Pickwick Publications.

Roon, Ger van. 1971. *German resistance to Hitler: Count Von Moltke and the Kreisau Circle*. London: Van Nostrand Reinhold Company.

Rowland, Antony. 1997. "Re-reading 'Impossibility' and 'Barbarism.' Adorno and Post-Holocaust poetics," *Critical Survey* 9(1): 57–69.

Rubenstein, Richard. 1966. *After Auschwitz: Radical Theology and Contemporary Judaism*. New York: The Bobbs-Merrill Company.

Sagrillo, Troy. 2015. "Shoshenq I and biblical Šîšaq: A philological defense of their traditional equation." In *Solomon and Shishak: Current perspectives from Archaeology, epigraphy, history and chronology*, edited by Peter James and Peter Gert van der Veen, 61-81. Oxford: Archeaopress.

Saliers, Don. 2011. "Reproaches (Improperia)," *Religion Past and Present*. http://dx.doi.org/10.1163/1877-5888_rpp_SIM_10324, accessed April 15, 2023.

Santucci, James. 2006. "Theosophical Society." In *Dictionary of Gnosis & Western Esotericism*, edited by Wouter Hanegraaff, 1114–23. Leiden: Brill.

Sarna, Nahum and Hirschberg, Haïm Zéw. 2007. "Nimrod." In *Encyclopaedia Judaica*, edited by Fred Skolnik, volume 15, 2nd edition, 269–70. Detroit: Thomson Gale.

Sax, Boria. 2000. *Animals in the Third Reich. Pets, scapegoats, and the Holocaust*. London: Continuum.

Schellenberg, Walter. 2006. *The Memoirs of Hitler's Spymaster*. London: Carlton.

Schrier, V. and Schleif, C. 2009. "The holy lance as late twentieth century subcultural icon." In *Cultural icons*, edited by K. Tomaselli and D. Scott. Walnut Creek: Left Coast Press.

Schiff, E., 1982. *From stereotype to metaphor: The Jew in contemporary drama.* Albany: State University of New York Press.

Schindler, Pesach. 1990. *Hasidic responses to the Holocaust in the light of Hasidic thought.* Hobroken: KTAV.

Scholem, Gershom. 2007. "Kabbalah." *Encyclopaedia Judaica*, edited by Fred Skolnik, volume 11, 2nd edition, 586–677. Detroit: Thomson Gale.

Schrank, Bernice. 2007. "Cutting off your nose to spite your race. Jewish stereotypes, media images, cultural hybridity." *Shofar* 25(4), 18–42.

Schulte, Jan-Erik. 2002. "Die SS in Wewelsburg. Weltanschauliche Hybris – terroristische Praxis: Auf dem Weg zu einer Gesamtdarstellung," in *Gedenkstättenarbeit und Erinnerungskultur in Ostwestfalen-Lippe: Ein abschließender Projektbericht für die Planungswerkstatt Erinnerungskultur: Geschichte in Ostwestfalen- Lippe 1933 - 1945. Wege der Erinnerung*, edited by Juliane Kerzel, 208–20. Büren: Planungswerkstatt Erinnerungskultur c/o Kreismuseum Wewelsburg.

Schulte, Jan-Erik (ed.) 2009. *Die SS, Himmler und die Wewelsburg.* Paderborn, München, Wien, Zürich: Ferdinand Schöningh.

Schweid, Eliezer. 1994. *Wrestling until day-break. Searching for meaning in the thinking on the Holocaust.* Lanham: University Press of America.

Scott, Mark. 2015. *Pathways in theodicy. An introduction to the problem of evil.* Minneapolis: Fortress Press.

Scott, Mark. 2022. "Cosmic Theodicy: Origen's Treatment of the Problem of Evil." In *The Oxford Handbook of Origen*, in Ronald E. Heine and Karen Jo Torjesen. Oxford: Oxford University Press.

Scullion, Chris. 2020. *The SNES encyclopedia. Every game released for the Super Nintendo Entertainment System.* Philadelphia: White Owl.

Segel, B. W. and Levy, Richard. 1995. *The lie and a libel. The history of the Protocols of the Elders of Zion.* Lincoln: University of Nebraska Press.

Seibert, Eric. 2009. *Disturbing divine behavior. Troubling Old Testament images of God.* Minneapolis: Fortress.

Shapira, Kalonymous. 2004. *Sacred Fire.* Lanham: Aronson.

Sharp, John. 2014. "Perspective." In *The Routledge companion to video game studies*, edited by Mark Wolf and Bernard Perron, 107–16. London: Routledge.

Shaw, Gregory. 2006. "Neoplatonism I: Antiquity." In *Dictionary of Gnosis & Western Esotericism*, edited by Wouter Hanegraaff, 834–37. Leiden: Brill.

Sheldon, Beau Jágr. 2021. "A new masculinity. The women of Wolfenstein." *BrieBeau.* March 31. Accessed May 6, 2022. https://briebeau.com/thoughty/the-women-of-wolfenstein.

Sherwin, Byron. 2006. *Kabbalah. An introduction to Jewish mysticism.* Lanham: Rowman & Littlefield.

Sherwin, Byron. 2007. "Golems in the biotech century." *Zygon* 42(1), 133–43.

Siepe, Daniela. 2002. "Wewelsburg und Okkultismus." In *Gedenkstättenarbeit und Erinnerungskultur in Ostwestfalen-Lippe: Ein abschließender Projektbericht für die Planungswerkstatt Erinnerungskultur: Geschichte in Ostwestfalen- Lippe 1933 - 1945. Wege der Erinnerung*, edited by Juliane

Kerzel, 376–398. Büren: Planungswerkstatt Erinnerungskultur c/o Kreismuseum Wewelsburg.

Siepe, Daniela. 2022. "The Sun Wheel as a 'Black Sun' in Wewelsburg Castle's Obergruppenführer Hall." In *Myths of Wewelsburg Castle*, edited by Kirsten John-Stucke and Daniela Siepe, 143–62. Leiden: Brill.

Sitelman, F. and Sitelman, R. 2000. "Ethics and culture. From the claim that God is dead, it does not follow that everything is permitted." In *Understanding cultural diversity. Culture, curriculum, and community in nursing*, edited by M. Kelley and V. Fitzsimons. Sudbury: Jones and Bartlett.

Sklar, Dusty. 1977. *Gods and Beasts: The Nazis and the Occult.* New York: Thomas Y. Crowell.

Skolnik, Fred. 2007 "Abraham's bosom." In *Encyclopaedia Judaica*, edited by Fred Skolnik, volume 1, 2nd edition, 316–17. Detroit: Thomson Gale.

Sölle, Dorothee. 1975. *Suffering.* Philadelphia: Fortress Press.

Stone, Jeff. 2005. "Germany in Film and Television (American) after World War II." In *Germany and the Americas. Culture, politics, and history*, edited by Thomas Adam, 338–40. Santa Barbara: ABC-CLIO.

Stulman, Louis and Paul Kim, Hyun Chul. 2011. *You are my people. An introduction to prophetic literature.* Nashville: Abingdon Press.

Sundquist, Eric (ed.). 2018. *Writing in witness. A Holocaust reader.* New York: State University of New York.

Sulles, Allen. 2019. *Germany's Underground.* Chicago: Eumenes Publishing.

Surin, Kenneth. 2004 [1986]. *Theology and the problem of evil.* Eugene: Wipf & Stock.

Pasi, Marco. 2006. "Westcott, William Wynn." In *Dictionary of Gnosis & Western Esotericism*, edited by Wouter Hanegraaff. Leiden: Brill, 1168–70.

Tate, Greg, Alexis Petridis, Lyndsey Winship, Priya Elan, Chuck Klosterman, Laura Snapes, and Simran Hans. 2019. "Too big to cancel. Can we still listen to Michael Jackson?" *The Guardian.* March 1. Accessed April 5, 2023. https://www.theguardian.com/music/2019/mar/01/leaving-neverland-is-it-still-ok-to-listen-to-michael-jackson.

Tautz, Johannes. 1990. *Walter Johannes Stein. A biography.* London: Temple Lodge Press.

Travers, Martin. 2001. "Introduction." In *European Literature from Romanticism to Postmodernism. A Reader in Aesthetic Practice*, edited by Martin Travers. London: Continuum.

Treffert, Darold. 2009. "The savant syndrome: an extraordinary condition. A synopsis: past, present, future." *Philosophical Transactions of the Royal Society of London.* Series B, Biological Sciences. 364 (1522): 1351–57.

Tymkiw, Michael. 2018. *Nazi exhibition design and modernism.* Minneapolis: University of Minnesota Press.

Vogel, Dan. 1980. *Emma Lazarus.* Boston: Twayne Publishers.

Vonberg, Judith. 2018. "Germany lifts ban on Nazi symbols in computer games." *CNN.* August 10. Accessed October 4, 2023. https://edition.cnn.com/2018/08/10/europe/germany-video-games-nazi-symbols-intl/index.html.

Waaijman, Kees. 2002. *Spirituality. Forms, foundations, methods*. Leuven: Peeters.

Watson, Alexander. 2008. *Enduring the Great War. Combat, morale and collapse in the German and British armies, 1914-1918*. Cambridge: Cambridge University Press.

Watson, Rebecca. 1971. *Chaos uncreated. A reassessment of the theme of "Chaos" in the Hebrew Bible*. Berlin: De Gruyter.

Weinreich, Uriel. 2007. "Yiddish language." In *Encyclopaedia Judaica*, edited by Fred Skolnik, volume 21, 2nd edition, 332-338. Detroit: Thomson Gale.

Weiss, Sheila. 2010. *The Nazi symbiosis. Human genetics and politics in the Third Reich*. London: University of Chicago Press.

Weiss, Tzahi. 2013. "Kabbalah." In *Encyclopedia of Jewish Folklore and Traditions*, edited by Raphael Patai and Jaya Bar-Itzhak, 287–91. London: M.E. Sharpe.

Westcott, William (ed.). 1996. *Sepher Yetzirah*, 4th edition. Edmonds: Holmes Publishing Group.

Widmann, Tabea. 2020. "Playing memories? Digital games as memory media." September 17. Accessed May 6, 2023. https://reframe.sussex.ac.uk/digitalholocaustmemory/2020/09/17/playing-memories-digital-games-as-memory-media.

Whitehead, Alfred North. 1978 [1929]. *Process and reality. An essay in cosmology*. New York: Free Press.

Winburne, Richard. 1998. *Providence and the problem of evil*. Oxford: Clarendon Press.

Winik, Akiva. 1954. "Jewish Life and Work in Chelm." *In Commemoration Book Chelm (Poland)*, edited by M. Bakalczuk, 179–202. Johannesburg: Jewishgen.

Wink, Walter. 1998. *The powers that be. Theology for a new millennium*. New York: Doubleday.

Wolfe, Danielle de. 2014. "MachineGames talk Wolfenstein." July 23. Accessed July 26, 2023. https://www.shortlist.com/news/machinegames-talk-wolfenstein.

Wright, Christopher. 2008. *The God I don't understand. Reflections on tough questions of faith*. Grand Rapids: Zondervan.

Yar, Sanam and Bromwich, Jonah. 2019. "Tales from the teenage cancel culture." *The New York Times*. October 31. Accessed April 5, 2023. https://www.nytimes.com/2019/10/31/style/cancel-culture.html.

Yenne, Bill. 2010. *Hitler's master of the dark arts. Himmler's black knights and the occult origins of the SS*. Minneapolis: Zenith Press.

Index

Ario-Christianity. *See* Ariosophy
Ariosophy, 2, 4, 15–23, 59–61, 161–63
Armamism. *See* Ariosophy

the Black Sun, 43, 51, 57, 60,
 66–68, 161
Blavatsky, Helena "Madame," 15–23,
 42, 54, 56, 58–59, 61, 67, 161–62
Blavatsky, Marianna, 43, 52, 57, 62, 68
Blazkowicz, William "B.J.," 1–2,
 13–14, 26, 35–46, 62–64, 68–69,
 76–77, 79–86, 88–91, 93, 95,
 97, 99–101, 103–5, 109–15, 117,
 119–23, 125–28, 131–40, 146–50,
 155–60, 163–64
Boone, Horton, 46, 120, 123, 149–
 50, 157

Caldwell, Norman, 46, 104–5, 120, 123
Camp Belica. *See* Jewish mysticism
Castle (Schloss) Wewelsburg, 22, 28,
 39, 51–54, 67–68, 161–62
Communication-Oriented Analysis, 3,
 5–7, 73–77, 136, 155–60
Chrétien de Troyes, 27

the Da'at Yichud, 2–3, 45–47, 56, 69,
 79, 82–83, 90–100, 103–5, 107, 109,
 111, 113, 148, 150–52, 163–65

Da'at. *See* Jewish mysticism
the Dagger of Warding, 42, 56, 68
deism, 95, 145, 150–52, 156

Eadgyth of England, 52, 64–66, 105
Essenbach, Wolfram von, 27

Frank, Anne, 86, 121, 162

the golem. *See* Jewish mysticism

Hass, Max, 102, 120, 123, 125–26
Heinrich I "the Fowler," 42–43, 62–64,
 68–69
Himmler, Heinrich, 17, 21–23, 28, 39,
 41–43, 52–54, 62–64, 67–69
Hitler, Adolf, 4, 19, 21–23, 25, 28–30,
 39–41, 47, 55–56, 59, 64, 66, 85,
 87–88, 99, 112, 130, 144, 148,
 150, 163

Jewish mysticism, 31–36; *Da'at*, 83, 96,
 101; the Golem, 97, 105–9, 162–64;
 Sefer Yetzirah, 34, 100, 102–3, 108;
 sephirot, 32, 34–35, 95–96, 101,
 144–45; *Yichud*, 83, 96, 101

Kabbala. *See* Jewish mysticism

the Kreisau Circle, 13, 38, 43, 45–46, 56–57, 97, 100, 109, 111, 113, 115, 117–23, 125–26, 128–31, 134, 136, 140, 148, 157, 164
Kreutz, Klaus, 120, 123, 125–26, 128

Liebenfels, Jörg Lanz von, 19–23, 28, 52, 59, 67, 83, 162
List, Guido von, 19–21, 59, 61, 67, 162

Nazism: Camp Belica, 2, 45–46, 79, 81, 83, 91, 109–16, 126, 133, 146, 156, 159; glorification, 2–4, 11–14, 71, 76–77, 157; occultism, 2, 4–5, 8, 15–23, 24–30, 42–43, 51, 61, 99, 161–62; the SS Ahnenerbe, 17, 28–29, 56, 68–69, 161; the SS Paranormal Division, 42–43, 51–70

Oliwa, Anya, 1, 45–47, 81–84, 86–90, 92, 95, 97, 123, 128, 130, 132, 157–59
the Order of the Golden Dawn, 33, 44, 60–61, 102
Ostara, 21–22, 28
Otto I "the Great," 44–45, 52, 55, 62–66, 68–69, 92, 94, 105–6, 108–9, 143, 161–62, 164

Prendergast (private), 139–42, 145, 157

Qabalah. *See* Jewish mysticism

Roth, Set, 2–3, 34, 41, 45–46, 52, 56, 79, 81, 83–84, 86, 90–104, 107, 109, 111, 113–14, 120–21, 123, 126, 133, 143, 146–48, 150–52, 155–57, 164

Sebottendorf, Rudolf von, 19–23, 59, 67, 162
Sefer Yetziah. *See* Jewish mysticism
the Spear of Destiny, 2, 7, 27–28, 37, 40–41, 51, 54–56, 60, 63, 66, 139, 155, 162
SS Ahnenerbe. *See* Nazism

SS Paranormal Division. *See* Nazism
the Statue of Liberty, 89–90
Streicher, Julius, 86–88
the swastika, 11, 19, 21, 43, 52, 59, 63, 66–68, 125

Tekla, 120, 123, 131–38, 139
theodicy, 2, 4–5, 44, 96, 139–52, 156
the Theosophical Society, 17–19, 58, 67
the Thule Society, 21–22, 51, 56–57, 59–60, 66, 161

Wagner, Richard, 21, 27–28, 39, 55
Wiligut, Karl Maria, 21–23, 42, 53, 119
Wolfenstein (the series): *Beyond Castle Wolfenstein*, 7, 37, 39, 44, 155, 162; *Castle Wolfenstein*, 7, 37, 39, 41, 44, 119, 162; *Return to Castle Wolfenstein*, 7, 14, 37–38, 42–45, 51–52, 56–57, 62–63, 68–69, 99, 119–21, 155, 162; *Spear of Destiny*, 7, 37–38, 40–41, 51, 54–56, 63, 119, 155, 162; *Wolfenstein (2009)*, 7, 14, 37–38, 43–45, 51, 56, 58, 60, 66–69, 102, 119–20, 155, 162; *Wolfenstein: Cyberpilot*, 7, 37, 44, 47, 158–59, 161–62; *Wolfenstein: Enemy Territory*, 7, 37; *Wolfenstein: The New Order*, 1–3, 5, 7–8, 37–38, 44–46, 69, 71, 76–77, 79, 80–81, 84–85, 89, 90, 95, 99–101, 105–7, 109, 113–14, 119–20, 123, 125–28, 130–33, 139, 145, 147–48, 155–56, 158–60, 162; *Wolfenstein: The Old Blood*, 7, 37, 44, 46, 51–52, 56, 62, 64–65, 68, 70, 80, 84, 86, 90, 105–6, 108, 119–21, 123, 133, 148, 155, 158, 161–62; *Wolfenstein RPG*, 7, 37; *Wolfenstein III*, 7–8; *Wolfenstein 3D*, 2, 7, 37–38, 40–44, 47, 51–52, 79, 99, 114, 134, 150, 155, 162; *Wolfenstein II: The New Colossus*, 2, 7, 37–38, 44, 46, 79, 84–86, 89–90, 93, 95, 97, 101, 104, 113, 116, 120, 126–29, 131,

133, 147–50, 155–57, 158, 162;
Wolfenstein: Youngblood, 7, 37–38, 39, 44, 46–47, 66, 120, 158–59, 162
Wotanism. *See* Ariosophy

Wyatt III, Probst, 100–104, 120, 123, 126–28, 139, 148, 156

Yichud. *See* Jewish mysticism

About the Author

Dr. Frank G. Bosman is a Dutch cultural theologian working as a senior researcher at the Tilburg School of Catholic Theology, Tilburg, the Netherlands. His popular and academic publications focus on the cultural persistence of the Christian rhetoric and aesthetic in our modern secular world. Bosman has published extensively on religion, theology, and video games, for example, *Gaming and the divine: A new systematic theology of video games* (2019), *The Sacred and the digital: Depictions of religions in video games* (editor, 2019), and, together with Archibald van Wieringen, *Video games as art: A communication-oriented perspective on the relationship between gaming and art* (2022). In 2011, he was chosen as the first Ambassador of Theology in the Netherlands.